Neil Young

THE VISUAL DOCUMENTARY
by John Robertson

OMNIBUS PRESS

Copyright © 1994 Omnibus Press
(A Division of Book Sales Limited)

Edited by Chris Charlesworth
Cover & Book designed by Mike Warry, 4i Limited
Picture research by David Brolan

ISBN: 0.7119.3816.4
Order No: OP 47568

Exclusive Distributors
Book Sales Limited, 8/9 Frith Street, London W1V 5TZ, UK.
Music Sales Corporation, 257 Park Avenue South, New York, NY 10010, USA.
Music Sales Pty Limited, 120 Rothschild Avenue, Rosebery, NSW 2018, Australia.

To the Music Trade only:
Music Sales Limited, 8/9, Frith Street, London W1V 5TZ, UK.

Photo credits:
Front And Back Cover: Aaron Rapoport/Retna; Back Cover: London Features
International; Richard E.Aaron/Star File: 76/77, 78, 79t, 80, 81, 82; Greg
Allen/Retna: 110/111; Atlantic Records: 22t&b, 26/27; Glenn A.Baker/
Redferns: 36l; Dick Barnett/Redferns: 20t&b, 21, 24b; Jay Blakesberg/Retna: 4t,
146b; Garry Brandon/Redferns: 136; Larry Busacca/Retna: 47b, 101, 114, 124;
Canadian Press Files: 23r; Liz Clark: 13; William Coupon/Retna: 97; Terry
Crosby: 121t; Dagmar/Star File: 57, 64, 65; Horst Ebricht Collection/National
Archives Of Canada: 51, 52, 53; John Einarson Collection: 6, 7, 8, 9, 10, 11,
12, 23l, 120t, 143; Dave Ellis/Redferns: 37b; Famous: 105; Francois Gaillard: 22c;
Armando Gallo/Retna: 116b, 117, 118; Garry Gershoff/Retna: 48, 110t; Mick
Gold: 62/63, 63r; Steve Granitz/Retna: 99; Bob Gruen/Star File: 149c; Liane
Hentscher: 141, 143b; Bob Johnson: 7; Larry Kaplan/Star File: 94b, 106b; Carey
Lauder: 122; Barry Levine/Redferns: 28/29; London Features International: 4,
15, 16t&b, 17t&b, 18, 19, 33, 34, 35, 36/37, 39, 40/41, 60/61, 62t, 67, 79,
93t&c, 106l&c, 109l&b, 119, 130t, 135b, 138, 139, 149t, 150b, 151t&b, 153,
160; Shirley Lord: 6, 7; Jeffrey Mayer/Star File: 154b; Anna Meuer/SIN: 152
(x3); Gordon Milne: 104, 105b; Susan Moore/Redferns: 5bl; Steve Morley/
Redferns: 42tl; Tony Mottram/Retna: 108t; Paul Natkin/Retna: 84; Dan Neil:
121b; Al Pereira/Star File: 125b, 131, 132t, 133t, 140, 148; David Peterson/
Retna: 107; Michael Putland/Retna: 69, 70, 72; Chuck Pulin/Star File: 44t, 96,
113, 116t, 125t, 134l&r, 145b; Aaron Rapoport/Retna: 46/47, 97b, 127, 150t;
R.B./Redferns: 40; David Redfern/Redferns: 37b, 85b, 86; Relay: 15b, 24t, 25,
32, 38, 44b, 44/45, 50, 85t, 87t&b, 88, 89t&b; Sid Rogers: 6; David Seelig/Star
File: 46l, 126b, 132/133; Gene Shaw/Star File: 5br, 143t; Scott Sheilds/Tom
Horricks: 11; Rex Features: 31, 45t, 98, 102 (x3), 108, 129, 143l, 146t, 155b;
Ebet Roberts/Redferns: 42b, 95, 101b, 103, 109t, 115, 126, 128, 130c,bl&r,
137, 142, 144, 147, 149b, 154t, 155t; Ed Sirrs/Retna: 5t; Star File: 43, 45b, 75,
145t; Peter Tangen/Retna: 3; Roy Tee/SIN: 112; Robert E.Teese/Star File: 94t;
Jay Telfer: 14; Jeff Tisman/Retna: 135t; Luciano Viti/Retna: 100; Western
Canada Pictorial Index: 90, 91; Vinnie Zuffante/Star File: 93r.
Every effort has been made to trace the copyright holders of the photographs in this
book but one or two were unreachable. We would be grateful if the photographers
concerned would contact us.

A catalogue record for this book is available from the British Library.

"It's better to burn out
than it is to rust."

Neil Young refuses to be stereotyped. You can recognise the people who've tried: they're the ones who arrive at a Crazy Horse gig expecting to hear 'Heart Of Gold', and have to run, cowering, for the exit, protecting their ears. Or the ones who come prepared for a night of fearsome rock'n'roll, and sit bewildered while Young rolls gently through a parade of acoustic ballads. Or the ones who snapped up albums like 'Trans', or 'Old Ways', or 'Hawks & Doves', and sold them a few days later, because the Neil Young on the record didn't sound like the Neil Young in their imagination.

Since 1969, when he began to lead a dual life as a sensitive hippie songwriter and a Rolling Stones-inspired hard rocker, Neil Young has been impossible to categorise or confine. He's made a career out of confounding expectations – delivering albums of country, blues or rockabilly, feigning incoherence or madness, always staying one step ahead of predictability.

"It's better to burn out than it is to rust," he sang provocatively in 1978. He's been accused of both in his time, but more than 30 years after he made his first record, he is still driven by the desire to create music that touches the emotions, whether that implies anger or romantic sadness. At both extremes, playing solo acoustic guitar or eardrum-battering electric rock'n'roll, Young has stayed true to his own wayward heart, even when it's led him into direct confrontation with his audience.

He first came to public attention with the California folk-rock band, The Buffalo Springfield, then achieved superstardom as a member of Crosby, Stills, Nash and Young. Since then, he's ploughed his own furrow, sometimes connecting perfectly with the world at large, sometimes baffling and irritating even his most loyal supporters.

But unlike some of his contemporaries – John Lennon and Keith Richards spring immediately to mind – Young has rarely featured in the non-rock media. There was a minor drugs bust in 1968, a muck-raking article in *People* magazine in 1983, and precious little else, before or after. Since his marriage to Pegi Morton, and the birth of their son Ben, Young has played his music, and kept the rest of his life out of the public eye.

A documentary of Young's life couldn't be a catalogue of scandals, then. As far as the outside world is concerned, Young's work is his life. No wonder that he attracts fans who are obsessed with his music rather than his image, who avidly collect and swap live tapes and bootleg albums, and whose gossip is restricted to the appearance of an unfamiliar song in a concert repertoire, rather than a string of night-club outings and drunken excesses.

So this book doesn't just document Young's movements from one band and one genre to the next: it's also intended as a musical history, listing every known recording session and live gig. Like Bob Dylan, Young continually re-invents his own material in concert, shedding new light on the most familiar songs by placing them in unusual contexts or arrangements.

It's these often subtle artistic shifts which delight his keenest followers, which is why I've tried, wherever possible, to chronicle the changing face of Young's live performances – both from one tour to the next, and within each individual tour. Anyone who's fascinated by Young's 'unofficial' recorded history will now be able to decide exactly which concert tapes they need to hear – or to drool over the fantasy of set-lists which were never committed to tape.

Young once quipped that he wrote a song every day. The prolific nature of his talent, plus his innate restlessness, make him a frustratingly inconsistent, but eternally compelling, performer. Thirty years into his professional career, it's still impossible to predict what he might do next. In an era when strategic marketing has robbed rock of its uncompromising raw edge, Neil Young is a musician and a writer to be treasured.

SCHOOL LIFE
1960 - 1961

GRADE NINE   EARL GREY JUNIOR HIGH SCHOOL   HOLLAND

ACKNOWLEDGEMENTS

Special thanks to Neil Young researcher supreme, John Einarson, both for his pioneering and tireless investigation of 'The Canadian Years', but also for his generous supply of information and rare photographs.

Endless thanks also to 'Broken Arrow', one of the world's great fanzines, without which no Neil Young project would be possible. Contact 'Broken Arrow' via the Neil Young Appreciation Society, 2A Llynfi Street, Bridgend, Mid Glamorgan, CF31 1SY, Wales.

Finally, grateful appreciation to the fellow collectors and fans who've kept me supplied with tapes and titbits over the last 20 years; to authors Johnny Rogan, Dave Zimmer and Scott Young, for their prose and perception; and to Neil, CSNY and the rest for the music.

JUNE 1940
Sports journalist Scott Young marries golfer and tennis-player Edna 'Rassy' Ragland in Winnipeg, Canada.

27 APRIL 1942
Their first child, Bob, is born in Toronto, Canada.

12 NOVEMBER 1945
Neil Young is born in Toronto General Hospital.

AUGUST 1949
The Young family move to the Ontario village of Omemee.

AUGUST 1951
Five-year-old Neil falls victim to the polio epidemic sweeping across Canada, which kills or cripples thousands of children. Young is hospitalised for several days, but recovers without any apparent ill-effects.

SEPTEMBER 1954
Scott and Rassy Young briefly separate, but are later reunited. Neil attends Brock Road School in Pickering.

1957
The Youngs move back to Toronto, where Neil switches to John Wanless School.

LATE 1958
Neil is given his first musical instrument – a plastic ukulele. The following year he buys an acoustic guitar, then an electric guitar in 1960.

MID-1960
Scott Young leaves his wife, remarrying Astrid Mead in May 1961. Rassy takes the boys back to Winnipeg (as chronicled in Young's song, 'Don't Be Denied'), where Neil attends Earl Gray Junior High School.

EARLY JANUARY 1961
On the first Friday after New Year Young makes his first ever public performance, playing rhythm guitar with his first band The Jades at the Earl Grey Community Club Teen Dance. It was The Jades' only gig. The other Jades were John Daniel on guitar and David Gregg on drums.

SPRING 1961
The Jades disband, so Young tries out with a local group called The Esquires, but is turned down because of his lack of experience.

YEAR BOOK STAFF

Seated: Jim Atkin, Joann Hagglund, Susan Kelso, Neil Young, Laurelle Hughes, June Hagglund, Ken Koblun. Standing: Mrs. Queen, Richard Clayton, Gerry Soucie, Shirley Lord, Mr. Patterson, Ruth Harris, Joe Vinci, Mrs. Mills.

SUMMER 1961
Young sees his name in print as a writer for the first time, for a short essay called 'Why I Chew Gum' in the Earl Gray School yearbook.

SEPTEMBER 1961
Young switches to Kelvin High School in River Heights (scene of The Squires' reunion in 1987). He continues to play with his Earl Gray classmate, Ken Koblun, and both of them rehearse with short-lived groups called The Stardusters and The Twilighters.

Opposite page: Young, once a member of the Canadian Freeloaders Society, with friends from Earl Grey Junior High School.

This page, top: Neil's mother, Edna 'Rassy' Young (bottom, centre) with her co-panellists on the Canadian TV show Twenty Questions; bottom left: Earl Grey Junior High School; bottom centre: Kelvin Technical High School; bottom right: Neil and his mother lived here, at Gray Apartments, Suite 5, between 1960 and 1962.

V

Allan Bates

Neil Young

45 RPM

V-109
Side A

Ken Smyth

"THE SULTAN"
by "The Squires"
Produced by Bob Bradburn

Above: Neil's first ever single, autographed by The Squires.

Below: Neil and his mother's home at 1123 Grosvenor Avenue, Winnipeg.

For three years, Neil Young ekes out a precarious living as the guitarist in a Winnipeg rock'n'roll band. Bass guitarist Ken Koblun becomes the first in a decade's worth of sidekicks – Bruce Palmer, Stephen Stills, Jack Nitzsche and Danny Whitten later took turns in the role – whose reassuring presence allows Young to shift quietly from centre-stage to the shadows of anonymity.

The Stardusters become The Classics, who become The Squires and then briefly The Castaways, but their fame never extends beyond the Canadian club circuit – first in Winnipeg, then in Fort William and finally (and briefly) in Toronto. Young is a self-confessed instrumental freak, buzzing on the metallic surf-guitar records of California's Dick Dale and the catchy hooks of England's Shadows, with the bespectacled Hank Marvin as his musical hero.

It is as a non-vocal combo that The Squires cut their first record, which is never given airplay beyond the Winnipeg city limits. But inspired by the composing exploits of The Beatles, Young begins to add lyrics to his creative skills. His thin, sometimes whining vocal style wins him few early admirers – "stick to instrumentals", one fan advises in 1964 – but his brief excursions into the spotlight prove to Young that he could hold an audience without compromising his ideals.

His earliest songs are little more than blues clichés, round which the band could jam. But on his 19th birthday, late in 1964, Young pens a tune that was still in his repertoire 30 years later – by which time its earnest adolescent naïveté makes him wince in wry amusement.

FEBRUARY 1962
Young and Koblun play a school gig with The Stardusters.

JUNE 1962
Neil's half-sister Astrid, the daughter of his father Scott Young and stepmother Astrid, is born. Young fails his Grade Ten school exams, and resolves to re-sit them later in the year. In the event, he elects to try and make a career as a musician, rather than continue his tortuous academic progress.

OCTOBER 1962
Neil Young forms The Classics with Ken Koblun.

17 NOVEMBER 1962
Young's first paid gig, as a member of The Classics, at Churchill High School, Winnipeg, Canada. The band — Young on lead guitar, plus Koblun (bass), Buddy Taylor (drums), Jack Gowenlock (rhythm guitar), Linda Fowler (piano) and vocalist John Copsey — share expenses of $5 between them.

24 NOVEMBER 1962
The Classics: Kelvin High School.

1 DECEMBER 1962
The Classics: Westworth Hi Club.

8 DECEMBER 1962
The Classics: Morse Place Community Club.

15 DECEMBER 1962
The Classics: Riverview Community Club.

29 DECEMBER 1962
The Classics play their final gig, at St. Ignatius CYO, Winnipeg. By this time, Young and Koblun have already formed a new band, The Squires.

JANUARY 1963
The Squires rehearse regularly in the basement of drummer Jack Harper's home.

1 FEBRUARY 1963
Neil Young plays his first show as a member of The Squires, at Riverview Community Club, Winnipeg. Further gigs follow approximately every two weeks, featuring the band's original line-up: Allan Bates (2nd guitar), Ken Koblun (bass) and Jack Harper (drums).

15 FEBRUARY 1963
The Squires: Grant Park High School.

2 MARCH 1963
The Squires: Crescentwood Community Club.

8 MARCH 1963
The Squires: Sir John Franklin Community Club.

22 MARCH 1963
The Squires: Grant Park High School.

29 MARCH 1963
The Squires: Glenlee Community Club.

APRIL 1963
Harper drops out of The Squires, and is replaced by Ken Smyth. Other musicians, like Greg Mudry, Jim Atkins and Jeff Waukert, also guest at the band's shows over the next few months.

19 APRIL 1963
The Squires: Westworth Hi Club.

26 APRIL 1963
The Squires take part in a Battle Of The Bands at Nelson MacIntyre High School and perform at the Sir John Franklin Community Club later in the evening.

27 APRIL 1963
The Squires: Sir Andrews High School.

10 MAY 1963
The Squires: Youth Council.

17 MAY 1963
The Squires: Sir John Franklin Community Club.

18 MAY 1963
The Squires: St Peter's Hi Club.

25 MAY 1963
The Squires: St Ignatius CYO.

7 JUNE 1963
The Squires: Earl Grey Community Club.

27 JUNE 1963
The Squires: Lipsett Hall CYO.

2 JULY 1963
The Squires: Crescentwood Community Club.

12 JULY 1963
The Squires audition at CKRC, a Winnipeg radio station, where DJ Bob Bradburn hears and approves them.

19 JULY 1963
The Squires are back at CKRC for a rehearsal.

23 JULY 1963
Neil Young's first recording session, as The Squires cut their only single, 'Aurora'/'The Sultan' – two instrumentals written by Young. The session is arranged by DJ Bob Bradburn.

30 JULY 1963
The Squires: Crescentwood Community Club.

7 AUGUST 1963
The Squires: Glenwood Community Club.

15 AUGUST 1963
The Squires: West End Memorial Community Club.

AUTUMN 1963
The Squires' début 45 is released on V Records, a local Winnipeg label. The band continue to play sporadic live gigs for the rest of the year.

2 SEPTEMBER 1963
The Squires play in a parking lot outside Topps Discount Store.

20 SEPTEMBER 1963
Young acquires his beloved orange Gretsch guitar and uses it for the first time at St Mary's CYO.

27/28 SEPTEMBER 1963
The Squires: The Celler.

5 OCTOBER 1963
The Squires: River Heights Community Club.

18 OCTOBER 1963
The Squires: Grant Park High School.

19 OCTOBER 1963
The Squires: West End Memorial Community Club.

Above: Neil on guitar at a Kelvin High School dance with unidentified friends.

26 OCTOBER 1963
The Squires: Our Lady Of Victory Church.

1 NOVEMBER 1963
The Squires: Portage La Prairie, Manitoba.

2 NOVEMBER 1963
The Squires: River Heights Community Club.

22 NOVEMBER 1963
The Squires: St Peter's Mission.

29 NOVEMBER 1963
The Squires: St Ignatius CYO.

6 DECEMBER 1963
The Squires: St Mary's CYO.

13 DECEMBER 1963
The Squires travel by bus to play at Dauphin, Manitoba.

20 DECEMBER 1963
The Squires: Charleswood Collegiate.

3 JANUARY 1964
The Squires' first gig of the New Year, at St. Ignatius CYO, Winnipeg. Young dares to sing in public for the first time, muttering his way through 'Money (That's What I Want)'. "Stick to instrumentals," is the apocryphal response.

24 JANUARY 1964
The Squires: Kelvin High School.

25 JANUARY 1964
The Squires' début performance at the Fourth Dimension, a Winnipeg folk club which becomes a regular haunt for the band. Young begins to increase the number of vocals in the band's set.

31 JANUARY 1964
The Squires: Miles McDonell Collegiate.

1 FEBRUARY 1964
The Squires: Glenwood Community Club.

5 FEBRUARY 1964
The Squires: Fourth Dimension.

7 FEBRUARY 1964
The Squires: Peterson's Ranch House.

8 FEBRUARY 1964
The Squires: Fourth Dimension.

9 FEBRUARY 1964
The Squires: St Paul Of The Apostle CYO.

14 FEBRUARY 1964
The Squires: Our Lady Of Victory Church.

21 FEBRUARY 1964
The Squires: Portage La Prairie, Manitoba.

22 FEBRUARY 1964
The Squires: McLean's United Church.

29 FEBRUARY 1964
The Squires: Fourth Dimension.

7 MARCH 1964
The Squires: Peterson's Ranch House.

14 MARCH 1964
The Squires: Glenwood Community Club.

26/28 MARCH 1964
The Squires: Person's Ranch House.

2 APRIL 1964
The second and last professional Squires recording session takes place at CKRC. Besides a couple of instrumentals, the band record several vocal tunes, including 'I Wonder' and 'Ain't It The Truth', which Young revives more than 20 years later with The Bluenotes. None of these tracks is released.

3 APRIL 1964
The Squires: Crescentwood Community Club.

4 APRIL 1964
The Squires: Norberry Community Club.

5 APRIL 1964
The Squires: St Paul Of The Apostle CYO.

11 APRIL 1964
The Squires: Peterson's Ranch House.

8 MAY 1964
The Squires: Winakwa Community Club.

25 MAY 1964
The Squires: Grandell Community Club.

9 JUNE 1964
The Squires: Notre Dame Auditorium.

12 JUNE 1964
The Squires: Maple Leaf Community Club.

15 JUNE 1964.
The Squires: Towers Town & Country Nightclub.

19 JUNE 1964
The Squires: Weston Community Club.

5 JULY 1964
The Squires: Proteen Club.

24 & 31 JULY 1964
The Squires: The Cellar.

4 AUGUST 1964
While on holiday in Falcon Lake, Young arranges for The Squires to play some shows at the resort. Two of the band refuse to travel so far out of town, and The Squires briefly split up, before Koblun and Young regroup with Bill Edmundson (drums) and Jeff Wuckert (piano).

6 AUGUST 1964
The Squires: Towers Town & Country.

23 & 30 AUGUST 1964
The Squires: Fourth Dimension.

11 & 18 SEPTEMBER 1964
The Squires: River Heights Community Club.

19 SEPTEMBER 1964
The Squires: St Paul The Apostle.

25 SEPTEMBER 1964
The Squires: Holy Cross Gymnasium.

3 & 9 OCTOBER 1964
The Squires: Glenwood Community Club.

10 OCTOBER 1964
The Squires: Murdock MacKay High School.

OCTOBER 1964
Young and The Squires leave Winnipeg for a long series of shows in Fort William. Young writes to his father: "I'm not particularly worried where we go right now, as long as we get paid and improve ourselves." They are paid $325 a week, which rises to $350 in November.

12 – 17 OCTOBER 1964
The first series of Squires shows at the Flamingo Club, Fort William, Ontario. The band also play afternoon sets at the local version of the Fourth Dimension club.

23 OCTOBER 1964
The Squires: West Kildonan Collegiate.

31 OCTOBER 1964
The Squires: River Heights Community Club.

2 – 14 NOVEMBER 1964
Flamingo Club, Fort William, Ontario. On the 12th Young celebrates his 19th birthday by writing 'Sugar Mountain' before The Squires' evening show at the Flamingo.

15, 20/21 NOVEMBER 1964
The Squires: Fourth Dimension, Fort William.

23 NOVEMBER 1964
The Squires record 'I'll Love You Forever', a song about Young's Winnipeg girlfreind Pam Smith, at CJLY in Fort William. It incorporates Young's voice double-tracked and background sounds of the sea.

DECEMBER 1964
Bill Edmundson leaves The Squires, and is replaced by a succession of temporary drummers — including Randy Peterson, with whom the band privately record two songs, 'I'm A Man' and 'I Can't Cry'.

12 DECEMBER 1964
The Squires: Fort William Coliseum.

15 – 20 DECEMBER 1964
The Squires: Twilight Zone Club.

23 DECEMBER 1964
The Squires: Selkirk Memorial Hall.

31 DECEMBER 1964
The Squires: Neepawa Drill Hall. The Squires are paid $200 for this New Years Eve gig.

DOC STEEN – Noon – 2 p.m.
Neil Young & Squires, Crescendos and Doc Steen out to UMSU Dance Friday, May 14.

Above: The Flamingo Club in Fort William.

Below: The Squires: Neil (with his orange Gretsch guitar), Bill Edmundson, Jeff Wuckert and bassist Ken Koblun.

Up in Fort William, The Squires run into an American folk combo, and Neil Young meets the man who will act, by turns, as a catalyst and a nemesis for the next 15 years or more. Stephen Stills is a sensitive extrovert, a Texan who's been schooled in Latin dance music and New York folk, who loves to sing harmony and yearns to play blues and rock'n'roll. In Young's raucous, edgy guitar-work and developing writing talent, Stills recognises a kindred spirit.

Within three months, The Squires have split up. Young toys with the idea of becoming a pop idol in Britain, and settles instead for the security of his father's floor in Toronto. A week or two later, he's vanished into Toronto's beatnik Bohemianism, from where he makes a brief visit to New York in search of Stills' bandmates. It is there that he records his first 'professional' demo tape, previewing some of the songs he will record over the next three years, unveiling a definite Dylan influence, and preparing a blueprint for the opening song on his 1975 album 'Zuma', in the shape of 'Don't Pity Me Babe'.

As early as 1965, Young is capable of bewildering transitions. He's arrived in New York as a folkie; within weeks he is signed to the legendary soul label Motown, as an integral part of a R&B/rock crossover band called The Mynah Birds. And by Christmas he is back in Toronto, waiting for the future to call.

Above: Neil, Ken Koblun and Geordie McDonald on their way to the gig in Vermont, October 1965.

Below: Neil and The Squires at Nelson Collegiate, February 1965.

2 JANUARY 1965
The Squires: Brandon Roller Rink.

3 JANUARY 1965
The Squires: St Paul the Apostle.

8 JANUARY 1965
The Squires: West End Memorial Community Club.

15 JANUARY 1965
The Squires: Churchill High School.

23 JANUARY 1965
The Squires: River Heights Community Club.

29 JANUARY 1965
The Squires: MacGregor, Manitoba.

30 JANUARY 1965
The Squires: Glenwood Community Club.

5 FEBRUARY 1965
The Squires: United College.

12 FEBRUARY 1965
The Squires: Glenlawn Collegiate.

13 FEBRUARY 1965
The Squires: Giroux, Manitoba.

14 FEBRUARY 1965
The Squires: Holy Cross CYO

19 FEBRUARY 1965
The Squires: Nelson MacIntyre High School.

26 FEBRUARY 1965
The Squires: Selkirk Memorial Hall.

27 FEBRUARY 1965
The Squires: River Heights Community Club.

5 MARCH 1965
The Squires: Selkirk Lutheran Hall.

7 MARCH 1965
The Squires: Fourth Dimension.

13 MARCH 1965
The Squires: River Heights Community Club.

19 MARCH 1965
The Squires: Riverview Community Club.

20 MARCH 1965
The Squires: Glenwood Community Club.

APRIL 1965
The Squires travel north to Churchill, Manitoba for a brief spell of gigs, and return to Fort William.

8 – 14 APRIL 1965
The Squires: Hudson Hotel, Churchill. On the 11th they double at Churchill's Navy Club.

18 APRIL 1965
Neil Young meets Stephen Stills for the first time at the Fourth Dimension coffee house in Fort William, where Young and The Squires share the bill with Still's group The Company. Stills and Young strike up an immediate friendship, and agree to keep in touch.

18 – 24 APRIL 1965
Fourth Dimension, Fort William (afternoon shows). On the 20th The Squires play Fort William's Polish Legion Club in the evening.

30 APRIL 1965
The Squires: Coliseum, Fort William.

1 MAY 1965
The Squires: Fourth Dimension, Fort William.

7 MAY 1965
The Squires: St Paul's Church, Port Arthur, Ontario.

8 MAY 1965
The Squires: Fourth Dimension, Fort William.

14 MAY 1965
The Squires: Aticokan, Ontario.

15 MAY 1965
The Squires: Fourth Dimension.

21 MAY 1965
The Squires: Westgate High School, Fort William.

22 – 30 MAY 1965
The Squires: Fourth Dimension, Fort William and, on most evenings, Smitty's Pancake House, Fort William.

12 & 16 JUNE 1965
The Squires' final gig, an afternoon performance at the Fourth Dimension. Koblun and Young briefly consider travelling to England in the hope of becoming pop stars, but settle their sights nearer to home, at Toronto. On the weekend of June 16/18 Young and his friends are on their way to Sudbury when Neil's beloved hearse Mort (aka Mortimor Hearseburg) breaks down in Blind River. The hearse is the inspiration for 'Long May You Run'.

Above: Neil and The Squires on stage at the 4-D, Fort William, May 1965.

Below: The Squires – Ken Koblun, Neil and Bob Clark – with Neil's beloved hearse, 'Mort', before they left for Fort William in April 1965.

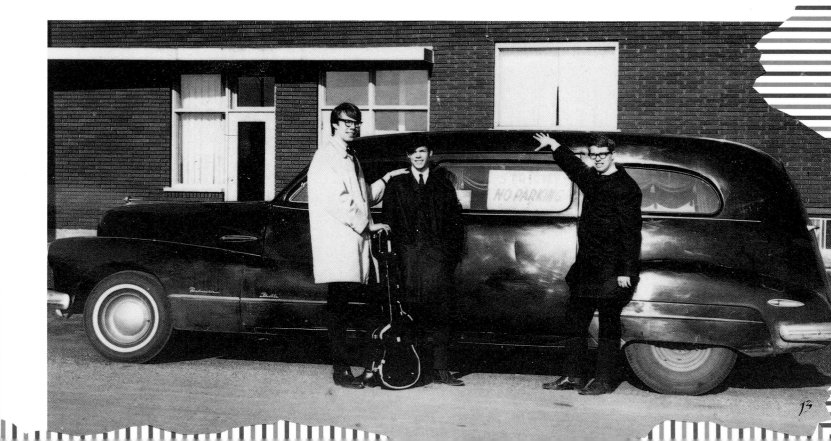

JULY 1965

Young hitches from Sudbury, Ontario, to stay with his father in Toronto. The Squires briefly reunite in the city, changing their name to The Castaways, but dissolve without playing any gigs there.

AUGUST 1965

Neil moves into Toronto's nearest equivalent to a Bohemian quarter, Yorkville, sharing an apartment with ex-Squire Ken Koblun. Booking agent Martin Onrot takes on Young as a client, but is only able to find him a handful of low-paying gigs, so Neil opts for a job as a stockroom worker in a bookstore. Carrying his guitar on the street one afternoon, he meets bass player Bruce Palmer. Around this time, Young writes 'Nowadays Clancy Can't Even Sing'.

30 OCTOBER 1965

Young, Ken Koblun and Geordie McDonald journey from Toronto to Killington, Vermont, for a gig at the Wobbly Barn ski resort that falls through after one night, whereupon Neil and Ken head for New York for three days. Neil meets Richie Furay, who was also in Stephen Stills' band The Company, and teaches him 'Nowadays Clancy Can't Even Sing'. Richie later takes the song to Stills in Los Angeles.

NOVEMBER 1965

The Mynah Birds travel to Detroit, where they succeed in being signed by the hottest soul label in America, Motown Records, and record eight tracks which Motown elect not to release.

Young: "We recorded five or six nights, and

SEPTEMBER 1965

Young and Koblun journey to New York where they search in vain for singer Richie Furay. Young is offered the opportunity to record his first demos at Elektra Studios, taping solo acoustic renditions of seven songs: 'Nowadays Clancy Can't Even Sing', 'Sugar Mountain', 'The Rent Is Always Due', 'Runaround Babe', 'Don't Pity Me Babe', 'Ain't Got The Blues' and 'When It Falls, It Falls On You'.

OCTOBER 1965

Back in Toronto, Bruce Palmer recruits Young for his new, multi-racial band, The Mynah Birds – led by Ricky James Matthews, a soul star 15 years later as Rick James.

if they thought we weren't strong enough, they'd Motown us! A couple of 'em would be right there, and they'd sing the part. Then everybody was grooving. And an amazing thing happened – we sounded hot. All of a sudden it was Motown. That's why all those records sounded like that."

DECEMBER 1965

Motown discover that Ricky Matthews is absent without leave from the US Navy, and persuade him to give himself up to the authorities. He is subsequently imprisoned, and The Mynah Birds disband, and return to Toronto.

Above: The Mynah Birds, with Ricky James Matthews (Ricky James) on vocals but without Neil.

Opposite page, inset: The Byrds visiting London in 1965 (left to right) are: Jim McGuinn, Gene Clark, Michael Clarke, Chris Hillman and David Crosby.

Buffalo Springfield is obviously meant to happen. Young travels south to California with his new soulmate, and fellow Mynah Bird, Bruce Palmer, in search of musical nirvana and Stephen Stills. Driving a hearse – what else? – Young and Palmer cross Stills' path on a California highway, and within a month the occupants of the two cars have formed a band, signed a deal with Sonny & Cher's managers, and played their first gig.

Young becomes lead guitarist in a group dominated by Stills' boundless energy and prolific writing talents. When the Springfield sign with Atlantic Records, and the label choose Young's 'Nowadays Clancy Can't Even Sing' as their début single, the tension comes close to fracturing the group. Not that the choice threatens to make Young a star: by democratic vote, his vocals aren't considered suitable for radio airplay, and Richie Furay sings Young's tune instead.

By the end of the year, Buffalo Springfield have recorded their first, self-titled album, and what proves to be their first hit single, Stills' 'For What It's Worth'. Neither record catches a hint of the raw, blues-tinged excitement of their early live shows, and the Springfield are immediately pigeonholed as a folk-rock combo in the tradition of The Byrds. Entirely true to form, it is Young's 'Burned' and 'Out Of My Mind' which come closest to denting the slickness of their public image.

Buffalo Springfield on a 1967 TV show: Ken Koblun (left) replaced the errant Bruce Palmer, alongside Richie Furay, Neil Young, Dewey Martin and Stephen Stills.

LATE FEBRUARY 1966

Young and Bruce Palmer drive towards California, once again in search of their friends from The Company. Meanwhile, in Los Angeles, Stephen Stills and Richie Furay are trying to contact Young to persuade him to join their band.

2 MARCH 1966

On a Los Angeles highway, Young and Palmer are leaving town in Neil's hearse, when they are spotted by Stills and Furay, driving in the opposite direction. The four men establish on-the-road contact, and agree to meet for a rehearsal the following day.

3 MARCH 1966

Drummer Dewey Martin joins Young, Stills, Palmer and Furay for the first rehearsal by The Buffalo Springfield.

late MARCH 1966

Buffalo Springfield's first gig, at the Orange County Fairgrounds, San Bernardino, California.
Around this time, Young suffers his first major epileptic seizure.

18 JULY 1966

Buffalo Springfield record 'Go And Say Goodbye' and Young's 'Nowadays Clancy Can't Even Sing' in Los Angeles.

25 JULY 1966

Buffalo Springfield appear at the Hollywood Bowl, supporting The Rolling Stones, The McCoys, The Standells, and The Tradewinds. They are billed as the first band to appear at the 20,000-seater venue without a hit record to their credit. Featured in their four-song set are 'Sit Down I Think I Love You' and 'My Kind Of Love'.

26 JULY 1966

Buffalo Springfield's managers, Charles Greene and Brian Stone, sign a deal for the group to make six appearances on the *Hollywood Palace* TV show.

OCTOBER 1966

Buffalo Springfield record their début album in Los Angeles, adding 'Sit Down I Think I Love You', 'Leave', 'Hot Dusty Roads', 'Everybody's Wrong', 'Flying On The Ground Is Wrong', 'Burned', 'Do I Have To Come Right Out And Say It', 'Baby Don't Scold Me', 'Out Of My Mind' and 'Pay The Price' to the two songs previously taped in July. Three songs are left over from the sessions, 'My Kind Of Love', 'Neighbor Don't You Worry' and 'Down Down Down'.

11 – 13 NOVEMBER 1966

Buffalo Springfield: Fillmore Auditorium, San Francisco, California, on the same bill as Country Joe & The Fish.

2/3 DECEMBER 1966

Buffalo Springfield: Avalon Ballroom, San Francisco, California, headlining at a Family Dog show over The Daily Flash and Congress Of Wonders.

5 DECEMBER 1966

Buffalo Springfield record 'For What It's Worth' at Columbia Studios in Los Angeles.

It is no coincidence that Young adopts the alias 'Bernard Shakey' in the late Sixties. As Buffalo Springfield take off in mid-1966, Young is struck by his first epileptic attack. Over the next three years, ill-health dogs the ascent of his career, as the after-effects of his childhood polio join forces with his increasing nervous instability.

After coupling The Stones' 'Satisfaction' riff to a startling examination of rock stardom on the brilliant single 'Mr Soul', Young lives out the psychic menace of the song by quitting the band on the verge of their biggest TV appearance to date. His decision forces the delay and then cancellation of 'Stampede', planned as the band's second album (though the bootleg of that name bears no resemblance to anything the Springfield might have considered releasing). Doug Hastings takes his place, aided at the prestigious Monterey festival in mid-summer by Byrds' front-man David Crosby.

Young, meanwhile, teams up with Jack Nitzsche, former right-hand-man to producer/genius Phil Spector. Nitzsche concocts moving orchestral arrangements for Young's increasingly personal songs, without at this stage any definite plans for the future. In the event, Young is persuaded back into the ranks in time to lend his new compositions to 'Buffalo Springfield Again', the brilliant album they completed by the end of the year.

But it is a tentative reunion. Canadian Bruce Palmer, in many ways the cohesive soul of the band, has been deported after a drugs bust, and though his replacement, Jim Messina, brought some much-needed studio nous to the line-up, the initial impetus of the Springfield has been lost.

Gene Clark fled The Byrds at the start of 1966, leaving David Crosby (far right) to bid for leadership of the band.

JANUARY 1967
'Buffalo Springfield', the group's début LP, is released by Atlantic, at the same time as the single, 'For What It's Worth'. As the latter becomes a hit, Atlantic withdraw the album, and reissue it with 'For What It's Worth' installed as the first track, replacing Stills' lacklustre 'Baby Don't Scold Me'.

9 JANUARY 1967
The tentative first version of 'Mr Soul' is recorded by Buffalo Springfield at Atlantic Studios in New York. The track is only released by mistake, on an Atlantic Oldies single in the 1970s. At the same session, the band record 'We'll See' and 'My Kind Of Love'.

25 JANUARY 1967
Buffalo Springfield: The Tempo, San Francisco, California. First show with Ken Koblun replacing Bruce Palmer, who has been arrested on drugs charges and deported home to Canada.

27 JANUARY 1967
Buffalo Springfield appear on the TV show *Hullabaloo*.

28 JANUARY 1967
Buffalo Springfield: Rolling Hills High School, Los Angeles, California.

1 FEBRUARY 1967
Buffalo Springfield appear on TV's *Where The Action Is*.

2 FEBRUARY 1967
A second appearance on *Hullabaloo*.

3/4 FEBRUARY 1967
Buffalo Springfield: Santa Barbara, California.

5 FEBRUARY 1967
Buffalo Springfield: Hollywood Palladium, Los Angeles, California.

6 FEBRUARY 1967
Buffalo Springfield: Cinnamon Cinder, Long Beach, California.

8 FEBRUARY 1967
Buffalo Springfield: Albuquerque, New Mexico.

9 FEBRUARY 1967
Buffalo Springfield: Santa Fe, New Mexico.

10 FEBRUARY 1967
Buffalo Springfield: Lubbock, Texas.

17 FEBRUARY 1967
'For What It's Worth' replaces 'Baby Don't Scold Me' on Buffalo Springfield's début album.

20 FEBRUARY 1967
Buffalo Springfield record a second version of 'Baby Don't Scold Me', to improve on the version dropped from their début album.

13 MARCH 1967
Buffalo Springfield record 'No Sun Today' and 'Who's The Next Fool' at Sound Recorders in Los Angeles.

8 APRIL 1967
The band tape the second version of Young's 'Mr Soul', subsequently issued as a single.

MID-APRIL 1967
The Springfield play a 10-night season at Ondine's in New York, joined on several nights by Otis Redding.
The band appear on the TV show *Hollywood Palace*, but Young vetoes an opportunity for them to perform on Johnny Carson's *Tonight Show*, fearing that the Springfield are losing their idealism.

LATE APRIL 1967
Buffalo Springfield: The Rock Garden, San Francisco.

28 APRIL 1967
Buffalo Springfield: Fillmore Auditorium, San Francisco, with The Steve Miller Blues Band and Freedom Highway.

29 APRIL 1967
Buffalo Springfield support The Supremes, Johnny Rivers, The Seeds, Brenda Holloway and The Fifth Dimension, at the Hollywood Bowl. Their set includes 'Pay The Price', 'Nowadays Clancy Can't Even Sing', 'For What It's Worth' and 'Mr Soul'. They then fly back to San Francisco to headline at the Fillmore Auditorium.

30 APRIL 1967
Final night at the Fillmore.

1 MAY 1967
Neil Young leaves Buffalo Springfield on the eve of their appearance on *The Tonight Show*. Doug Hastings is recruited as his replacement.

6 MAY 1967
Young records two instrumentals, 'Whiskey Boot Hill' and 'Slowly Burning', at Sunset Sound in Los Angeles. The tracks aren't issued at the time, but are delivered to Atlantic in 1971 as part of a batch of unissued Buffalo Springfield material.

The classic original Buffalo Springfield line-up, pictured between drug busts in 1967. Clockwise from top left: Dewey Martin, Stephen Stills, Neil Young, Bruce Palmer and Richie Furay.

6 JUNE 1967
Buffalo Springfield mix their new single, 'Bluebird'/'Mr Soul'.

16 JUNE 1967
Buffalo Springfield appear without Neil Young at the Monterey International Pop Festival. David Crosby is drafted in from The Byrds to take his place.

30 JUNE 1967
Young's 'Down, Down, Down' and Richie Furay's 'Nobody's Fool' are recorded by Buffalo Springfield – without Young's involvement. 'Down, Down, Down' and 'Whiskey Boot Hill' (see 6 May 1967) are later incorporated into the 'Déjà Vu' CSNY track, 'Country Girl'.

1 AUGUST 1967
Buffalo Springfield begin six consecutive nights of shows at the Fillmore Auditorium, San Francisco, California, supporting Muddy Waters.

24 AUGUST 1967
'Expecting To Fly', effectively a Neil Young solo recording, is completed in New York.

30 AUGUST 1967
Young rejoins Buffalo Springfield to record 'Rock'n'Roll Woman' and 'A Child's Claim To Fame' at Sunset Sound in Los Angeles.

1 SEPTEMBER 1967
Buffalo Springfield record an unused version of 'Hung Upside Down' at Sunset Sound. During these sessions, Sunset engineer Jim Messina assists Young in remixing the solo tapes he'd cut during his summer absence from the band. Messina is subsequently asked to replace Bruce Palmer in the Springfield.

6/7 OCTOBER 1967
Buffalo Springfield: Denver, Colorado, for The Family Dog, with Eighth Penny Matter supporting.

9 OCTOBER 1967
Work is completed on a batch of songs for Buffalo Springfield's second album, including 'Everydays', 'Hung Upside Down', 'Sad Memory', 'Good Time Boy' and 'Broken Arrow'.

14 NOVEMBER 1967
The initial recording of Young's 'On The Way Home' is done, for the third Buffalo Springfield album.

DECEMBER 1967
The second Springfield album, 'Buffalo Springfield Again', is released. One perceptive reviewer comments on the band's

lack of "blend; only a rather obvious alienation among the compositions". But the LP is still rated as a vast improvement over their début.

21 DECEMBER 1967
Buffalo Springfield: Fillmore West, San Francisco, California, headlining over The Collectors and Hour Glass.

22/23 DECEMBER 1967
Buffalo Springfield: Fillmore East. Before the show, the band hold a press conference.

29 DECEMBER 1967
Buffalo Springfield: The Cheetah, Venice, California, on a bill with The Seeds and The Lollipop Shoppe.

30/31 DECEMBER 1967
Buffalo Springfield: The Cheetah, Venice, California.

Bruce Palmer's deportation left the four original Springfield members without a bassist. They subsequently enlisted engineer Jim Messina.

1968

After a year of promise and another of chaos, 1968 brings a slightly depressed stability to Young's career. Buffalo Springfield slide slowly into dissolution by the Spring, Young acknowledging the inevitable by jumping ship shortly before the final collapse.

A controversial drugs bust sees the band out in no sort of style, and once the story vanishes from the pages of *Rolling Stone* in May, Neil Young effectively disappears from public view. But he's still managed to make one of the most important contacts of his life, signing with Joni Mitchell's manager, Elliot Roberts, who in turn negotiates him a solo deal with Reprise.

In exhausting sessions that stretch from summer into autumn, Young and Jack Nitzsche assembled a gentle, often mournful, and equally often inspired solo album. 'Neil Young' escapes gently onto the shelves by the end of the year, its commercial prospects ruined by a tentative mix that buries Young's voice deep beneath the instrumental ornamentation. His solo acoustic shows at the end of the year show the same self-effacement, his features masked by swathes of hair as he hunches over the microphone.

Meanwhile, two of Young's former Springfield colleagues are adopting a higher profile. Richie Furay has formed a country-rock band, Poco; while Stephen Stills has taken part in the much-hyped 'Super Session' project with Al Kooper, and caught the imagination of the fledgling underground press by announcing the formation of 'a group that's not a group' with two other late Sixties mavericks: David Crosby of The Byrds and Graham Nash of The Hollies. Young is left to celebrate another kind of union: his marriage to Susan Acevedo, which presents him with an instant family.

2 JANUARY 1968
A batch of Buffalo Springfield recordings are mixed for possible use on their third album. They include two instrumentals, 'Raga No. 1' and 'Raga No. 2', plus 'Whatever Happened To Saturday Nite' and two song-segments, 'Theme Jazz' and 'Ball Park'.

6 JANUARY 1968
Buffalo Springfield: The Earl Warren, Santa Barbara, California, supported by Charles Lloyd and Turquoise.

c. JANUARY 1968
Buffalo Springfield support The Beach Boys on a brief West Coast tour.

15 FEBRUARY 1968
Months of sporadic sessions result in the delivery to Atlantic of a collection of Buffalo Springfield tracks for the group's third album. Songs completed include two versions of 'In The Hour Of Not Quite Rain', 'Questions', 'Four Days Gone',

'Merry-Go-Round', 'Pretty Girl Why', 'I Am A Child', 'Special Care', 'Kind Woman', 'Uno Mundo', and three songs that remain unissued by the band, 'Carefree Country Day' (2 versions), 'What A Day' and 'Fa-Fa-Fa'.

26 FEBRUARY 1968
Buffalo Springfield record 'Can't Keep Me Down' at Sunset Sound.

9 MARCH 1968
'Can't Seem To Get Movin' ' is submitted to Atlantic for consideration on the next Buffalo Springfield album.

MID-MARCH 1968
Young announces his intention to leave Buffalo Springfield at the end of their current touring commitments. "I just couldn't handle it towards the end," he explains later. "My nerves couldn't handle the trip. It wasn't me scheming for a solo career, it wasn't anything but my nerves." He contacts Joni Mitchell's manager, Elliott Roberts, and asks him to become his manager.

"Neil was resenting the fact that I was starting to play lead guitar," Stephen Stills mused later on the Springfield split. "I was the arranger, and all of a sudden I was treading on his territory, so he started getting into mine."

20 MARCH 1968
Young is one of a dozen people arrested in a private home in Toganga Canyon, Los Angeles; the others include Richie Furay, his wife, Jim Messina and Eric Clapton. They all face charges of "being at a place where it is suspected marijuana is being used", and are bailed after 12 hours in police custody.

Young (1988): "I used a few drugs. I smoked a lot of grass in the Sixties, continued to smoke grass into the Seventies and dabbled around in other drugs. But I never got hooked... never got out of hand with the harder drugs I experimented with, but I think I'm basically a survivor."

David Crosby, Stephen Stills and Graham Nash were refugees from top Sixties bands, who combined at the end of 1968 to form "a group that isn't a group".

26 MARCH 1968

The initial court hearing in the drug-use case. The proceedings are adjourned until the end of May, though police warn that, if they're found guilty, the defendants face a $500 fine and a six-month jail sentence.

APRIL 1968

The American magazine *Teen Set* runs the first major feature story on Young – ironically coinciding with his final weeks in the Springfield.

Young: "Our problems have hurt us, no doubt about that. I can't even say how much, no-one will know for another year, but we've never hidden our problems from anyone. We've always been pretty honest about how mixed up we were."

MAY 1968

Two further Buffalo Springfield songs are completed around the time of their split, 'On The Way Home' and 'It's So Hard To Wait'.

Another teenage magazine, *Song Hits*, follows *Teen Set*'s lead and publishes a feature on Young.

5 MAY 1968

Final Buffalo Springfield gig, at the Long Beach Arena, Long Beach, California.

29 MAY 1968

A planned six-night season of Buffalo Springfield gigs at the Fillmore West in San Francisco has to be cancelled after the group refuse Bill Graham's pleas that they re-form.

LATE MAY 1968

The charges against Young from the Topanga Canyon incident in March are reduced to "disturbing the peace", an offence for which he is found guilty, and receives a small fine.

Elliott Roberts succeeds in negotiating a solo deal for Young with Reprise Records, and Neil uses the advance as down-payment on a house in Topanga Canyon.

MID-1968

Neil Young supplies music for the Hal Bartlett movie, *Changes*, alongside tracks by Judy Collins, Tim Buckley and Kim Weston.

JUNE 1968

Young begins work on his first solo album, with the help of Jack Nitzsche. One track in particular, 'The Old Laughing Lady', requires "months of recording" to complete.

AUGUST 1968

The third and final Buffalo Springfield album, 'Last Time Around', is released.

23 AUGUST 1968

Recording of 'The Emperor Of Wyoming' completed.

24 AUGUST 1968

'The Loner' is given its final mix.

28 SEPTEMBER 1968

Young finishes recording 'What Did You Do To My Life'.

30 SEPTEMBER 1968

'Birds' and Young's first recording of 'Everybody Knows This Is Nowhere' are completed.

1 OCTOBER 1968

Young records the lengthy surrealistic acoustic cut, 'The Last Trip To Tulsa'.

2 OCTOBER 1968

'Here We Are In The Years' is completed.

7 OCTOBER 1968

Recording of 'If I Could Have Her Tonight' finishes.

9 OCTOBER 1968

'I've Been Waiting For You' is completed and mixed.

17 OCTOBER 1968

Final work on 'The Old Laughing Lady', 'I've Loved Her So Long' and 'String Quartet From Whiskey Boot Hill' completes the recording sessions for Young's first solo album.

23 – 28 OCTOBER 1968

The Bottom Line, New York, sharing the bill with Joni Mitchell.

29 OCTOBER – 4 NOVEMBER 1968

The Bottom Line, New York, solo.

9 NOVEMBER 1968

'Sugar Mountain' is recorded live in concert by Reprise during a show at the Canterbury House, Ann Arbor, Michigan.

12 NOVEMBER 1968

Young's début album, 'Neil Young', is released in the States. Both the cover design and album mix are subsequently altered from this original version. Reprise are sufficiently unaware of their new artist to spell his name 'Neal Young' on the special promotional records sent to radio stations.

DECEMBER 1968

Release date of Young's first solo single, 'The Loner'/'Sugar Mountain'.

1 DECEMBER 1968

Neil Young marries Susan Acevedo in Topanga Canyon, California; the couple set up home with Susan's seven-year-old daughter, Tia.

RIVERBOAT
COFFEE HOUSE
134 YORKVILLE AVE. 922-6216
EVERY NIGHT

Maurey Haydn

BUDDY GUY
JAN. 14–26   CHICAGO BLUES BAND

MIKE SEEGER
JAN. 28–FEB. 2

NEIL YOUNG
FEB. 4–9   THE BUFFALO SPRINGFIELD

DOC WATSON
FEB. 11–16

JOHN HAMMOND
FEB. 18–23

SPIDER JOHN KOERNER
FEB. 25 – MARCH 2

JERRY JEFF WALKER
MARCH 4 – 9

Lenny Breau
MARCH 11–16

GORDON LIGHTFOOT
MARCH 29, 30, 31

Young begins 1969 as an obscure solo folkie; he ends it as a member of the most prestigious American rock band of the age. Capitalising on the moment, as he has throughout his career, Young uses the publicity he gains from joining Crosby, Stills, Nash and Young as a platform for his solo career. While his three new colleagues pledge to place CSNY before all other considerations, Young never forgets that he had another musical option.

After the personal antagonism that helped split Buffalo Springfield, Young isn't Stephen Stills' first choice when Crosby, Stills and Nash need back-up musicians for their début tour. In fact, Stills has to be persuaded by Atlantic's Ahmet Ertegun to approach Young, after he has been turned down by both Steve Winwood and Mark Naftalin. He rationalises the decision by hiring Young as a keyboardist and guitarist; Young insists, in fact, that it took a month for CSN to agree to give him co-billing. As the initial press coverage confirms, Young is joining as very much the junior partner.

CSNY's initial burst of activity – once they've hired and then fired Young's friend, Bruce Palmer, and then played their first live shows in August 1969 – catches the band at their peak. Their second gig is at Woodstock, where their tightrope-walking harmonies and all-for-one spirit epitomise what is seen as the central vibe of the festival. As ever, Young's involvement in the hippie dream is only tentative: CSNY don't appear in the movie as a quartet because Young refuses to be filmed. His spirit, and that of the age, are always separated by a wall of irony.

If CSNY's prestige entails that his name will always be linked with theirs, another liaison forged in 1969 proves to be more durable. Early in the year, he begins to work with members of the California band, The Rockets. He renames them Crazy Horse, and utilises their no-frills musical fundamentalism to the full on the sparse, compelling 'Everybody Knows This Is Nowhere' album. Crazy Horse rarely sparkle, and they sing even more out of tune than CSNY are sometimes apt to manage on stage; but their simplicity echoes Young's own preferences.

'Everybody Knows This Is Nowhere' only starts to sell after CSNY go out on the road; then Crazy Horse are sidelined while CSNY began work on 'Déjà Vu'. Those tortuous sessions are fractured by personal traumas: David Crosby's girlfriend is killed, while the others' relationships (including Young's marriage) are also foundering. The album is effectively complete by Christmas, however, and the quartet approach the New Year with optimism, little realising that their most unified and creative months are already behind them.

MID-JANUARY 1969
Young plays a week of acoustic shows at the Bitter End, New York.

28 JANUARY – 3 FEBRUARY 1969
Le Hibou, Ottawa, Canada. Among the songs Young performs at these shows are 'The Loner', 'Down By The River' and 'Cowgirl In The Sand', all played acoustic.

4 – 9 FEBRUARY 1969
Young's solo residency at The Riverboat, Yorkville, Toronto, Canada.

LATE FEBRUARY 1969
Young jams with a band called The Rockets during several shows at the Whisky-A-Go-Go in Los Angeles.

Billy Talbot of The Rockets: "He asked if he could come and sit in. We said 'sure'. But we first met Neil when he came to LA, working on the first Buffalo Springfield album. After that, we used to see him on and off. He came around while the Springfield were breaking up and jammed at our house."

Atlantic issue 'Retrospective', a compilation of material by Buffalo Springfield.

MARCH 1969
Reprise briefly issue the original version of

Young's week-long residency at the Riverboat in Yorkville facilitated a reunion with his proud father, Scott.

Buffalo Springfield wasn't the only band with bassist problems. Crosby, Stills, Nash and Young had a steady drummer in 1969, Dallas Taylor (top right), but a brief experiment with Bruce Palmer on bass didn't work out.

'Everybody Knows This Is Nowhere' as a single in the States – its only official release.

MID-MARCH 1969
Young invites The Rockets to record with him: three of the band, guitarist Danny Whitten, bassist Billy Talbot and drummer Ralph Molina, agree to his request. Young writes three songs while suffering from flu – 'Cinnamon Girl', 'Cowgirl In The Sand' and 'Down By The River' – and fixes up a recording session with the trio, whom he dubs Crazy Horse.

20 MARCH 1969
In his first session with Crazy Horse, Young records 'Cinnamon Girl'.

21 MARCH 1969
'Cowgirl In The Sand' is recorded, virtually live-in-the-studio.

24 MARCH 1969
'Running Dry', 'Everybody Knows This Is Nowhere' (version 2) and 'Round And Round' are all recorded with Crazy Horse.

26 MARCH 1969
Crazy Horse assist in the recording of the country tune, 'The Losing End'.

29 MARCH 1969
Young and Crazy Horse cut 'Down By The River', the centrepiece of his second solo album.

EARLY APRIL 1969
Young plays a week of concerts at the Whiskey-A-Go-Go in Los Angeles, accompanied by Crazy Horse. Ex-Buffalo Springfield colleague Stephen Stills attends several of the shows.
David Crosby, Graham Nash and Stephen Stills – alias Crosby, Stills and Nash (or CSN) – consider augmenting the trio-plus-drummer format of their début album for a possible American tour in the summer.

MAY 1969
Young is spotted on several occasions in night-clubs on Sunset Boulevard, accompanied by Stephen Stills. Atlantic's Ahmet Ertegun suggests to Stills that Young might be an ideal support member for CSN on tour. The trio subsequently approach Young with a tentative offer; he refuses, until CSN agree that his name will be added to the title of the group – who become Crosby, Stills, Nash and Young (alias CSNY). The quartet becomes a six-piece with the addition of drummer Dallas Taylor and bassist Bruce Palmer, another former member of The Buffalo Springfield.
Neil Young: "Playing with Stephen is

special. David is an excellent rhythm guitarist and Graham sings so great... I knew it would be fun. I didn't have to be out front. I didn't have to be me all the time."
'Everybody Knows This Is Nowhere' is released in the States.

6 MAY 1969
Buffalo Springfield's recording of Young's 'Down To The Wire' is belatedly mixed and delivered to the Atlantic Records tape vault.

JUNE 1969
Reprise issue an edited version of Young's 'Down By The River' as a US single.

11 JUNE 1969
At the first full CSNY recording session, the band work on a song written by Terry Reid, 'Horses Through A Rainstorm' (eventually issued as 'Man With No Expression'). They also rehearse a new arrangement for 'Helplessly Hoping', and jam with drummer Buddy Miles.

15 JUNE 1969
At Sunwest Studios in Los Angeles, CSNY record the 'remake' of 'Helplessly Hoping' issued 22 years later on the 'CSN' boxed set.

17 JUNE 1969
CSNY start to record a new Stephen Stills song, 'Bluebird Revisited' at Wally Heider's studio in San Francisco. During the sessions, they also jam on two Four Tops hits, '(It's The) Same Old Song' and 'Reach Out, I'll Be There', besides starting work on Stills' 'So Begins The Task' and two unknown numbers, listed on the session boxes as 'Far On' and 'Boat Song'.

26 JUNE 1969
Another CSNY session, with three Stills songs on the agenda – 'Go Back Home', 'Change Partners' and 'Sugar Babe'. The group also attempt The Beatles' 'Blackbird', which CSN had previously recorded without Young for their début album.

16 JULY 1969
Stephen Stills records '4+20' for CSNY's album.

19 JULY 1969
CSNY regroup at Wally Heider's studio to record 'Everyday We Live' and a new Young song, 'When You Dance I Can Really Love'. Neither recording is completed or released.

25 JULY 1969
CSNY are scheduled to play their first live shows, at the Fillmore East in New York, but the concerts are postponed when Graham Nash is diagnosed as suffering from nodules

on his throat, and is advised not to sing for two weeks.

1 AUGUST 1969
CSN are billed to appear at the Atlantic City Pop Festival, billed beneath Iron Butterfly and Johnny Winter, but cancel the gig.

2 AUGUST 1969
Young records 'Oh Lonesome Me' with Crazy Horse, at the start of a run of sessions for his third solo album – scheduled at this point to be a mix of live and studio recordings.
Bruce Palmer is sacked by CSNY, and replaced by Greg Reeves. "We tried to work it out with Bruce," says David Crosby, "but he's into Indian or neo-Indian music." Crosby also comments on press speculation about possible tensions between Young and Stills: "Only rarely do Neil and Stephen play guitar together, and when they do, it's interlocking parts. They're not at war at all."

3 AUGUST 1969
The Crazy Horse sessions continue as Young records the country ballad, 'Wondering'.

4 AUGUST 1969
Two versions of 'I Believe In You' are recorded.

7 AUGUST 1969
Young tapes an experimental version of 'Birds' with Crazy Horse, but the recording isn't completed.

10 AUGUST 1969
'Everybody's Alone' completes an erratic week of sessions with Crazy Horse.

11-15 AUGUST 1969
CSNY rehearse at Stephen Stills' house in Studio City, Los Angeles.

16 AUGUST 1969
The first CSNY show finally takes place, at the Chicago Auditorium, Chicago, Illinois. Joni Mitchell is the support act.

17 AUGUST 1969
CSNY fly by private jet and then helicopter to Max Yasgur's farm in White Lake, New York – site of the three-day Woodstock festival. Young and Jimi Hendrix commandeer a pick-up truck for an unofficial tour of the festival site.

18 AUGUST 1969
At 3am, CSN – joined after a few songs by Young – take the stage at Woodstock. Their set is later greeted by the press as the highlight of the festival, but no CSNY performances are included in the film of the event: Young refuses to allow the cameras on

CSNY rehearse for their first live show at the Chicago Auditorium.

stage while he is playing. Among the highlights of the CSNY set are a lengthy jam on 'Down By The River', a rowdy but enthusiastic performance of Young's 'Sea Of Madness', which ends up on the 'Woodstock' soundtrack LP, and a rare Stills/Young acoustic version of 'Mr Soul'.

20-25 AUGUST 1969
CSNY play six nights of shows at The Greek Theater, Los Angeles, California. The season is briefly cancelled after Graham Nash is diagnosed as still suffering from nodules on his vocal cords, then scheduled once again against medical advice. Joni Mitchell is the support act. Young performs 'I've Loved Her So Long' at these shows.
On August 25, they perform an astonishing version of 'Down By The River', captured alongside several other Young tracks on the 'Old Country Road' bootleg.
David Crosby: "I preferred our version of that song. I didn't like Crazy Horse. I thought they were dull."

SEPTEMBER 1969
CSNY record *The Tom Jones Show* and *The Music Scene*, both for ABC TV.

2 SEPTEMBER 1969
CSNY return to the studio and 'Horses Through A Rainstorm'. Neil Young leads the band through two songs, 'Sea Of Madness' and 'Birds'.

3 SEPTEMBER 1969
CSNY record rough versions of Young's 'Sea Of Madness' and Graham Nash's 'Our

House' at Wally Heider's studio in San Francisco, besides rehearsing several songs for future live performances.

6 SEPTEMBER 1969
Plans for CSNY to play their début UK performance at a free concert in London's Hyde Park are aborted.

13/14 SEPTEMBER 1969
CSNY turn down a lucrative offer to appear on the TV show *Hollywood Palace,* and instead choose to perform at the Big Sur folk festival – closing the proceedings on both nights, before a group of around 12,000 people at Esalen Institute, California. Part of their Sunday set – including electric performances of Young's 'Sea Of Madness' and 'Down By The River' – are captured in the *Celebration At Big Sur* movie, which remains the finest visual record of CSNY's career.
   Young also performs 'Birds' during the acoustic set, while the second, electric set also features 'Pre-Road Downs', 'Long Time Gone', 'Bluebird Revisited' and 'Wooden Ships'. Bootlegs: 'Big Sur Folk Festival'/ 'Old Cop'.

15/16 SEPTEMBER 1969
CSNY play two nights at the Winterland Ballroom, San Francisco.

19-21 SEPTEMBER 1969
CSNY play three nights at the Fillmore East, New York. On the final night, Stephen Stills elects to impress the audience (which includes Bob Dylan) with an elongated solo acoustic set, immediately before the intermission. CSNY argue for 45 minutes backstage, before returning to deliver one of their finest electric sets.

30 SEPTEMBER 1969
David Crosby's girlfriend, Christine Hinton, is killed in a car accident north of San Francisco.

2 OCTOBER 1969
Planned first night of a four-night stay at the Fillmore West, San Francisco, aborted because of the death of Christine Hinton.

EARLY OCTOBER 1969
The band's first album as a quartet is reported to be ready for release in December, under the title 'Crosby, Stills, Nash And Young'.

9 OCTOBER 1969
Young returns to Crazy Horse for one unsatisfactory session, taping Danny Whitten's 'Look At All The Things' and his own 'Helpless'.

14 OCTOBER 1969
'Woodstock' dominates the CSNY sessions for the day, though the group also attempt

Crosby's 'Song With No Words', Nash's 'Right Between The Eyes', Young's 'Round And Round', and three more mysterious titles: 'Cologne', 'He Died For Mary' and 'When You Were Asleep'.

MID-OCTOBER 1969
Reprise reissue Young's début album, highlighting his links with CSNY with an advertising campaign that uses the slogan "——, ——, —— & Young".
   The revamped album retains the title 'Neil Young', despite earlier plans to rename it 'Neil Young's First Album Again'; it brings Young's vocals and guitar further forward in the mix.

20 OCTOBER 1969
'20 Dollar Fine' is the subject of today's CSNY recording work.

23 OCTOBER 1969
CSNY work on 'Teach Your Children' and a backing track for Young's 'Helpless'. Young: "I had to play 'Helpless' with them until about four o'clock in the morning, doing it over and over and over again, to get everybody tired enough so that they would stop doing this extra stuff where everyone was playing too much. Finally we got one where they were half asleep and they didn't know they were doing it."

24 OCTOBER 1969
Two Stephen Stills songs, 'Sugar Babe' and 'So Begins The Task', are attempted during the day's CSNY sessions, plus David Crosby's 'Laughing' and 'Almost Cut My Hair' and Neil Young's 'Everybody's Alone'.

25 OCTOBER 1969
CSNY appear on *The Tom Jones Show*, performing 'You Don't Have To Cry' and (with their host) 'Long Time Gone'.

27 OCTOBER 1969
CSNY return to '20 Dollar Fine', and also work on 'Woodstock' and 'Our House'.

30 OCTOBER 1969
A lengthy CSNY session produces working versions of Stills' 'Questions' (shortly to evolve into 'Carry On'), two Crosby songs, 'Déjà Vu' and 'Almost Cut My Hair', and the mysterious 'You're Wrong Baby'.

1 NOVEMBER 1969
CSNY cut a basic version of 'Teach Your Children'.

3 NOVEMBER 1969
David Crosby's 'Déjà Vu' is the main focus of the day's CSNY recording session at Wally Heider's, while his 'Almost Cut My Hair' is also reprised.

Crosby, S

Nash & Young

5 NOVEMBER 1969
Work continues on Graham Nash's 'Our House' and Neil Young's 'Country Girl'. CSNY also perform 'Woodstock', mixed later that day and included in the 1991 boxed set 'CSN'.

'Woodstock' was recorded live by the full band, but Stills subsequently overdubbed a new vocal for the 'Déjà Vu' album version, to Young's displeasure: "The track was magic. Then they were in the studio nitpicking. Sure enough, Stephen erased the vocal and put another one on that wasn't nearly as good."

6 NOVEMBER 1969
More sessions at Wally Heider's, producing recordings of 'Blackbird' and 'Sugar Babe', followed by overdubs on 'Questions', 'Almost Cut My Hair', 'Our House' and Stills' 'Black Queen'. Later, Young works on 'Country Girl' and 'Helpless'.

7 NOVEMBER 1969
An untitled jam and a working version of Stephen Stills' 'Change Partners' emerge from CSNY's latest session. The group also have a second shot at Stills' 'Sugar Babe', revive '20 Dollar Fine' and 'Woodstock', and experiment briefly with The Beatles' 'You've Got To Hide Your Love Away'. Other unissued songs, like 'Master My Fear', 'She Can't Handle It' and 'Whole People', are also attempted during the session. The final harmonies for 'Helpless' are laid down, completing the track. Finally, the group begin work on 'Everybody I Love You', a Stills/Young co-composition.

c 10 NOVEMBER 1969
Young performs at the Civic Auditorium, Santa Monica, California, with Crazy Horse.

12 NOVEMBER 1969
CSNY return to The Beatles' 'Blackbird' and attempt a new Crosby composition, 'Sea Song'. The release date for their now untitled album is pushed back to February 1970.

13 – 16 NOVEMBER 1969
CSNY: Winterland, San Francisco, California, supported by Cold Blood, Joy Of Cooking and Lamb. On the 15th Crosby loses his voice early in the show and Stills comments: "We were bored out there tonight."

17 NOVEMBER 1969
Crosby's title track for the 'Déjà Vu' album is completed at Wally Heider's.

DECEMBER 1969
CSNY's 'Carry On' is submitted to Atlantic as a possible single, but the group ultimately reject the track.

2 DECEMBER 1969
Stephen Stills records '4+20' for CSNY's 'Déjà Vu' album, while the band also attempt 'Everyday We Live'.

6 DECEMBER 1969
CSNY: Altamont Speedway, on the bill of The Rolling Stones' infamous free concert; then Pauley Pavilion, UCLA, Los Angeles, California, supported by Taj Mahal. Part of the Pauley Pavilion show is captured on the first CSNY bootleg LP, 'Wooden Nickel'.

Stephen Stills: "David and I pushed for us to do Altamont. But I sensed real danger the minute we got there. I was literally flinching on stage. When we finished our set, I started barking orders. We cleared the area in ninety seconds flat." During The Rolling Stones' closing set, Hells Angels stab to death audience member Meredith Hunter, who seemed to have pulled a gun close to the stage. The day's eerie events are captured in the movie, *Gimme Shelter*.

9 DECEMBER 1969
CSNY: University of California, Santa Barbara, California, supported by Sweetwater and Steve Miller. In an attempt to simulate democracy, the group are billed for their December shows as 'Crosby, Stills, Nash & Young with Taylor & Reeves'.

14 DECEMBER 1969
CSNY: Cobo Hall, Detroit, Michigan. Young performs a solo acoustic version of 'Country Girl', plus 'Helpless' and the expected 'Down By The River'. Bootleg: "Live In Detroit".

21 DECEMBER 1969
CSNY: Balboa Stadium, San Diego, California.

22 DECEMBER 1969
Stills and the rest of CSNY have a final attempt at recording 'So Begins The Task'.

28 DECEMBER 1969
CSNY complete recording work on Terry Reid's 'Horses Through A Rainstorm', issued in 1991 on the 'CSN' boxed set, and 'Carry On' – though Young does not contribute to the later track. The group also cut a backing track for David Crosby's 'The Lee Shore', vocal overdubs for which are finally added (without Young) in August 1991.

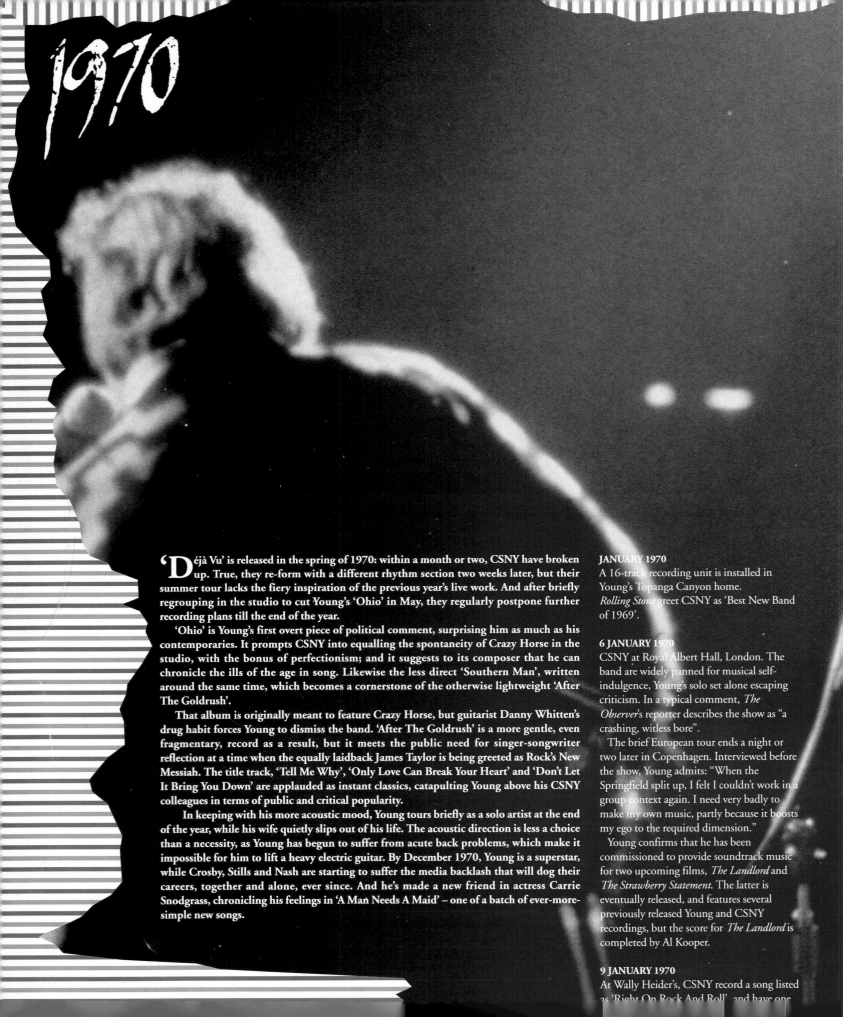

1970

'Déjà Vu' is released in the spring of 1970: within a month or two, CSNY have broken up. True, they re-form with a different rhythm section two weeks later, but their summer tour lacks the fiery inspiration of the previous year's live work. And after briefly regrouping in the studio to cut Young's 'Ohio' in May, they regularly postpone further recording plans till the end of the year.

'Ohio' is Young's first overt piece of political comment, surprising him as much as his contemporaries. It prompts CSNY into equalling the spontaneity of Crazy Horse in the studio, with the bonus of perfectionism; and it suggests to its composer that he can chronicle the ills of the age in song. Likewise the less direct 'Southern Man', written around the same time, which becomes a cornerstone of the otherwise lightweight 'After The Goldrush'.

That album is originally meant to feature Crazy Horse, but guitarist Danny Whitten's drug habit forces Young to dismiss the band. 'After The Goldrush' is a more gentle, even fragmentary, record as a result, but it meets the public need for singer-songwriter reflection at a time when the equally laidback James Taylor is being greeted as Rock's New Messiah. The title track, 'Tell Me Why', 'Only Love Can Break Your Heart' and 'Don't Let It Bring You Down' are applauded as instant classics, catapulting Young above his CSNY colleagues in terms of public and critical popularity.

In keeping with his more acoustic mood, Young tours briefly as a solo artist at the end of the year, while his wife quietly slips out of his life. The acoustic direction is less a choice than a necessity, as Young has begun to suffer from acute back problems, which make it impossible for him to lift a heavy electric guitar. By December 1970, Young is a superstar, while Crosby, Stills and Nash are starting to suffer the media backlash that will dog their careers, together and alone, ever since. And he's made a new friend in actress Carrie Snodgrass, chronicling his feelings in 'A Man Needs A Maid' – one of a batch of ever-more-simple new songs.

JANUARY 1970
A 16-track recording unit is installed in Young's Topanga Canyon home. *Rolling Stone* greet CSNY as 'Best New Band of 1969'.

6 JANUARY 1970
CSNY at Royal Albert Hall, London. The band are widely panned for musical self-indulgence, Young's solo set alone escaping criticism. In a typical comment, *The Observer*'s reporter describes the show as "a crashing, witless bore".

The brief European tour ends a night or two later in Copenhagen. Interviewed before the show, Young admits: "When the Springfield split up, I felt I couldn't work in a group context again. I need very badly to make my own music, partly because it boosts my ego to the required dimension."

Young confirms that he has been commissioned to provide soundtrack music for two upcoming films, *The Landlord* and *The Strawberry Statement*. The latter is eventually released, and features several previously released Young and CSNY recordings, but the score for *The Landlord* is completed by Al Kooper.

9 JANUARY 1970
At Wally Heider's, CSNY record a song listed as 'Right On Rock And Roll', and have one

final attempt at Stills' 'So Begins The Task'. They also tape the live-in-the-studio version of 'Almost Cut My Hair' included on the 'Déjà Vu' album, and in its unedited form on the 'CSN' boxed set.

19 JANUARY 1970
The final mix of the 'Déjà Vu' album is prepared at Wally Heider's Studio in San Francisco.

19 FEBRUARY 1970
Young & Crazy Horse film at KQED TV.

24 FEBRUARY 1970
Public Auditorium, Cleveland, Ohio.

25 FEBRUARY 1970
Ludlow's Garage, Cincinnati, Ohio: solo acoustic set ('On The Way Home', 'Broken Arrow', 'I Am A Child', 'Helpless', 'Dance Dance Dance', 'Sugar Mountain', 'Don't Let It Bring You Down' and 'The Old Laughing Lady') plus electric set with Crazy Horse ('The Loner', 'Everybody Knows This Is Nowhere', 'Winterlong', 'C'mon Baby Let's Go Downtown', 'Wonderin'', 'It Might Have Been', 'Down By The River' and 'Cinnamon Girl'). Bootlegs: 'Acoustic Token'/'Electric Prayers'/'Collectors' Item'/'Neil Young & Crazy Horse'/ 'Winterlong'/'Young'n'Old'.

28 FEBRUARY 1970
Electric Factory, Philadelphia, Pennsylvania. Young performs a rare version of 'Flying On The Ground Is Wrong'.

1 MARCH 1970
Boston Tea Party, Boston, Massachusetts.

2 MARCH 1970
Young is interviewed for his first major solo piece in *Rolling Stone*.

6 MARCH 1970
Fillmore East, New York, New York (2 shows). All four Fillmore East shows, with very similar set-lists to the Cincinnati show in February, are recorded by Reprise for a possible live album. The performance of 'C'mon Baby Let's Go Downtown' from the 7 March shows eventually appears on 'Tonight's The Night'. Bootlegs: 'Everybody Knows'/'Fillmore East'/'Blankness'/'Sunset Cowboy'.
    Young is supported at the Fillmore East by Miles Davis and The Steve Miller Blues Band. "Neil Young was exquisite," gushes one reviewer. "He made me want to redefine soul music."

7 MARCH 1970
Fillmore East, New York, New York (2 shows). Bootlegs: 'Fillmore East'/'Blankness'.

13 MARCH 1970
Contra Costa Junior College, Contra Costa (with Crazy Horse). 'The Loner' has shifted from the electric to the acoustic set, but otherwise Young's March shows duplicate the Cincinnati line-up in February.

14 MARCH 1970
Contra Costa Junior College, Contra Costa (with Crazy Horse).

21 MARCH 1970
Young completes work on a batch of songs recorded over the previous few weeks: 'Only Love Can Break Your Heart', 'Winterlong', 'Come On Baby, Let's Go Downtown' (a live recording with Crazy Horse), 'After The Goldrush', 'Till The Morning Comes', 'Tell Me Why', 'Don't Let It Bring You Down' and 'Southern Man'.
    Young: "'Southern Man' was recorded downstairs at my house in Topanga Canyon. That whole record has a kind of home recording quality to it."

28 MARCH 1970
Civic Auditorium, Santa Monica, California. First known live performance of 'Everybody's Alone', while 'Birds' and 'I Believe In You' act as a taster for Young's next album.

APRIL 1970
In an interview with radio station KSAN-FM, Young reveals: "I'm not working with Crazy Horse any more. I've got a new group behind me. You know, I just go through different bags." And he confirms that his decision – sparked by guitarist Danny Whitten's increasing heroin use – means the scrapping of a planned Young/Crazy Horse LP, leaving their recording of Don Gibson's 'Oh Lonesome Me' as the sole completed track for the project.

The first *Rolling Stone* Neil Young interview is published.

'Wooden Nickel' becomes the first bootleg CSNY LP. "It's a burn on everybody," says the ever-radical David Crosby.

14 APRIL 1970
Stephen Stills breaks his wrist in a Laurel Canyon car accident, forcing CSNY's upcoming US tour to be delayed for a week, from 5 to 12 May.

30 APRIL 1970
CSNY regroup to rehearse for their upcoming tour.

MAY 1970
Young mixes the live take of 'C'mon Baby Let's Go Downtown', but elects not to include it on his forthcoming album.

3 MAY 1970
Young adds the song fragment 'Crippled Creek Ferry' to the running order of his third solo album.

4 MAY 1970
Four students are killed and eleven injured on the campus of Kent State University, Kent, Ohio, by National Guardsmen. The incident follows a student protest against the escalation of the conflict in South-East Asia.

10 MAY 1970
Stephen Stills tears a knee ligament and is forced to wear a cast for the next fortnight.

11 MAY 1970
CSNY bassist Greg Reeves is sacked for daring to suggest he be allowed to perform his own songs on stage. Fuzzy Samuels takes his place, just 24 hours before the first show.

12 MAY 1970
CSNY begin their tour a week late in Denver, Colorado. Much of the tour is filmed, for a proposed documentary, which (says Elliott Roberts) captures "all the shit that came down with the individual cats".

The Denver show is a disaster: Fuzzy Samuels folds under the pressure of performing with the band at such short notice; Crosby and Nash both suffer vocal problems from rehearsing too strenuously; and the remainder of the band resent Stills using the walking stick he adopts for the performance as a conductor's baton, as if they were merely his supporting cast.

14 MAY 1970
CSNY are scheduled to play the Chicago Auditorium, but before the show the band argue violently about their chaotic performance in Denver, and split up. Graham Nash: "We broke up in Chicago. We couldn't relate to each other on a rational level. So we all flew home."

15 MAY 1970
Tempers assuaged after their flight home from Chicago, CSNY briefly regroup in Los Angeles – long enough to fire drummer Dallas Taylor – before Young and Crosby travel on to Pescadero for a week's vacation.

19 MAY 1970
Fired by magazine reports on the Kent State shootings, Young writes his 'protest' song, 'Ohio'. David Crosby contacts Stills and Nash to organise an immediate recording session.

20 MAY 1970
The *Woodstock* movie is premièred in London; the soundtrack album, featuring CSNY's 'Sea Of Madness' and 'Wooden Ships', is also released this week.
Young and Crosby return to Los Angeles.

21 MAY 1970
CSNY record and mix 'Ohio' and 'Find The Cost Of Freedom' in Los Angeles, for immediate release; the tapes are delivered to Atlantic in New York that night. Young's explanation for the song: "I don't know, man. I never wrote anything like this before. But there it is..."

24 MAY 1970
Local students organise a boycott of CSNY's planned show at the Metro Sports Center, St. Paul, Minnesota, as a protest against the extortionate ticket prices – $10 is being charged for the best seats. CSNY and their management disclaim responsibility, and say they'll attempt to have the prices dropped. In the event, the show is cancelled.

29 MAY 1970
CSNY: Boston. The first night of the revamped tour schedule, with Fuzzy Samuels and ex-Turtles drummer Johnny Barbata completing the band. Before the show, CSNY assure the press that they'll be starting work on their second album in September.

30 MAY 1970
CSNY: Civic Center, Baltimore.

JUNE 1970
In an interview in which he also reveals that CSN re-recorded their 'live' vocals for the *Woodstock* movie, Robbie Robertson of The Band is reported as singling out Neil Young as CSNY's sole redeeming factor, and claiming: "Young is out looking for a job. He asked me if I ever leave The Band to recommend him for the job." Robertson later retracts his comments.

2 JUNE 1970
The opening night of CSNY's week-long stay at the Fillmore East in New York is taped by Atlantic – as is the entire run of New York shows. Young joins Crosby, Stills and Nash on acoustic renditions of 'On The Way Home', 'Teach Your Children' and 'Tell Me Why', before offering a solo set which includes 'Birds' (marked on the tape box as 'Neil's Song') and 'Only Love Can Break Your Heart'. The entire band then play an electric set of 'Pre-Road Downs', 'Long Time Gone', 'Helplessly Hoping', 'Ohio', 'As I Come Of Age', 'Southern Man' and 'Carry On', plus encores of 'Find The Cost Of Freedom' and 'Woodstock'.

Interviewed prior to the first show, Young admits that he is becoming scared of performing in the USA, because of the volatile political situation. Meanwhile, an Atlantic Records source suggests that CSNY will record their second studio album immediately after their June tour.

3 JUNE 1970
CSNY's second night at Fillmore East, with Young replacing 'Birds' with 'Down By The River' in his solo set. Bootlegs: 'America's Children'/'Long Time Gone'/'Live At Fillmore East'.

4 JUNE 1970
'Ohio'/'Find The Cost Of Freedom' is released as CSNY's new single. At the third CSNY show at Fillmore East, Young retains 'Down By The River', while 'Woodstock' is dropped from the encore.

5 JUNE 1970
'Find The Cost Of Freedom', 'Southern Man' and 'Ohio'. 'Down By The River' is augmented in a medley with 'Cinnamon Girl' in Young's Fillmore East solo set, while 'Woodstock' also returns to the repertoire.

6 JUNE 1970
Fifth night at Fillmore East, with the Atlantic tape machines still rolling: Young's acoustic set consists of the medley, with 'The Loner' added to 'Cinnamon Girl' and 'Down By The River'. Bootleg: 'On The Right Track'.

7 JUNE 1970
Last night at the Fillmore East, where Young performs 'Don't Let It Bring You Down', and then repeats the previous night's acoustic medley.

9 JUNE 1970
CSNY: Providence, Rhode Island.

MID-JUNE 1970
CSNY are forced to cancel several shows because Graham Nash is suffering from a throat complaint.

16 JUNE 1970
CSNY: Memorial Coliseum, Portland, Oregon.

19 JUNE 1970
CSNY: Oakland Coliseum, Oakland, California.

26 JUNE 1970
CSNY: The Forum, Los Angeles, California. Young performs 'On The Way Home', 'Tell Me Why', 'Don't Let It Bring You Down', 'Southern Man' and 'Ohio'. Bootlegs: 'The All American Phonograph Record Album'/'Live At The Los Angeles Forum'/'Live At L.A. Forum'/'Best Of CSNY Live In Concert'/'American Dreamland'/'Neil Young In Concert'.

27 JUNE 1970
CSNY: The Forum, Los Angeles, California.

28 JUNE 1970
CSNY: The Forum, Los Angeles, California. Young performs his acoustic medley of 'The Loner', 'Cinnamon Girl' and 'Down By The River'. Bootlegs: 'Memorial'/'Long Time Gone'/'Red Woods'/'Everybody Knows'.

JULY 1970
Jack Nitzsche signs Crazy Horse and Nils Lofgren to his new record label, North Star.

4/5 JULY 1970
CSNY: Auditorium Theater, Chicago, Illinois. Both the Chicago shows are taped on the instructions of the band, who have "good vibes in advance" about the quality of these concerts. Their hopes are mostly fulfilled, and plans to fill the band's live album with performances solely from the Fillmore East are stalled.

9 JULY 1970
The last official CSNY show for four years, in Minneapolis, Minnesota.

31 JULY 1970
'Ohio' is released in Britain; meanwhile, several American radio stations have banned it from airplay, because of its anti-Government message.

5 AUGUST 1970
'When You Dance I Can Really Love' and 'Birds' are the final tracks to be completed for 'After The Goldrush'.

6 AUGUST 1970
David Crosby, Graham Nash and Neil Young record 'Music Is Love'. The song is briefly scheduled as a Crosby, Nash and Young single, before finally surfacing on Crosby's first solo album.

mid-AUGUST 1970
Young completes the final overdubbing and mixing of the 'After The Goldrush' album.

20 AUGUST 1970
Young is in the audience for a Little Richard show at the Whisky-A-Go-Go in Hollywood.

29 AUGUST 1970
Young accompanies Joni Mitchell to the Isle Of Wight festival. He plans to make an unannounced solo appearance, but cancels the idea after Mitchell is booed and disturbed by members of the audience leaping on stage during her set. Young leaves the island for London without waiting for Joni to complete her performance – his swift departure is also apparently fuelled by the news that manager Elliott Roberts, driving from London to the Isle of Wight in a Rolls-Royce, has been arrested on drugs charges.

17 SEPTEMBER 1970
Release date of 'The Strawberry Statement' 2-LP soundtrack, featuring 'The Loner' and 'Down By The River' by Neil Young, and 'Our House' and 'Helpless' by CSNY.

OCTOBER 1970
Atlantic Records deny prevalent rumours that CSNY will be returning to London in

December to play at the Lyceum Ballroom. Their next tour, the label explains, won't take place until May 1971.

'After The Goldrush' is released. In *Rolling Stone*, critic Langdon Winner raises a rare sceptical voice: "Neil Young devotees will probably spend the next few weeks trying desperately to convince themselves that 'After The Goldrush' is good music. But they'll be kidding themselves."

2 NOVEMBER 1970
'After The Goldrush' qualifies for a gold record on US sales.

17 NOVEMBER 1970
Young records the piano ballad 'Soldier' at his Topanga Canyon home. Around this time, Young's marriage to Susan Acevedo collapses, and he moves out to the Château Marmont in Hollywood, prior to purchasing a new

home in San Mateo County.

He also begins to suffer from severe back pain after slipping a disc, and is advised by doctors to rest and wear a back brace. His injury prevents him from playing stand-up electric guitar for the next year, restricting him to solo acoustic gigs.

21 NOVEMBER 1970
Neil Young is featured on the front cover of *Melody Maker* for the first time, under the headline: "Neil Young Goldrush Is On". Young was originally booked to perform at the Royal Festival Hall on this date, but the booking was passed to Joni Mitchell, who shares Young's management company. The reason given for the alteration is that Young is in San Francisco, working on an album of entirely solo performances as a follow-up to 'After The Goldrush'.

LATE NOVEMBER 1970
While in Los Angeles to seek medical advice, Young contacts actress Carrie Snodgrass, entranced by her performance in the movie *Diary Of A Mad Housewife.*

30 NOVEMBER 1970
Cellar Door, Washington DC. All three Cellar Door shows are recorded by Reprise.

DECEMBER 1970
Crazy Horse are reported to have completed their first album without Young. One bizarre publicity release from Reprise suggests that "Crazy Horse's Danny Whitten will be the lead vocalist on the next Neil Young album."

1/2 DECEMBER 1970
Cellar Door, Washington DC.

4 DECEMBER 1970
Carnegie Hall, New York. Young's father and brother attend the show – the latter reviewing the performance for *Maclean's* magazine.

5 DECEMBER 1970
Reprise record Young's show at Carnegie Hall, New York. The songs featured include 'Down By The River', 'Cinnamon Girl', 'I Am A Child', 'Expecting To Fly', 'The Loner', 'Helpless', 'Wonderin' ', the first known performance of 'Bad Fog Of Loneliness', 'Southern Man', 'Nowadays Clancy Can't Even Sing', 'On The Way Home', 'Only Love Can Break Your Heart', 'After The Goldrush', 'Flying On The Ground Is Wrong', 'Old Man', 'Don't Let It Bring You Down', 'Cowgirl In The Sand', 'Birds', 'Ohio', 'See The Sky About To Rain' and 'Sugar Mountain'. Bootlegs: 'See What A Fool I've Been'/'The 1970 Carnegie Hall Show'/'Carnegie Hall'/'Citizen Kane Junior Blues' (1 track)/'Love Art Blues' (1 track).

Young: " 'Old Man' was about this guy on my ranch, Louie Avella, who used to drive me around."

7 DECEMBER 1970
Fillmore East, New York.

MID-DECEMBER 1970
Young performs at the Berkeley Community Theater, California; he is then hospitalised in L.A. because of his back problems.

LATE DECEMBER 1970
Melody Maker journalists choose 'After The Goldrush' as the best LP of 1970.

Neil Young

35

Three stages in the fiery relationship between Neil Young and Stephen Stills: Buffalo Springfield in 1967, CSNY in 1970, and the CSNY reunion in 1974.

40

Young with Crazy Horse, the band with whom he's enjoyed an on-off working relationship since 1969: (left to right) Ralph Molina, Billy Talbot, Frank Sampedro and Neil Young.

Neil Young

42

Neil Young

Neil Young

Neil Young

Young with his blues big band, The Blue Notes.

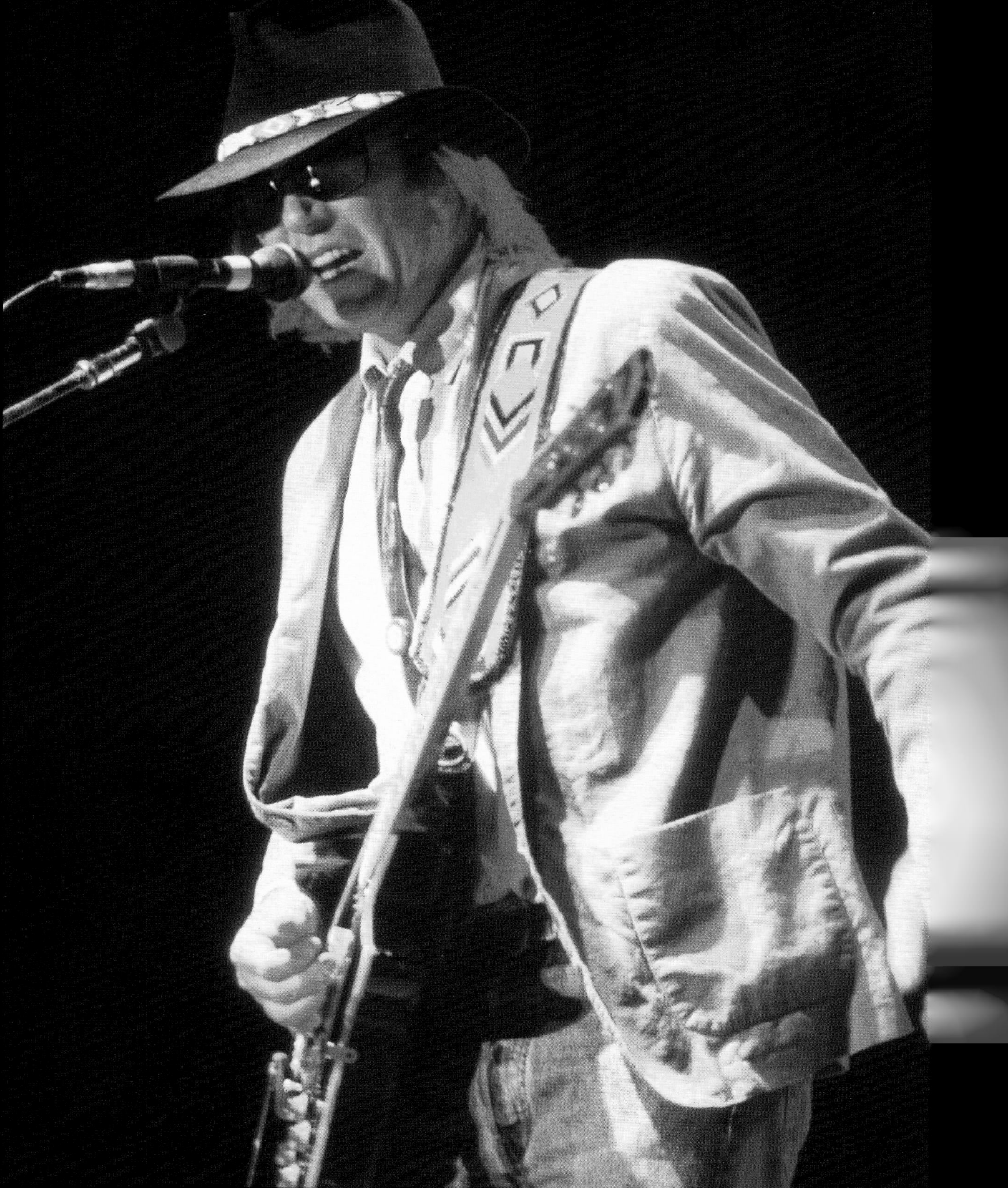

The stunning acoustic shows that Young played in the early weeks of 1971 — in which he previewed most of 'Harvest', and revisited almost his entire back catalogue — ensured that he maintained the momentum he'd generated over the previous year. After filming an eccentric but likeable *In Concert* show for BBC TV, though, he effectively retired from the public eye for the rest of the year.

Sessions in Nashville and then on his California ranch completed work on 'Harvest', another disappointingly low-key album destined to be a million-seller. Plans for a live double-LP, documenting the solo gigs, were scrapped, under the expectation that 'Harvest' would soon be ready for release. But Young's perfectionist attitude towards the album packaging delayed the project into the following year.

Otherwise, 1971 was notable for what didn't happen — like a CSNY reunion, or a return to Crazy Horse, or anything more productive than the back surgery Young underwent in the summer, and the stop-gap release of CSNY's own double in-concert set.

JANUARY 1971
Neil Young is rumoured to have played piano during the recording of Graham Nash's 'I Used To Be A King' at Wally Heider's in San Francisco, taped this month.

6 JANUARY 1971
Neil Young plays his major Canadian concert as a solo artist, when he appears at the Queen Elizabeth Theater, Vancouver. Young débuts several new songs, including 'A Man Needs A Maid', interlocked in a medley with 'Heart Of Gold'.
Young: "I was on the road doing an acoustic tour, and I had many new songs. I got reviews, mentioning that the new songs, 'Old Man', 'Heart Of Gold' and 'A Man Needs A Maid', lacked the depth of the earlier work that I did. They signified that it was the end of my career."

7 JANUARY 1971
Portland, Oregon.

9 JANUARY 1971
Seattle, Washington.

10 JANUARY 1971
University of Oregon, Eugene, Oregon.

12 JANUARY 1971
Edmonton, Canada.

13 JANUARY 1971
Winnipeg, Canada.

14 JANUARY 1971
Guthrie Theater, Minneapolis, Minnesota.

16 JANUARY 1971
Auditorium Theater, Chicago, Illinois (2 shows). First known performance of 'Love In Mind'.

17 JANUARY 1971
Detroit, Michigan.

19 JANUARY 1971
Massey Hall, Toronto, Canada (2 shows).

21 JANUARY 1971
Boston Music Hall, Boston, Massachusetts. Young performs 'There's A World', played at only a handful of live shows.

22 JANUARY 1971
Shakespeare Theater, Stratford, Connecticut. German TV film part of this show for *Swinging With Neil Young*, a 30-minute documentary aired later in the year.

23 JANUARY 1971
Details are released of Young's forthcoming album, which is reported to be a live double-LP. Besides performances of 'Down By The River', 'Wondering' and 'Everybody Knows This Is Nowhere' with Crazy Horse (from a show at the Fillmore East in New York), it is intended to include acoustic versions of the following songs, culled from gigs at the Cellar Door club in Washington and Carnegie Hall in New York: 'I Am A Child', 'Expecting To Fly', 'Flying On The Ground Is Wrong', 'Nowadays Clancy Can't Even Sing', 'Cowgirl In The Sand', 'Ohio', 'Old Man', 'Dance Dance Dance', 'Sugar Mountain', 'See The Sky About To Rain', 'The Needle And The Damage Done' and 'Bad Fog Of Loneliness'. The album is set for release in March: a spokesman adds, "all that has to be completed is some of the mixing, which was delayed by his slipped disc".
'The Needle And The Damage Done', tipped at this point as a possible single, is the only one of these recordings included on Young's actual next LP, 'Harvest' — though the performance used there was taped on 30 January.
Young: "I wrote that about Danny Whitten. He'd gotten so wasted, so strung out, that he ODed and almost died."

24 JANUARY 1971
St. Louis, Missouri.

27 JANUARY 1971
University Of Colorado, Boulder, Colorado. Young's set comprises 'On The Way Home', 'Tell Me Why', 'Old Man', 'Journey Through The Past', 'Love In Mind', 'Heart Of Gold', 'A Man Needs A Maid', 'The Needle And

The Damage Done', 'Ohio', 'See The Sky About To Rain', 'Don't Let It Bring You Down', 'Dance Dance Dance', 'Sugar Mountain', 'Cowgirl In The Sand' and 'I Am A Child'. Bootlegs: 'Live'/'The Loner'/ 'Boulder, Colorado'/'Rocky Mountain Review'.

29 JANUARY 1971
Pasadena, California.

30 JANUARY 1971
Royce Hall, Los Angeles, California. Admission for this special show for UCLA students is set at a minimal $2. 'The Needle And The Damage Done' and 'Love In Mind' from this show are subsequently given an official release.

31 JANUARY 1971
Community Theater, Berkeley, California.

FEBRUARY 1971
CSNY's double-live album, 'Four Way Street', is released, comprising performances from the previous summer's tour.

1 FEBRUARY 1971
Dorothy Chandler Pavilion, L.A. Music Center, Los Angeles, California. Bootlegs: 'I'm Happy That Y'all Came Down'/'In Concerto'/'At The Los Angeles Music Center'/'Neil Young'/'Glühend Morgendammerung'/'The Complete Neil Young'/'Live On Sugar Mountain Vols. 1 & 2'/'Niel (sic) Live'/'Young Man's Fancy'. 'Young Man's Fancy' is available under the counter within three weeks of this concert. Young ends this tour suffering from a second slipped disc, which is aggravated during his Nashville recording sessions.

5 FEBRUARY 1971
In Nashville, Young tapes a guest spot on *The Johnny Cash Show*, where he performs 'Old Man'.

6 FEBRUARY 1971
Young records 'Old Man' and 'Bad Fog Of Loneliness' at Quadraphonic Sound Studios in Nashville, with Linda Ronstadt, James Taylor, Kenny Buttrey, Ben Keith, Tim Drummond and (playing lead guitar on 'Bad Fog Of Loneliness') Tony Joe White. Young: "I was in Nashville to do the Cash show, and James and Linda were there too. We figured, since we've got all these people around, perhaps we could cut some things and have them sing on them. It was just a total accident, the whole thing. We tried it out, and it worked."

7 FEBRUARY 1971
Recording: 'Dance, Dance, Dance' in Nashville, though this track isn't completed.

8 FEBRUARY 1971
Recording: 'Heart Of Gold' in Nashville. Young: "This song put me in the middle of the road. Travelling there soon became a bore, so I headed for the ditch. A rougher ride, but I saw some interesting people there."

14 FEBRUARY 1971
Another proposed date for Young's solo début in London is cancelled.

21 FEBRUARY 1971
Young arrives in London for two weeks of performances and recording; he also writes 'Harvest' during this time. While he's in the city, he stays with Graham Nash, who's holidaying here from California.

23 FEBRUARY 1971
BBC recording of a 30-minute *In Concert* in London. First known performance of 'Out On The Weekend', opening a set that also includes 'Old Man', 'Journey Through The Past', 'Heart Of Gold', 'Don't Let It Bring You Down', 'A Man Needs A Maid', 'Love In Mind' and 'Dance Dance Dance'. Bootlegs: 'The BBC Broadcast'/'Neil At The Beeb'/'November Fog'.

27 FEBRUARY 1971
Royal Festival Hall, London, with a set including three Buffalo Springfield revivals, 'I Am A Child', 'Nowadays Clancy Can't Even Sing' and 'Expecting To Fly', plus 11 songs officially unreleased at that point. Tickets for the show sell out in less than two hours.

1-3 MARCH 1971
Young records 'A Man Needs A Maid' and 'There's A World' with the London Symphony Orchestra at Barking Town Hall. During these sessions, Young rests for much of the time in a bed set up alongside the orchestra, to avoid aggravating the slipped disc he suffered recently in California. Young: "I wanted to add a little extra to the sound of the album."

early MARCH 1971
Young is asked to leave the London apartment where he has been staying, after numerous complaints about excessive noise in the early hours of the morning. He returns home to California, several days ahead of schedule.

1 APRIL 1971
Recording: 'Alabama'.

2 APRIL 1971
Recording: 'Out On The Weekend'.

4 APRIL 1971
Recording: 'Harvest'.

6 APRIL 1971
Recording: the first, unreleased version of 'See The Sky About To Rain'.

23 APRIL 1971
Crazy Horse release their version of Young's 'Dance, Dance, Dance' as a single.

late APRIL 1971
CSNY regroup at David Crosby's California home, for an evening of polite conversation and music, during which they firm up plans to tour America — but not until February 1972.

30 APRIL 1971
CSNY's 'Four Way Street' is released in Britain.

22 MAY 1971
A proposed 28-day Young/Crazy Horse US tour, with The Strawbs as their support act, which is supposed to begin in San Francisco on this date, is cancelled on doctor's orders, after Young's back condition fails to improve.

30 JUNE 1971
Reprise Records reveal that Young's next album, provisionally titled 'Harvest', will not be released in August as originally scheduled. Recording work has been postponed until Young's back condition is eased.

11 AUGUST 1971
Young undergoes surgery for his back problems, forcing the cancellation of a planned August gig at the Troubadour in Hollywood, which Reprise would have recorded for a live album.

mid-AUGUST 1971
Stephen Stills pens a pithy self-biography as part of a promotional media pack for his

second solo album. Commenting on the addition of Neil Young to CSN, he writes: "Stephen felt they needed someone in the group proficient enough not as a composer or singer but rather as a lead guitarist for him to hit from." His disparaging comments do nothing to heal his fragile relationship with Young.

18 SEPTEMBER 1971
Melody Maker readers follow the paper's writers by choosing 'After The Goldrush' as the best LP of the past year, and voting Young the world's best male singer.

23 SEPTEMBER 1971
Young returns to his home recording studio, to work on 'Words (Between The Lines Of Age)' and 'Are You Ready For The Country'.
Young: "That was in my barn. We recorded there with a truck and it sounded good. You can see those sessions in the movie."

24 SEPTEMBER 1971
Young re-records 'Alabama', with assistance from Crosby and Nash.

26 SEPTEMBER 1971
More recording work, on 'Are You Ready For The Country' and 'Alabama'. This session, plus the following day's, is filmed for use in the movie *Journey Through The Past*.

27 SEPTEMBER 1971
Young and The Stray Gators record 'Words', with Stephen Stills and Graham Nash.

30 SEPTEMBER 1971
The mysterious 'Gator Rag #2' is the sole product of this session.

OCTOBER 1971
Young is reported to have refused to allow his partner, Carrie Snodgrass, to attend the Oscar ceremony in Hollywood, where she was nominated for an award for her role in *Diary Of A Mad Housewife*.

1 OCTOBER 1971
Two further tracks date from the day's Stray Gators session: 'Gator Stomp' and 'Gator Rag'.

4 OCTOBER 1971
Young joins Stephen Stills as a guest at an acoustic Crosby & Nash show at Carnegie Hall, New York. The show is taped for a possible CSNY live album, but the quartet elect against following 'Four Way Street' with another in-concert set.

14 OCTOBER 1971
A partial CSNY reunion at the Community Theater, Berkeley, California, as Neil Young guests during a Crosby & Nash concert.

16 OCTOBER 1971
Reports from California suggest that Crosby, Stills, Nash and Young have re-formed, more than a year after their last official show together. They are rumoured to have scheduled recording sessions for December, with an American tour to follow in February and March.
Meanwhile, Reprise announce that 'Harvest' has been delayed until the New Year, as Young has decided to replace two tracks on the album. Crazy Horse record their 'Loose' album, without any input from their supposed leader, Neil Young.

The release of 'Harvest' re-established Young as a first-division rock luminary — a reputation that was steadily demolished over the next three years. Instead of touring, or reviving CSNY, the singer spent much of the year assembling his first feature film, an extremely personal, conceptual project entitled Journey Through The Past. As a work-in-progress, it simply added to Young's mystique; but the release of the over-indulgent soundtrack album, without the film, at the end of 1972 was widely criticised.

In between, Young recorded just one song, which passed almost unnoticed by the general public. Two years earlier, the musical journalism of 'Ohio' had caught the mood of the times. In 1972, Young (like John Lennon) was discovering that the radical unity of the Woodstock era had dissolved. Young's single, 'War Song', was intended to support the doomed presidential ambitions of George McGovern: the single flopped, and so, at the end of the year, did George. Nixon won the election, while the man who'd slammed him in 'Ohio' watched in gloom.

The depression was heightened by another November drama: the death of Crazy Horse guitarist, and former Young sidekick, Danny Whitten, of a heroin overdose. Young had recalled the band for tour rehearsals, then sent Whitten packing with the money for his fare after his drug abuse rendered him inoperative as a musician. Whitten spent the money on smack, and Young assumed private guilt for his demise.

The birth of Young's first son, Zeke, should have lifted the cloud: instead, after a few months it became apparent that the boy was stricken with cerebral palsy, making any real communication with him difficult, to say the least. The illness undoubtedly put severe strain on his relationship with Carrie Snodgrass.

JANUARY 1972

Another release date for the 'Harvest' album comes and goes, after Young insists that the cover for the LP should be made out of oatmeal paper, delaying production.
Young spends much of the next two months editing the rushes of his movie, *Journey Through The Past*.

10 FEBRUARY 1972

The orchestral pieces, 'Handel's Messiah' and 'The King Of Kings Theme', are recorded for *Journey Through The Past*.

15 FEBRUARY 1972

'Harvest' is finally released, having chalked up more than three million advance orders worldwide. Thousands of faulty copies are returned to British stores: UK Reprise blame their American parent company, who manufactured the pressings that were imported into Britain to meet the massive demand.
Young: "I think 'Harvest' was probably the finest record that I've made, but that's really a restricting adjective for me. It's really *fine*... but that's all."

18 FEBRUARY 1972

'Harvest' qualifies for gold-album status in the USA.

18 MARCH 1972

Young tops the US singles and LPs chart simultaneously, with 'Heart Of Gold' and 'Harvest'.

23 MARCH 1972

A film of Young performing 'Heart Of Gold' is shown on BBC-TV's *Top Of The Pops*.

26 MARCH 1972

Once again, Young guests at a Crosby & Nash show, at Winterland, San Francisco, California, performing 'Harvest', 'Only Love Can Break Your Heart', 'Heart Of Gold' and 'The Needle And The Damage Done'.

APRIL 1972

Young joins David Crosby and Graham Nash in the studio as they help Joni Mitchell record her 'For The Roses' album, though he isn't featured on the finished album.

6 APRIL 1972

Top Of The Pops repeats the 'Heart Of Gold' clip.

MAY 1972

Young writes 'War Song' as a gesture of support for the anti-Vietnam War campaign of Presidential candidate George McGovern, and records it on his ranch with Graham Nash (who receives co-billing on the subsequent single), Kenny Buttrey, Tim Drummond and Ben Keith. The single is released to coincide with the Democratic Party's California primary, with proceeds going to help meet McGovern's expenses. Young is rumoured to have agreed to produce the next Linda Ronstadt album.

21 MAY 1972

'Let Me Call You Sweetheart' is the final piece of music to be recorded for *Journey Through The Past*.

JUNE 1972

Publication of Tom Clark's poetry collection, *Neil Young*, which is dominated by the lengthy title poem — every line of which is borrowed from one of Young's songs.
Young confirms that he will be fit to resume live performances in January, when he intends to tour with the band he used on 'Harvest'. He also expresses an interest in playing an outdoors live show in Hyde Park, London, in January, before being advised that weather conditions might not be suitable.

JULY 1972

Cementing their break from Young, Crazy Horse leave their shared record label, Reprise, and sign with Epic.
Speaking on Los Angeles radio, Stephen Stills drops hints about a possible album collaboration between himself and his ex-Buffalo Springfield colleagues Neil Young and Richie Furay.

16 JULY 1972

Young makes a brief, unexpected appearance at the Mariposa Folk Festival in Toronto, Canada, performing solo renditions of 'Helpless', 'Harvest', 'Sugar Mountain' and 'Heart Of Gold'. Folkies resent the fact that he draws fans away from the 'real' folk musicians playing simultaneously on another stage.

late JULY 1972

Neil joins Stephen Stills, Manassas and Graham Nash onstage at Berkeley Community Theater, for a ragged but spirited performance of 'Helpless', 'Carry On' and 'Find The Cost Of Freedom'. "It was more like hopeless than 'Helpless'," frowns a *Melody Maker* reviewer.

8 SEPTEMBER 1972

Carrie Snodgrass gives birth to her and Neil's son, Zeke Snodgrass Young, on Young's California ranch.

26 OCTOBER 1972

Young guests at a Crosby/Nash concert at Winterland, San Francisco, California, performing 'Harvest', 'Only Love Can Break Your Heart', 'Heart Of Gold' and 'The Needle And The Damage Done'. Bootleg: 'Waterbrothers'.

NOVEMBER 1972

Neil Young, John Lennon and Yoko Ono are among the guests at a celebrity party as a third Record Plant studio is opened in Sausalito, California.
Young regroups with The Stray Gators to begin rehearsals for the lengthy world tour that has been on hold since he began to suffer severe back-pain in 1970.

18 NOVEMBER 1972

Guitarist Danny Whitten, formerly Young's sidekick in Crazy Horse, dies of a heroin overdose at a friend's home in Los Angeles at the age of 29. He'd been given $50 and a plane ticket by Young's management, after being fired from the band during rehearsals for the upcoming U.S. tour. Young: "He just couldn't cut it. He was too out of it. I had to tell him to go back to L.A. He split. That night the coroner called me from L.A. and told me he'd OD'ed. That blew my mind."

8 DECEMBER 1972

The soundtrack double-LP for Young's as-yet unissued film, *Journey Through The Past*, is released in Britain — without any mention in Reprise's promotional ads that the album is anything less than a new album of Young songs. *Melody Maker* greets the patchy set of live recordings and studio out-takes with a review headed, "Neil, Was The Journey Really Necessary?", and comments: "It smacks of self-indulgence and laziness".

After two years of creative stasis, Neil Young enters one of his most productive periods, just in time to be dismissed by the world at large as an embarrassing relic of the Woodstock era. 1973 is bookended by, on the surface, disastrous tours. In between, his movie venture flops; a CSNY reunion collapses; one new album sells poorly and another is abandoned; and Young himself is widely reported to have died of a drugs overdose. It is that kind of year.

The 'Time Fades Away' tour breaks away from the acoustic whimsy of 'After The Goldrush' and 'Harvest', defying audience expectations. What is viewed at first as eccentricity is soon interpreted as a tragedy in the waiting, once Young's voice begins to suffer under the strain of a three-month tour, forcing him to enlist support from Crosby and Nash.

Having survived that, he travels to Detroit for the poorly-attended – and received – première of *Journey Through The Past*. The movie is scarcely seen in public thereafter, except in Boston, which is where Young is reported to have died in October. The public impression that Neil is an imminent drug casualty is enhanced by the nature of the 'Tonight's The Night' tour, during which he appears to casual observers to have no awareness of which continent he is playing in, and to be racked by the drug-raddled ghosts of Danny Whitten and ex-CSNY roadie Bruce Berry.

Like Bob Dylan in 1966, some of Young's finest live shows are greeted with disgust and despair. It takes the belated release of the startling 'Tonight's The Night' album, cut in '73 but delayed at record company suggestion for two years, to reveal that far from being a rambling wreck on this tour, Young is actually playing out a complex, tragi-comic psychodrama, investing his darkest demons with fresh life night after night, and then slaying them with the naked energy of his music.

Much the same sense of raw emotion is apparent on 'Time Fades Away', the album of new material pulled from the early-'73 tour. The raucous guitar thrashing of 'Last Dance' is a far cry from 'Heart Of Gold', which is what a substantial proportion of Young's audience want him to repeat.

Between two such personal projects, the CSNY reunion proves to be almost an irrelevance – for 1973, at least. The rehearsals pass in a vacation spirit of mutual tolerance, but once they have to clock in at a studio on a daily basis, CSNY soon dissolve into four antagonistic camps. The latest split does nothing to improve the group's tattered media image.

JANUARY 1973

Reprise suggest that Young is about to release another album, to divert attention from the poor response of *Journey Through The Past*. The label are not apparently discouraged by the fact that Young has only recorded one new track, 'War Song', since finishing 'Harvest'.

Young announces a series of British concerts from May 9 to 14, in Manchester and London.

4 JANUARY 1973

What comes to be known as the 'Time Fades Away' tour opens at Dane County Coliseum, Madison, with The Stray Gators – Tim Drummond, Ben Keith, Johnny Barbata and Jack Nitzsche – backing Young.

The set-list features: 'Tell Me Why', 'Cowgirl In The Sand', the first performance of 'L.A.', 'A Man Needs A Maid', 'I Am A Child', 'Sugar Mountain', the first-ever 'Borrowed Tune', 'Old Man', 'Harvest', 'Heart Of Gold', 'Time Fades Away', 'Everybody Knows This Is Nowhere', the first performances of 'Lonely Weekend', 'Last Dance' and 'Lookout Joe', and 'Are You Ready For The Country'.

5 JANUARY 1973

Milwaukee Auditorium, Milwaukee, Wisconsin.

7 JANUARY 1973

Metropolitan Sports Center, Minneapolis, Minnesota.

8 JANUARY 1973

Cobo Hall, Detroit, Michigan. Young adds 'Alabama' to the set-list, and débuts 'Don't Be Denied'.

9 JANUARY 1973

Cobo Hall, Detroit, Michigan.

10-12 JANUARY 1973

Arie Crown Theater, Chicago, Illinois.

14 JANUARY 1973

War Memorial Auditorium, Buffalo, New York.

15 JANUARY 1973

Maple Leaf Gardens, Toronto, Canada. After this show, 'Borrowed Tune' is dropped from the set-list.

16 JANUARY 1973

Civic Center, Ottawa, Canada.

18 JANUARY 1973

The Forum, Montreal, Canada.

19 JANUARY 1973

Civic Center, Baltimore, Maryland. 'Lonely Weekend' is performed for the final time.

21 JANUARY 1973

Young and The Stray Gators perform an "earsplittingly loud" show at Carnegie Hall, New York, New York, after a pre-concert delay of almost two hours. The audience receive a rare live outing for 'Cripple Creek Ferry'.

22 JANUARY 1973

Nassau Coliseum, Hampstead.

23 JANUARY 1973

Madison Square Garden, New York.

A cease-fire is declared in the Vietnam War. During his concert with The Stray Gators, Young is handed a message about the declaration during his show. He announces "Peace has come", is greeted by hysterical cheering from the audience, and proceeds to perform 'Southern Man'. Also performed during this show are 'On The Way Home', 'Here We Are In The Years', 'L.A.', 'Soldier', 'On The Weekend', 'Harvest', 'Old Man', 'Heart Of Gold', 'The Loner', 'Time Fades Away', 'New Mama', 'Alabama', 'Don't Be Denied', 'Cinnamon Girl', 'Lookout Joe', 'Southern Man', 'Last Dance' and 'Are You Ready For The Country'.
Bootleg: 'In Concert'.

24 JANUARY 1973
Stray Gators' performances of 'Time Fades Away' (2 versions), 'L.A.' and 'The Last Trip To Tulsa' are delivered to Atlantic in New York, for consideration as part of Young's next album – though none of these tracks is eventually used.

25 JANUARY 1973
Coliseum, Newhaven.

26/27 JANUARY 1973
The Spectrum, Philadelphia, Pennsylvania.

28 JANUARY 1973
JFK Center, Washington DC. Bootlegs: 'Coming Home'/'Springfield Slaughter Tour 1973'/'Extra Special, The 1973 Tour'.

29 JANUARY 1973
Scope Arena, Norfolk, Virginia. Bootlegs: 'A Bit More'/'Coming Home'/'Springfield Slaughter Tour 1973'/'Extra Special, The 1973 Tour'.

31 JANUARY 1973
Omni Auditorium, Atlanta, Georgia.

FEBRUARY 1973
Johnny Barbata, a veteran of the final CSNY shows, replaces Kenny Buttrey in Young's band during February.
   Rumours spread that Buffalo Springfield will shortly be re-forming, after Young and Stills' managers, Elliott Roberts and David Geffen, sign Poco, featuring fellow ex-Springfield vocalist Richie Furay.

1 FEBRUARY 1973
Sports Stadium, Orlando, Florida.

2 FEBRUARY 1973
Show at the Sportatorium, Hollywood, Florida is cancelled.

3 FEBRUARY 1973
Bayfront Center Arena, St. Petersburg, Florida.

5 FEBRUARY 1973
University Of Alabama, Tuscaloosa, Alabama.

7 FEBRUARY 1973
Civic Center, Roanake.

8-10 FEBRUARY 1973
Boston Garden, Boston, Massachusetts.

11 FEBRUARY 1973
Public Hall, Cleveland, Ohio. 'Journey Through The Past' from this show is used on 'Time Fades Away'.

13 FEBRUARY 1973
Convention Center, Indianapolis, Indiana.

14 FEBRUARY 1973
Cincinnati Gardens, Cincinnati, Ohio.

15 FEBRUARY 1973
Convention Center, Louisville, Kentucky.

17 FEBRUARY 1973
Show at Loyola University, New Orleans, Louisiana is cancelled.

18 FEBRUARY 1973
Louisiana State University, Baton Rouge, Louisiana. The show's startlingly powerful electric arrangement of 'Last Trip To Tulsa' is issued as a single B-side later in the year.

19 FEBRUARY 1973
Memorial Coliseum, Shreveport, Louisiana.

20 FEBRUARY 1973
Municipal Auditorium, Mobile, Alabama.

21/22 FEBRUARY 1973
Memorial Auditorium, Dallas, Texas.

23 FEBRUARY 1973
Show at Tarrant County Civic Center, Fort Worth, Texas is cancelled, and replaced by a third show at the Memorial Auditorium, Dallas.

24 FEBRUARY 1973
Coliseum, Houston, Texas.

26 FEBRUARY 1973
Memorial Auditorium, Kansas City.

28 FEBRUARY 1973
Tarrant County Convention Center, Fort Worth, Texas.

1 MARCH 1973
The Myriad, Oklahoma City, Oklahoma. 'Time Fades Away' and 'L.A.' from this show are included on the 'Time Fades Away' LP.

3 MARCH 1973
University Of New Mexico, Albuquerque, New Mexico.

4 MARCH 1973
Community Center, Tucson, Arizona. David Crosby and Graham Nash fly in to join Young's band, to help cover for Young's increasing vocal problems on the tour, which have been attracting consistently poor reviews. They appear for the second half of the show, which usually features 'The Loner', 'L.A.', 'New Mama', 'Don't Be Denied', 'Look Out Joe', 'Last Dance' and 'Cinnamon Girl', with an encore of 'Southern Man' and

'Are You Ready For The Country'. Young opens with an acoustic set of 'Sugar Mountain', 'Tell Me Why', 'After The Goldrush', 'Old Man' and 'Heart Of Gold'.
   David Crosby: "He said it wasn't going very well and that he needed our help. He called me and asked me to come."

5 MARCH 1973
Coliseum, Phoenix, Arizona. Young adds an extra verse to 'Don't Be Denied'; part of this performance is included on 'Time Fades Away'.
   Young's management cancel the British dates scheduled for May, pleading that Young is experiencing serious throat problems on tour. The British pop paper *Disc* misinterprets the news, and announces that Young is suffering "a serious heart condition".

8 MARCH 1973
Civic Auditorium, Sacramento, California. 'The Bridge' is recorded at this show for 'Time Fades Away'.

9 MARCH 1973
'Love In Mind'.

10 MARCH 1973
Civic Auditorium, Santa Cruz, California.

12/13 MARCH 1973
Coliseum, Denver, Colorado.

15 MARCH 1973
Coliseum, Portland, Oregon.

17 MARCH 1973
The Coliseum, Seattle, Washington. The first-ever performance of 'Yonder Stands The Sinner' is taken from this show for 'Time Fades Away'.

18 MARCH 1973
Coliseum, Vancouver, Canada.

20 MARCH 1973
Civic Auditorium, Bakersfield, California. The only known performance of Young's strange song for Joni Mitchell, 'Sweet Joni'. Bootleg: 'The Last Album'/'Time Fades Away'/'Young'n'Old'.

21/22 MARCH 1973
Winterland, San Francisco, California. On the second night, while performing 'Old Man', Young's voice effectively gives out, and the gig is salvaged only by the support vocals of Crosby and Nash.

23 MARCH 1973
The Forum, Los Angeles, California. The ensemble flirt with a spoof version of 'Mr Tambourine Man'.

24 MARCH 1973
Long Beach Arena, Long Beach, California.

25 MARCH 1973
Convention Center, Anaheim, California.

27 MARCH 1973
Memorial Auditorium, Sacramento, California.

28 MARCH 1973
Coliseum, Phoenix, Arizona.

29 MARCH 1973
Sports Arena, San Diego, California. The performance of 'Last Dance' from this show appears on 'Time Fades Away'.

31 MARCH 1973
Coliseum, Oakland, California. During the final song, 'Southern Man', Young leaves the stage, after mumbling: 'I can't do it with what's going on out there.'

Young (1974): "I was singing away, you know, 'Southern man, better keep your head'. This guy in the front row, he jumped up and went, 'Right on, right on, I love it'. He felt really good, I could tell. All of a sudden, this black cop just walks up to him, and he just crushed him. I just took my guitar off, put it on the ground, got in the car and went home. Ever since then I've never sung the song, I don't know why."

APRIL 1973
In an attempt to counter British criticism

that Young continued to perform in the States several weeks after cancelling his upcoming UK shows, manager Elliott Roberts comments: "Neil has nodes on his throat. He was in great pain during some of the concerts, and now we are waiting for a doctor's report on whether he will need an operation or not."

8 APRIL 1973
Journey Through The Past is premièred at the US Film Festival in Dallas. After the showing, which takes place before a paltry audience at the Memorial Auditorium, part of Dallas Convention Center, Young sidesteps most of the queries in a question-and-answer session.

Young: "It's hard to say what the movie means. I think it's a good film for a first film. It does lay a lot of shit on people, though."

12 APRIL 1973
Rolling Stone reports that The Buffalo Springfield may be about to re-form. "It's all up to Neil right now," guitarist Richie Furay is quoted as saying.

MAY 1973
Another round of CSNY reunion rumours sweep through the California music business. Graham Nash: "All of us had been planning to take summer vacations in Hawaii. The timing seemed right." The quartet rehearse at a house on Maui, which Young is renting,

and make plans for full-scale sessions the following month at Young's ranch. Graham Nash takes the proposed cover photo for the CSNY LP, provisionally titled 'Human Highway'. During the rehearsals, informal versions of several songs are recorded, including 'Sailboat Song' and 'Pardon My Heart'. The former eventually surfaces on 'Zuma' as 'Through My Sails'.

LATE JUNE 1973
CSNY regroup at Young's California home, with Tim Drummond (bass) and Johnny Barbata (drums). They record Stephen Stills's 'See The Changes' (on 28 June, as issued on the 'CSN' boxed set), plus Young's 'Human Highway' and two Nash songs, 'So It Goes' and 'Prison Song'.

JULY 1973
The CSNY reunion sessions are reported to have been abandoned ("It just turned into a piece of shit," explains Graham Nash); instead, the quartet are rumoured to be preparing for a US tour in August.
The British Board of Film Censors bans Young's film, *Journey Through The Past*, from any public screening in the UK, because of its explicit scenes of drug use.
Around this time, former CSNY roadie Bruce Berry dies of a drug overdose, inspiring Young to write an anguished song called 'Tonight's The Night'.

11 AUGUST 1973
Corral Club, Topanga Canyon, California (2 shows). The first warm-up concerts for what becomes the 'Tonight's The Night' tour – though this song is not completed until after the Topanga dates. Young performs with an extended Crazy Horse line-up (Ralph Molina, Ben Keith, Billy Talbot and Nils Lofgren), rather than (as the media had predicted) CSNY. Among the songs played at these brief shows are 'Mellow My Mind', 'World On A String', 'Speakin' Out', 'Albuquerque', 'New Mama', 'Roll Another Number For The Road', 'Tired Eyes' and 'Cowgirl In The Sand'.
Young announces his decision to concentrate on club dates rather than stadium shows in future. "I can't project what I am to 18,000 people at a concert which resembles a circus," he says. "The time when I could only see myself miles from an audience, singing to a cop in the front row, is finished."

12 AUGUST 1973
Corral Club, Topanga, California (2 shows).

20 AUGUST 1973
Young begins work on what becomes the 'Tonight's The Night' album, taping 'Lookout Joe' and 'Borrowed Tune'.

Young: "I never hit 'Lookout Joe' the way I wanted to."

21 AUGUST 1973
Two versions of 'Tonight's The Night' are recorded.
Young: "We'd get really high – drink a lot of tequila, get right out on the edge. We'd just wait until the vibe hit us and do it. It blew my mind when I saw what was happening."

22 AUGUST 1973
Young tapes two more songs, 'Albuquerque' and 'Roll Another Number For The Road'.

23 AUGUST 1973
'Tired Eyes' is recorded.

24 AUGUST 1973
'Everybody's Alone' is cut during the 'Tonight's The Night' sessions, though it doesn't make the final album.

25 AUGUST 1973
'Mellow Your Mind'.
Young: "This is a song about wanting to stop. After a long tour you just want to be able to slow down. Even when it's over, you can't stop."

9 SEPTEMBER 1973
Young records 'Walk On', which he uses on the 'On The Beach' LP.

11 SEPTEMBER 1973
'Speaking Out' is recorded for 'Tonight's The Night'.

12 SEPTEMBER 1973
'New Mama' is recorded on the final day of the 'Tonight's The Night' sessions.

15 SEPTEMBER 1973
'Time Fades Away' is issued in the U.S.

20-23 SEPTEMBER 1973
Young performs two shows a night during the opening four nights at the Roxy Theater, in Los Angeles, California (2 shows); support acts are Graham Nash and Cheech & Chong. 'Tonight's The Night' is performed live for the first time (twice!), alongside several other new songs: 'Mellow My Mind', 'World On A String', 'Speakin' Out', 'Albuquerque', 'New Mama', 'Roll Another Number For The Road' and 'Tired Eyes'. The encore of 'Cowgirl In The Sand' is the only familiar number in the show.
Young confidently predicts that an album featuring these songs will be in the shops by February. And for the first time, he breaks into his 'Welcome to Miami Beach' rap, omnipresent for the rest of the '73 shows.
Young: "I would just talk away to people,

tying songs together with these raps that I'd make up as I went along. I got to act. I had a part in the show instead of it being me; the pressure was off me a little bit."
'Time Fades Away' is released. *Rolling Stone* greets it as "a startlingly unorthodox album... a revealing self-portrait".
Young: "Nobody expected 'Time Fades Away' but I'm not sorry I put it out. You gotta keep changing. It stood for where I was at during that period. I was nervous and not quite at home in those big halls."
During one of the shows on September 22, Young promises a silver boot to the first woman to appear topless on stage; his partner, Carrie Snodgrass, wins the prize.

1 OCTOBER 1973
McMaster University, Hamilton, Canada.

2 OCTOBER 1973
Waterloo University, Waterloo, Canada.

3 OCTOBER 1973
Guelph University, Guelph, Canada.

4 OCTOBER 1973
Young flies home from Canada in time for CSNY to reunite during a Stephen Stills/Manassas show at the Winterland Ballroom, San Francisco, California. Before the show, the quartet rehearse at Graham Nash's house; afterwards, they talk briefly to the press, promising an acoustic tour of the States before Christmas. Asked about the possibility of CSNY playing in Europe, Stills comments: "The cost would be prohibitive, unless we could get a show at Wembley, and I can't see that happening."

MID-OCTOBER 1973
As Young attends the opening of his movie *Journey Through The Past* in Boston, rumours spread from an American press agency that he has died of a drug overdose. The story is actually announced as fact on BBC radio news before official denials are obtained.

27 OCTOBER 1973
'Time Fades Away' enters the official UK LP chart at No. 20, its highest position.

28 OCTOBER 1973
McMaster University, Hamilton, Canada.

29 OCTOBER 1973
Laurier University, Waterloo, Canada.

30 OCTOBER 1973
Guelph University, Guelph, Canada.

3 NOVEMBER 1973
Palace Theater, Manchester. The 'Tonight's The Night' UK tour begins with a set list that

comprises all the new songs débuted in Topanga in August, plus the live première of 'Human Highway'. 'Flying On The Ground Is Wrong', 'Helpless', 'Don't Be Denied' and 'Cowgirl In The Sand' are the only 'old' songs performed at the show. "Play something good," screams one aggrieved fan as Young launches into another unfamiliar tune.

The tour was originally advertised as featuring Young supported by Crazy Horse; however, on the flight to Britain, Young renames the band The Santa Monica Flyers, and all the posters outside the halls have to be amended.

4 NOVEMBER 1973
Hippodrome, Bristol. Young performs 'Tonight's The Night' three times during this show, in which he also adds 'The Losing End' to the brief menu of familiar songs. By now, 'Tonight's The Night' has become a psychodrama, incorporating Young's mock dialogue between himself and the late CSNY roadie Bruce Berry.

5 NOVEMBER 1973
Rainbow Theatre, London. Audience response is lukewarm, especially when Young quips, "I probably won't be seeing you for another two years, so I can do what I like." Catcalled for talking too much between songs, he adds: "I play more than I talk, so the more I talk, the more I play."

6 NOVEMBER 1973
Empire Theatre, Liverpool.

8 NOVEMBER 1973
Apollo Theatre, Glasgow. 'The Losing End' is added to the set-list.

9 NOVEMBER 1973
City Hall, Newcastle. In a belated bid to satisfy audience requests for more familiar material, Young performs 'Cinnamon Girl' and 'Southern Man', but only after many of the audience have left the theatre during the lengthy preamble of new material.

10 NOVEMBER 1973
Royal Festival Hall, London. 'I Am A Child' is performed for the first time on this tour (preceded by Young borrowing a camera from a fan, and taking a photo of the audience), as well as the triple-play of 'Tonight's The Night'. Richard Williams of *Melody Maker* reviews the show as "a lifeless performance which left many people heading for the bar or an early train home".

After the RFH show, Young turns up as a surprise guest at the London Speakeasy, and performs a short set with the band.

11 NOVEMBER 1973
Young eventually persuades the bouncers that he is who he says he is, and manages to gets backstage for a Who gig at the Lyceum Ballroom.

15 NOVEMBER 1973
Golden Auditorium, Queens College, New York (2 shows). Young revises the set for the American leg of the tour, opening with 'Don't Be Denied' instead of 'Tonight's The Night', which is now played twice separated by just three songs. Several of the 'new' numbers are dropped, to be replaced by 'When You Dance I Can Really Love', 'The Needle And The Damage Done' and 'I Believe In You'. The second show also features a remarkable 'Cowgirl In The Sand'. Bootleg: 'Goodbye Waterface'.

16 NOVEMBER 1973
Boston Music Hall, Boston, Massachusetts. Nils Lofgren sings 'Happy Birthday' to Young during the show, despite the fact that Young's birthday had been four days earlier.

18 NOVEMBER 1973
Columbus, Ohio.

19 NOVEMBER 1973
Cleveland, Ohio.

20 NOVEMBER 1973
Chicago Auditorium, Chicago, Illinois. The closing performance of 'Tonight's The Night' on this final night of the tour stretches for some 35 minutes.

23 NOVEMBER 1973
Young joins Crazy Horse for their show at the Berkeley Community Center, Berkeley, California.

DECEMBER 1973
Young is persuaded not to release the original version of the 'Tonight's The Night' album, which incorporated the songs recorded in August/September, linked by drunken studio chatter.

Atlantic release a double-LP retrospective of Buffalo Springfield's career, featuring a previously unissued long version of 'Bluebird'.

7 DECEMBER 1973
Young joins Crosby and Nash onstage at the Civic Auditorium, San Francisco, California. Among the songs performed by the trio are 'Only Love Can Break Your Heart', 'New Mama', 'Prison Song', 'Almost Cut My Hair', 'Pre-Road Downs', 'Military Madness', 'Immigration Man', 'Ohio' and 'Teach Your Children'.

1974

Writing and releasing the troubled, yet quite brilliant, 'On The Beach' album just six months after completing the equally dark 'Tonight's The Night' proves that Young is at his artistic zenith. Small wonder that he dominates the summer's long-awaited CSNY reunion tour: while his colleagues mostly retread old glories, Young casually drops staggering songs like 'Revolution Blues' and 'Ambulance Blues' into the set, alongside a handful of tunes that are destined never to be released.

Among them is 'Pushed It Over The End', a stark (if muddle-headed) glimpse of the post-Germaine Greer sex war, which is débuted with much of the 'On The Beach' material during a brief but compelling acoustic show at New York's Bottom Line just prior to the CSNY excursion.

But it is the supergroup reunion which dominates the headlines. CSNY view themselves as the world's most popular band, and the scale of their on-the-road venture suggests they might be right. Only in retrospect do Crosby and Nash start making cracks about 'The Doom Tour', complaining that the sheer vastness of the arenas and stadiums fatally compromises CSNY's emotional link with their audience, and that the band has sacrificed their ideals for greenbacks. Interestingly, Young elects not to travel by plane from show to show with the rest of the entourage; instead, he drives from town to town in his camper-truck, accompanied by Carrie Snodgrass, one roadie and his dog.

Young is fingered as a prime mover in the tour, but somehow, as usual he emerges with his reputation intact, while CSN suffer for the quartet's inability to follow the concerts with a suitably superb album. Any album, in fact, would have been welcome: instead, another batch of reunion sessions dissolve into claim and counter-claim, Young jumping ship as soon as the waters became stable. CSN could be forgiven for wondering whether his involvement in the tour has more to do with promoting 'On The Beach' and subsidising a follow-up than in any great desire on Young's part to continue the CSNY experiment into the mid-70s. In the weeks when the quartet should have been completing their 'Human Highway' album, Young instead devotes himself to a sparse, romantically doomed set of mostly acoustic tunes, planned for early 1975 release as 'Homegrown' (or 'Mediterranean', depending on his biorhythms). The record is sparked by the disintegration of his relationship with Carrie Snodgrass, though a final separation isn't confirmed until the following year.

JANUARY 1974
Graham Nash's 'Wild Tales' album is released, with Young guesting under the pseudonym 'Joe Yankee'.

FEBRUARY 1974
Questioned about the delayed CSNY reunion, Stephen Stills notes: "No-one's saying no."

14 FEBRUARY 1974
Young attends the final show of Bob Dylan and The Band's US tour, at the Forum, Los Angeles. David Crosby is also there, and tells a reporter that the planned CSNY reunion has been "sacrificed at the altar of ego". Both

men also show up at the end-of-tour party in the early hours of the 15th.

EARLY MARCH 1974

Stephen Stills climaxes a solo show in Chicago by announcing, "CSNY are getting back together this summer for a big tour, and we'll make another album in the fall."

8 MARCH 1974

Young records 'For The Turnstiles' with Ben Keith.

26 MARCH 1974

Young plays two benefit shows for Red Wind Indians at Luesta College, San Louis Obispo. Supported by The Eagles, he raises $8,000 to help the group build a cultural centre. During the afternoon set, he played four songs with The Eagles, including 'Helpless', 'Vampire Blues' and 'Down By The River'; in the evening, he performs a solo acoustic set which includes 'Revolution Blues' and 'Ambulance Blues', before being joined by The Eagles for Chuck Berry's 'Carol', 'Down By The River' and their 'Chug All Night'.

29 MARCH 1974

Young re-records 'See The Sky About To Rain', originally attempted for the 'Harvest' album.

EARLY APRIL 1974

'Ambulance Blues', 'Revolution Blues' (with David Crosby on guitar), 'Vampire Blues', 'On The Beach' (with Graham Nash on piano) and 'Motion Pictures' are recorded. Together with the two songs taped in March, and 'Walk On' from the previous summer, they make up the 'On The Beach' album.

CSNY manager Elliott Roberts confirms that the band will be re-forming, but that they will not be playing any festival bills. He also promises a reunion album by the end of 1974, which will incorporate material recorded during the previous year's brief union.

16 MAY 1974

The Bottom Line, New York. Young's set at this remarkable acoustic concert comprises 'Pushed It Over The End' (introduced as 'Citizen Kane Junior Blues'), 'Long May You Run', the traditional folk song 'Greensleeves', 'Ambulance Blues', 'Helpless', 'Revolution Blues', 'On The Beach', 'Roll Another Number', 'Motion Pictures', 'Pardon My Heart', 'Dance Dance Dance'.
Bootlegs: 'First Plane Outta Here'/'All Night Long'/'Citizen Kane Junior Blues'/'Love Art Blues' (1 track).

JUNE 1974

CSNY rehearse for their upcoming tour on Young's ranch in Santa Cruz. Bassist Tim Drummond, drummer Russ Kunkel and percussionist Joe Lala are enlisted for the concerts. The group also hold some im- promptu recording sessions, taping their only four-way co-composition, 'Little Blind Fish'.

JULY 1974

Young's epic 'On The Beach' LP is released, being greeted by *Rolling Stone* as "his best album since 'After The Goldrush'... one of the most despairing albums of the decade, a bitter testament from one who has come through the fire and gone back into it".

9 JULY 1974

CSNY: The Coliseum, Seattle, Washington. Young plays 'Love Art Blues', 'Traces', 'Cowgirl In The Sand', 'Ohio', 'Human Highway', 'Long May You Run', 'A Man Needs A Maid', 'Don't Be Denied', 'Revolution Blues' and 'Pushed It Over The End' during a show that lasts for almost four hours, and doesn't finish until 1.37am. The original opening dates of the tour, at the L.A. Coliseum on 6/7 July, are cancelled.

10 JULY 1974

CSNY: Vancouver, Canada. David Crosby is almost unable to sing after the over- exuberance of the previous show.

13 JULY 1974

CSNY: Oakland Stadium, Oakland, California. Support acts are The Band, Joe Walsh and Jesse Colin Young. Neil Young dominates the show: he performs 'Traces', 'Ohio', 'Human Highway', 'Pushed It Over The End', 'Long May You Run', 'Only Love Can Break Your Heart', 'Ambulance Blues', 'On The Beach' and 'Revolution Blues'.
Bootlegs: 'We Waited 3 Years For This'/'Traces'.

14 JULY 1974

CSNY: Oakland Stadium, Oakland, California.

16 JULY 1974

CSNY: Tempe, Arizona.

19 JULY 1974

CSNY: Royals Stadium, Kansas City, Missouri.

21 JULY 1974
Milwaukee County Stadium, Milwaukee, Wisconsin, with CSNY. During his acoustic set, Young gives 'Homefires' its first public airing, and also performs 'Walk On'.

22 JULY 1974
CSNY: Civic Center Coliseum, St. Paul.

25 JULY 1974
CSNY: Mile High Stadium, Denver, Colorado. Support acts include The Beach Boys. Young performs 'Sugar Mountain', 'Ambulance Blues', 'Revolution Blues', 'Pushed It Over The End', 'Only Love Can Break Your Heart', 'Don't Be Denied' and 'Ohio'. Bootleg: 'Reunion Concert July 25, 1974'.

28 JULY 1974
CSNY: Houston, Texas.

31 JULY 1974
CSNY: Dallas, Texas.

AUGUST 1974
Atlantic capitalise on the CSNY tour with a compilation album, 'So Far'.
CSNY: Atlantic City, New Jersey, during a violent rainstorm.

5/6 AUGUST 1974
Boston Garden, Boston, Massachusetts, with CSNY.

8 AUGUST 1974
CSNY: Roosevelt Stadium, Jersey City, New Jersey.

11 AUGUST 1974
CSNY: Rich Stadium, Buffalo, New York.

14/15 AUGUST 1974
CSNY: Nassau Coliseum, Hampstead, Long Island.
  On the 15th Young performs 'Love Art Blues', 'Down By The River', a strange medley of 'Pardon My Heart' and 'The Old Homestead', 'Only Love Can Break Your Heart', 'On The Beach', 'Walk On' and 'Ohio'. Bootleg: "Nice To See You".

17 AUGUST 1974
CSNY: Forman Field, Norfolk, Virginia.

18 AUGUST 1974
CSNY: JFK Stadium, Philadelphia, Pennsylvania.

19 AUGUST 1974
CSNY: Capitol Center, Largo, Maryland.

20/21 AUGUST 1974
CSNY: Capitol Center, Largo, Maryland.

23 AUGUST 1974
CSNY: Tampa Stadium, Tampa, Florida.

25 AUGUST 1974
CSNY: Bush Stadium, Memphis, Tennessee.

27-29 AUGUST 1974
Chicago Stadium, Chicago, Illinois, with CSNY. Young's 'Pushed It Over The End', taped on the 27th, is subsequently overdubbed in the studio by CSN. It is eventually released, in Italy only, in 1982. All three of the Chicago concerts are taped by His Master's Wheels mobile studios, for a planned CSNY live album.

31 AUGUST 1974
CSNY: Municipal Stadium, Cleveland, Ohio.

2 SEPTEMBER 1974
CSNY: Varsity Stadium, Toronto, Canada.

8 SEPTEMBER 1974
CSNY: Roosevelt Raceway, Westbury, Long Island. Young performs 'Helpless', 'Walk On', 'Only Love Can Break Your Heart', 'Long May You Run', 'Ambulance Blues', 'Old Man', 'Don't Be Denied', 'Revolution Blues', 'Ohio', 'Hawaiian Sunrise', 'Pushed It Over The End' and 'Love Art Blues' during this show. Bootleg: 'Love Art Blues' (2 tracks)/'Old Country Road' (10 tracks).

14 SEPTEMBER 1974
CSNY: Wembley Stadium, London, with Joni Mitchell and The Band heading the supporting cast. 'Hawaiian Sunrise' is performed by Young for the final time, and 'Star Of Bethlehem' for the first. Part of this show is apparently filmed by the BBC.

After the show, CSNY attend a party at Quaglino's in Piccadilly, where Young and Stills jam with members of The Band and Led Zeppelin, performing 'Vampire Blues' and 'On The Beach' among other songs.

'On The Beach' reaches No. 16, its peak position on the US LP chart in *Billboard*.

21 SEPTEMBER 1974
The scheduled final show of the CSNY tour, at the September Jam staged at the Ontario Speedway, California, is cancelled. Instead, Young and Nash spend several days in Amsterdam.

OCTOBER 1974
Stephen Stills says that CSNY plan to perform at the L.A. Forum in November, begin work on an LP in December, and then tour indoor arenas in the spring.

18 OCTOBER 1974
Young records 'World On A String', to complete the track listing for 'Tonight's The Night'.

NOVEMBER 1974
Young and Carrie Snodgrass separate: Young rents a house in Malibu Beach.
CSNY begin recording the 'Human Highway' album at the Record Plant in Sausalito. 'Homeward Through The Haze', 'Wind On The Water' and 'Human Highway' are among the songs completed between November and January 1975, with the aid of Russ Kunkel, Bill Kreutzmann of The Grateful Dead and Leland Sklar. David Crosby notes: "It would have been the best one, man. You should have heard us. We smoked and burned!" But the sessions are marred by arguments, notably between Stills and Young. Having commented earlier in the proceedings that he "feels like he's somewhere else", Young puts that feeling into practice and departs without warning the others, who briefly attempt to complete the album without him before the sessions dissolve in chaos.

A tape of Buffalo Springfield performing an unissued song called 'Ash On The Floor' is discovered and delivered to the Atlantic Records tape vault.

2 NOVEMBER 1974
CSNY's 'So Far' compilation tops the US LP chart for one week.

9 NOVEMBER 1974
'So Far' reaches No. 1 on the UK LP chart.

2 DECEMBER 1974
The recording of 'Separate Ways' marks the beginning of a set of sessions for an album of sparsely arranged, emotionally bleak songs, provisionally entitled 'Homegrown'.

3 DECEMBER 1974
Recording: 'White Lines'.

4 DECEMBER 1974
Recording: 'Star Of Bethlehem', with Emmylou Harris.

5 DECEMBER 1974
Recording: 'Try'.

7 DECEMBER 1974
Recording: 'Daughters'.

8 DECEMBER 1974
Recording: 'Deep Forbidden Lake'.

9 DECEMBER 1974
Recording: 'Homegrown', 'Love Is A Rose' and 'We Don't Smoke It No More'.

13 DECEMBER 1974
Recording: 'Vacancy'.

16 DECEMBER 1974
CSNY record David Crosby's 'Homeward Through The Haze' at the Record Plant, Sausalito. After that session, Young records his own 'Give Me Strength'.

LATE DECEMBER 1974
Young meets Pegi Morton in California.

'**H**omegrown' is never released; Young reckons it is too similar in mood to 'On The Beach'. Instead, he delves back to 1973 for the drunken, scabrous 'Tonight's The Night'. With 'On The Beach' and the CSNY tour as proof that Young hasn't been temporarily insane during his late 1973 concerts, critics are free to acknowledge 'Tonight's The Night' as a cathartic masterpiece.

Meanwhile, Young has renewed his links with Crazy Horse, who've survived a series of increasingly lacklustre album projects and recruited a new guitar foil for Young, Frank Sampedro. With the original rhythm section of Ralph Molina and Billy Talbot still intact, Crazy Horse join Young to record 'Zuma', a much more stable and simplistic batch of songs than those on his recent records. Issued at the end of 1975, the album attracts those who like the idea of Young as an eccentric depressive more than the reality.

With Crazy Horse, Young stages a brief tour of Northern California bars at year's end, earlier ventures having been ruled out by surgery for his continued throat problems. But it is his unexpected gigs with Stephen Stills that excite the media, plus the promise of a full-scale duet project the following year.

3 JANUARY 1975
Young resumes work on the 'Homegrown' album, taping 'Love Art Blues', 'Home Fires' and 'The Old Homestead'.

4 JANUARY 1975
Young records 'Long May You Run'.

7 JANUARY 1975
Recording: 'The Tie Plate Yoddle #3'.

21 JANUARY 1975
Recording: 'Little Wing'. With 'Homegrown' complete, Young elects to shelve the album in favour of the two-year-old 'Tonight's The Night'.

Young: "Listening to those two albums back to back at a party, I started to see the weaknesses in 'Homegrown'. I took 'Tonight's The Night' because of its overall strength in performance and feeling. 'Homegrown' was the darker side of 'Harvest'. A lot of songs had to do with me breaking up with my old lady. It was a little too personal... it scared me."

23 MARCH 1975
Neil Young appears at Kezar Stadium, Golden Gate Park, San Francisco, California, during a benefit concert for SNACK (Students Need Athletic and Cultural Kicks). With his constant sidekicks, Ben Keith and Tim Drummond, three members of the Band, Rick Danko, Garth Hudson and Levon Helm, and Bob Dylan, Young contributes to an eight-song set.

Young performs 'Are You Ready For The Country', 'Looking For A Love', and a medley of his own 'Helpless' and Dylan's 'Knockin' On Heaven's Door'. He also plays piano and guitar behind Dylan on 'I Want You', and Danko/Helm renditions of 'Ain't That A Lot Of Love', 'Loving You Is Sweeter Than Ever' and 'The Weight'.
As an encore, Young and Dylan perform an acoustic version of 'Will The Circle Be Unbroken'. The entire concert is broadcast live by local radio station KIOI-FM, and raises $200,000 for the San Francisco school system. Bootlegs: 'SNACK'/'Dollar Snack'/'Live In San Francisco 1975'/'The Prophet And The Clown'.

Stephen Stills tells reporter Barbara Charone: "Neil Young backs me up better than anyone in the world. What I want to do is make an album with him. We'd terrorise the industry."

APRIL 1975
Young is reported to be mixing a new album at Wally Heider's Studio in San Francisco: the record in question is 'Tonight's The Night'.

18 JUNE 1975
Graham Nash and David Crosby record

'Cowboy Of Dreams', a song about Neil Young.

LATE JUNE 1975
'Tonight's The Night' is finally released, almost two years after sessions for the album began.

Young: " 'Tonight's The Night' didn't come out right after it was recorded because it wasn't finished. It just wasn't in the right order, the concept wasn't right. I had to get the colour right, so it was not so down that it would make people restless. I had to keep jolting every once in a while to get people to wake up so they could be lulled again."

EARLY JULY 1975
Young begins his first full set of recording sessions with Crazy Horse since 1970. The band are now a trio, with Billy Talbot and Ralph Molina joined by new guitarist Frank Sampedro. 'Don't Cry No Tears' (a reworking of a song from Young's 1965 acoustic demo tape) and 'Pardon My Heart' are two of the first songs to be completed.
Young: "I'm recording a lot of long instrumental guitar things now."

9 JULY 1975
Young and Crazy Horse record 'Stupid Girl'.

11 JULY 1975
'Cortez The Killer', 'Barstool Blues' and 'Ride My Llama' are recorded.

Young on 'Cortez The Killer': "It's about the Incas and the Aztecs. It takes on another personality. It's like being in another civilisation."

On 'Barstool Blues': "I was very drunk. I was so drunk that I woke up the next morning and it was like someone had left it for me. I couldn't remember writing it or anything but I had the chords written out, and when I started to play it I realised that whoever wrote it sang higher than I did."

12 JULY 1975
'Danger Bird' and 'Drive Back' complete the sessions for the 'Zuma' album, less than 10 days after they began.

The album is originally planned for release as 'In My Llama', then 'In My Neighbourhood' – both references to 'Ride My Llama', which is eventually dropped from the running-order.

25 JULY 1975
Young joins The Stephen Stills Band onstage at the Greek Theater, Berkeley, California. Unable to sing because of throat problems, Young plays guitar behind Stills, who returns the compliment by performing Young compositions like 'On The Beach', 'The Loner' and 'New Mama'.

The Stills/Young collaboration
began with some impromptu live
shows, and turned into an album,
a tour and a psychodrama. "We're
gonna terrorise the industry," Stills
predicted before the venture. When
the partnership collapsed, he
admitted: "I have no future".

AUGUST 1975
Young records the epic 'Like A Hurricane' for the first time.

9 AUGUST 1975
'Tonight's The Night' reaches its peak position of No. 25 on the *Billboard* US LP chart.

14 AUGUST 1975
Rolling Stone magazine runs a cover-story interview with Young, carried out by Cameron Crowe.

28 AUGUST 1975
NBC TV's *Midnight Special* runs a Young interview.

SEPTEMBER 1975
Recording: 'Powderfinger' and 'Captain Kennedy' (both solo).

5 SEPTEMBER 1975
Recording: 'Pocahontas' (solo) and 'Lookin' For A Love' (with Crazy Horse).

6 SEPTEMBER 1975
Young re-records 'Human Highway' in a solo arrangement, the CSNY version having been shelved.

OCTOBER 1975
Neil attends a Roxy Theater show by Toots & The Maytals.

13 OCTOBER 1975
In a Los Angeles hospital, Young undergoes a throat operation, to remove a benign growth from his vocal cords.

19 NOVEMBER 1975
Recording: 'Homegrown' (version 2) with Crazy Horse.

22 NOVEMBER 1975
Roscoe Maples Pavilion, Stanford University, Palo Alto, California, with Stephen Stills Band. Young joins Stills for the acoustic set, duetting on 'Everybody's Talkin' ', 'Long May You Run', 'Do For The Others' and 'Human Highway'. He remains onstage for the second electric set,

23 NOVEMBER 1975
Another Stills/Young collaboration, at Pauley Pavilion, UCLA. During the electric set,

Stills is moved to exclaim: "The spirit of The Buffalo Springfield is back!"

26 NOVEMBER 1975
Recording: 'Like A Hurricane' (version 2), with Crazy Horse.

27 NOVEMBER 1975
Recording: the second version of 'White Lines', replacing the bleak feel of the 'Homegrown' take with a more ragged arrangement from Crazy Horse.

28 NOVEMBER 1975
Recording: 'Lotta Love' and the first, pre-punk version of 'Sedan Delivery' with Crazy Horse.

DECEMBER 1975
'Zuma' is released.

12 DECEMBER 1975
Inn At The Beginning, Cotati, California, with Crazy Horse. This show begins a series of low-key, effectively unannounced shows at small California clubs, under the banner of the 'Northern California Bar Tour'.

13 DECEMBER 1975
Marshall Tavern, Point Reyes, California.

19 DECEMBER 1975
Inn At The Beginning, Cotati, California, with Crazy Horse. The show features 'Country Home', 'Don't Cry No Tears', 'Cowgirl In The Sand', 'I'm Just A Man', Billy Talbot's 'New Orleans', 'Cinnamon Girl', 'Homegrown', 'Down By The River', 'She's Hot' (sung by Frank Sampedro), 'Like A Hurricane', 'Looking For A Love', Crazy Horse's 'Lost And Lonely Feeling', 'Drive Back', 'White Line' and 'Southern Man'. Bootleg: 'Northern Sky' (1 track).

22 DECEMBER 1975
Marshall Tavern, Point Reyes, California. Young and Crazy Horse play two 45-minute sets. The songs débuted at these December shows were briefly intended for release on an album to be called 'Ranch Romance', which would include both Crazy Horse and Young compositions.

31 DECEMBER 1975
Alex's, Woodside, California, with Stephen Stills. The two men play a lengthy acoustic set to see in the New Year.

1976 is the year when Young undertakes a majestic tour with Crazy Horse; guests at The Band's all-star farewell concert; and acquires a reputation for utter unpredictability by preparing a three-album retrospective of his career, and then cancelling the project just before the proposed release date.

But one event – or rather non-event – dominated the year, and comes close to undercutting Young's improved media profile since 1973. As promised, he teams up with Stephen Stills for an album, and then a tour. But both ventures end in farce. Midway through the sessions for 'Long May You Run', Young invites David Crosby and Graham Nash to add vocals and songs; the second CSNY studio album was, it seemed, a reality.

Instead, Crosby and Nash have some unfinished duet business of their own to complete. During what is supposed to be an absence of days rather than months, Stills and Young elect to wipe their friends' contributions from the tapes, and revert to their original concept. This single action splits CSNY down the middle, to the point that the four men don't record together again as a unit for more than a decade. Worse still, the Stills/Young Band's album is a stale, lacklustre affair, easily outclassed by the Crosby/Nash record issued at the same time.

A few sparks of the old Buffalo Springfield/CSNY fire are rekindled when Stills and Young go out on the road. But Young is still suffering with his throat and, more vitally, with his spirit. Midway through the schedule, he drives home rather than to the next gig, abandoning Stills without a hint of apology. Riding his luck, as ever, Young survives with his image, if anything, enhanced; for Stills, meanwhile, the trauma cements the impression that he is yesterday's man.

3 MARCH 1976
Aichiken Taiikukan, Nagoya, Japan. First known performance of 'Don't Say You Win, Don't Say You Lose', which becomes a standard part of the opening acoustic set on this Japanese and European tour. Also featured in this set are 'Tell Me Why', 'Mellow My Mind', 'After The Goldrush', 'Too Far Gone', 'Only Love Can Break Your Heart', 'A Man Needs A Maid' and 'Heart Of Gold'.

The electric set with Crazy Horse is also fairly standard throughout the tour: 'Country Home', 'Don't Cry No Tears', 'Down By The River', 'Lotta Love', 'Like A Hurricane' (a showstopper every night, with a giant fan brought on stage to imitate the force of a howling gale), 'The Losin' End', 'Drive Back', 'Southern Man', 'Cinnamon Girl' and 'Cortez The Killer' (although this last song isn't featured in the first show at Nagoya).

Young: "It was my first time in Japan, and it was amazing to see people had come to the shows and copied even the way I dress, the patterned trousers."

4-6 MARCH 1976
Festival Hall, Osaka, Japan.
Young drops a rare version of 'Let It Shine' into his acoustic set on the 6th.

8 MARCH 1976
Kyudenkinen Taiikukan, Fukoka, Japan.

10/11 MARCH 1976
Budo Kan, Tokyo, Japan. David Briggs records the Budo Kan shows for Young. 'Let It Shine' reappears at the last Japanese show, as well as an electric version of 'Cowgirl In The Sand'.

15 MARCH 1976
Ekerberghallen, Oslo, Norway. First known performance of 'Day And Night We Walk These Aisles', which Young uses as a surprise opening number – followed by 'Old Man', a regular inclusion in the European shows.

Young hires a documentary film crew to capture the European tour – both on- and off-stage – though the footage remains unseen.

16 MARCH 1976
Falkonertreatret, Copenhagen, Denmark.

18 MARCH 1976
Rhein-Necker-Halle, Heidelberg, W. Germany. 'Cowgirl In The Sand' re-emerges, this time in the acoustic set, while the Crazy Horse set is revamped for the night to include 'Helpless', 'Let It Shine' and 'Barstool Blues'. 'Day And Night We Walk These Aisles' appears for the third and final time on this leg of the tour. 'The Needle And The Damage Done' makes its first appearance on this tour, while the acoustic set also includes 'Ohio'.

19 MARCH 1976
Stadthalle, Offenbach, W. Germany. 'Ohio' is played for the second and last time on this trip, while the electric set includes a one-off 'Barstool Blues'.

20 MARCH 1976
Sporthalle, Cologne, W. Germany. 'The Losing End' is added to the electric set.

21 MARCH 1976
Congress Centrum, Hamburg, W. Germany. 'Last Trip To Tulsa', played with Crazy Horse, features for the only occasion on this tour. Bootleg: 'Live At The Roman Colosseum'.

23 MARCH 1976
Pavilion de Paris, Paris, France.

24 MARCH 1976
Ahoy Hall, Rotterdam, Holland.

25 MARCH 1976
Vorst National Stadium, Brussels, Belgium.

26 MARCH 1976
Japp-Eden Hall, Amsterdam, Holland.

28-31 MARCH 1976
Hammersmith Odeon, London. Again, these shows are recorded by David Briggs. Young débuts 'Midnight On The Bay' in the acoustic set on the 29th. After opening almost every show with 'Tell Me Why' and 'Mellow My Mind', Young replaces them with 'On The Way Home' and 'Human Highway' on the 30th. The final night sees the first known performance of 'Stringman', while the acoustic set now opens with 'The Old Laughing Lady', complete with lyrical adaptations. This set is recorded, and 'Stringman' is nearly released on the 'Chrome Dreams' album.

2 APRIL 1976
Apollo Theatre, Glasgow. The final set of the tour ends with Young and Crazy Horse performing 'Homegrown'.

APRIL 1976
During lengthy sessions at Criteria Studios in Miami, Florida, the Stills/Young Band (featuring Joe Lala, George Perry, Joe Vitale and Jerry Aiello) record at least working versions of the following songs: 'Long May You Run', 'Human Highway', 'One Way Ride', 'Fountainbleu', 'Ocean Girl', 'Traces', 'Let It Shine', 'Separate Ways', 'Midnight On The Bay' (all by Young); 'Make Love To You', 'Guardian Angel', 'Black Coral', 'Beaucoup Gumbo', 'Tree Top Flyer' (all by Stills); 'No-One Seems To Know', 'Western Witches', 'Talk Too Much', 'Walk Before You Run' (composers unknown).

During the sessions, David Crosby and Graham Nash are invited to join the proceedings. As a foursome, CSNY attempt or complete recording work on the following songs: 'Taken It All' (by Crosby/Nash; date erroneously listed as 1/4/76 on 'CSN' boxed set), 'Time After Time' (by Crosby), 'Make Love To You', 'Black Coral', 'Beaucoup Gumbo', 'Tree Top Flyer', 'I Wanna Make Love To You', 'Christopher's Jam' (all by Stills), 'Mutiny' (by Nash), 'Separate Ways', 'Traces', 'Will To Love', 'Human Highway', 'Ocean Girl', 'Midnight On The Bay', 'One Way Ride' (all by Young), 'Little Blind Fish' (the only song co-written by all four members of CSNY), and several songs of indeterminate authorship: 'Talk To Me', 'After Hours', 'Talk Too Much', 'Secrets', 'My Girl', 'Last Hundred Yards Of Freedom', '10 90', 'Western Witches', 'Let Me Down', 'No-One Seems To Know', and 'Sleep'.

Finished versions of several songs, including 'Midnight On The Bay' and 'Make Love To You', are prepared; but Crosby and Nash are forced to interrupt the sessions to complete work on their own new album, 'Whistling Down The Wire'. During their absence, Young and Stills elect to keep safety copies of the CSNY recordings, before wiping Crosby and Nash's harmonies off the existing tracks. The Stills/Young recordings are then mixed for release on the 'Long May You Run' album.

This incident sparks a severe breakdown in the CSNY relationship: both Crosby and Nash are quoted as saying that they will never work with Stills or Young again.
Graham Nash: "I must admit I was surprised to hear from Neil. But I was intrigued by this project he was doing with Stephen. When he came by my house and played me and David a tape of some of the things they'd done – 'Black Coral', 'Midnight On The Bay', 'Human Highway' – they sounded great. Then Neil said, 'Isn't there somethin' missing?' Crosby goes, 'Yeah, us.' So the next morning we were on a plane to Miami."
Stephen Stills: "Neil and I were almost finished with the album. When David and Graham had to leave, we had to get on with it. We couldn't wait. It was Neil's idea to take David and Graham's vocals off our tracks."
Graham Nash: "Fuck 'em. I will not work with them again."

MAY 1976
After failing to record the song satisfactorily with CSNY, Young tapes his solo version of 'Will To Love'.

23 JUNE 1976
The Stills/Young Band open their first and only US at the Pine Knob Theater,

Young during his remarkable Hammersmith Odeon show in 1976, taped by Reprise for a possible live album.

Clarkston. The set-list features a mix of songs by both men, with two electric sets separated by acoustic interludes midway through. The opening show has Young performing 'The Loner', 'Long May You Run', 'Old Man', 'Southern Man', 'On The Way Home', 'Heart Of Gold', 'Ohio', the first known performance of 'Evening Coconut', 'Let It Shine' and 'Cowgirl In The Sand'.

24 JUNE 1976
The Stills/Young Band play a shortened set at the Cobo Hall, Detroit, Michigan. 'Helpless' is Young's only addition to their repertoire.

26 JUNE 1976
Boston Garden, Boston, Massachusetts: Stills/Young Band. 'Stringman', a song Young wrote about Stills, is an appropriate inclusion in this show, plus 'Too Far Gone' (its sole performance on the tour).

27 JUNE 1976
Stills/Young Band: Civic Center, Springfield, Massachusetts.

28 JUNE 1976
Young spends the day at Criteria in Miami, mixing the Stills/Young album.

29 JUNE 1976
Stills/Young Band: The Spectrum, Philadelphia, Pennsylvania. Young introduces 'After The Goldrush' into the set-list. Bootleg: 'For What It's Worth'.

1/2 JULY 1976
Stills/Young Band: Nassau Coliseum, Hampstead, Long Island.

4 JULY 1976
Stills/Young Band: Convention Center, Niagara Falls, New York. Stills chooses to end proceedings with a cacophonous electric guitar rendition of 'The Star-Spangled Banner', celebrating Independence Day.

5 JULY 1976
Stills/Young Band: Civic Center, Rochester, New York.

7 JULY 1976
Stills/Young Band: Civic Center, Providence, Rhode Island. In the longest show of the tour, Young performs 'Sugar Mountain', a one-off Stills/Young version of 'Midnight On The Bay', and Buffalo Springfield's 'Mr Soul'.

9/10 JULY 1976
Stills/Young Band: Capitol Center, Largo, Maryland. 'Stringman' reappears in Young's solo set.

11 JULY 1976
Stills/Young Band: Hartford, Connecticut.

12 JULY 1976
Young returns to Criteria for another mixing session.

13 JULY 1976
Stills/Young Band: Richfield Coliseum, Cleveland, Ohio. Young performs 'I Believe In You' for the first time on the tour, at a show reckoned to be the pinnacle of the Stills/Young Band venture.

14 JULY 1976
Stills/Young Band: Riverfront Coliseum, Cincinnatti, Ohio. 'Ocean Girl' makes the set-list for the first time

15 JULY 1976
Stills/Young Band: Pittsburgh, Pennsylvania.

17 JULY 1976
Stills/Young Band: Greensboro'.

18 JULY 1976
Stills/Young Band: The Coliseum, Charlotte, Virginia. The final Stills/Young Band show: after this concert, Young vanishes into the night, sending Stills – waiting in Atlanta for the next show – a laconic telegram: "Dear Stephen, funny how some things that start spontaneously end that way. Eat a peach. Neil." Young's management suggest he is suffering from throat problems, and claim that the singer was acting on doctor's orders; Stills can only respond, "I have no future". "All I know," he explains in more stable mood the following year, "is that Neil turned left at Greensboro'."

AUGUST 1976
The Stills/Young Band's 'Long May You Run' is released.

29 AUGUST 1976
Neil Young joins the re-formed Spirit onstage in Santa Monica, California, to perform 'Like A Rolling Stone' – unbeknown to guitarist Randy California, who attempts to have Young thrown off the stage until he realises his identity. At the same show, Young also performs 'Just Like Tom Thumb's Blues' with the opening act, Firefall. Bootleg: 'Old Man's Fancy'/'Northern Sky'.

OCTOBER 1976
Reprise prepare for the imminent release of 'Decade', a three-LP retrospective of Young's career, by manufacturing test pressings of the set. These include the full-length version of 'Campaigner', which is edited when the albums are finally issued exactly a year later. Young requests 'Decade' to be postponed while he gets ready another new album, provisionally entitled 'Chrome Dreams', supposedly due for November release.

16 OCTOBER 1976
'Long May You Run' reaches No. 12, its peak position on the UK LP chart.

NOVEMBER 1976
Recording: 'Look Out For My Love' (with Crazy Horse), 'Hold Back The Tears' (solo), and 'Too Far Gone' (with Frank Sampedro).

1 NOVEMBER 1976
Dorothy Chandler Pavilion, Los Angeles, California, at the start of a US tour with Crazy Horse.

2 NOVEMBER 1976
The Community Center, Berkeley, California. First known performance of 'Give Me Strength'.

4 NOVEMBER 1976
The Forum, Los Angeles, California. Young performs 'Campaigner', 'Human Highway', 'After The Goldrush', 'Pocahontas', 'Too Far Gone', 'Old Man', 'A Man Needs A Maid', 'Sugar Mountain', 'Country Home', 'Don't Cry No Tears', 'Down By The River', 'Lotta Love', 'Like A Hurricane', 'Drive Back', 'Cinnamon Girl' and 'Cortez The Killer'. Bootlegs: 'Old Man's Fancy'/'Northern Sky'.

6 NOVEMBER 1976
Balch Fieldhouse, Boulder, Colorado. 'Homegrown' makes a rare appearance in the set-list.

7 NOVEMBER 1976
Balch Fieldhouse, Boulder, Colorado.

9 NOVEMBER 1976
Austin, Texas.

10 NOVEMBER 1976
Tarrant County Convention Center, Fort Worth, Texas.

11 NOVEMBER 1976
Houston, Texas.

14 NOVEMBER 1976
Dane County Coliseum, Madison, Wisconsin. During the acoustic set, Young briefly starts to play 'Don't Say You Win, Don't Say You Lose', then explains: "This is not the night for that song, folks, it's too sad!". It *is* that kind of night, as it turns out: after his guitar amp malfunctions, Young performs much of 'Like A Hurricane' on piano.

15 NOVEMBER 1976
Arie Crown Theater, Chicago, Illinois. Bootlegs: 'Love Art Blues' (4 songs), 'Depression Blues' (1 song).

18-20 NOVEMBER 1976
The Palladium, New York, New York. 'Give Me Strength' is performed again on the 18th, for the penultimate time.
'Long May You Run' hits its peak position of No. 25 on the US LP chart in *Billboard*.

22 NOVEMBER 1976
Boston Music Hall, Boston, Massachusetts. (2 shows). The final performance of 'Give Me Strength' is heard during this evening, which also includes a radical reworking of 'The Old Laughing Lady'.

24 NOVEMBER 1976
Atlanta, Georgia (2 shows).

25 NOVEMBER 1976
Young appears as one of The Band's guests at their stellar 'farewell' concert, The Last Waltz, at the Winterland Palace, San Francisco, California. He performs 'Four Strong Winds' and 'Helpless' during the main show, joins Joni Mitchell (who sings back-up on 'Helpless') to play harmonica on her 'Furry Sings The Blues', and then takes part in the all-star finale of 'I Shall Be Released', and the subsequent instrumental jam.
Young: "I was fried for the Last Waltz. I was gone, you know? I'm not proud of it. They just caught me at a bad time. I had been on the road for 45 days and I'd done two shows the night before in Atlanta and I just got carried away, and we just blew it out the window. So I was still up."

2 DECEMBER 1976
The Bodega, Santa Cruz, California, guesting with Crazy Horse.

Young ends 1976 amid a flurry of media plaudits for his live work with Crazy Horse. Rather than capitalise on that attention with a new electric album, he prepares a mostly solo set called 'Chrome Dreams' – a strange mixture of rowdy rock songs and delicate, ultra-personal ballads – and then, erratic as ever, cancels it.

Instead, he picks four of the 'Chrome Dreams' tunes and combines them with five good-time honky-tonk rockers, cut in a single rehearsal session with Linda Ronstadt and a woman who has caught Young's eye for more than purely artistic reasons, Nicolette Larson. The result is the almost schizophrenic 'American Stars'n'Bars', a slightly disappointing offering which is soon overshadowed by the delayed release of the mighty 'Decade' compilation.

Maintaining his eclectic reputation, Young turns up in Santa Cruz late in the year as part of a bar band called The Ducks – an impromptu aggregation who play fierce R&B before crowds numbering in tens rather than thousands. As soon as the national press realise what he is doing, Young calls the fun to a halt. Having purged his electric needs for a few months, he begins work on a lush, country-flavoured record, provisionally titled 'Gone With The Wind' – on which Nicolette Larson, coincidentally enough, just happens to play a vital role.

12 JANUARY 1977
Despite critical disappointment and personal friction, the Stills/Young Band's 'Long May You Run' LP achieves gold-record status in the USA.

16 MARCH 1977
Acetates of the completed 'Chrome Dreams' album are cut in New York by Warner Brothers. The projected line-up for the album is (Side 1) 'Pocahontas', 'Will To Love', 'Star Of Bethlehem', 'Like A Hurricane', 'Too Far Gone'; (Side 2) 'Hold Back The Tears', 'Homegrown', 'Captain Kennedy', 'Stringman', 'Sedan Delivery', 'Powderfinger', 'Look Out For My Love'.

LATE MARCH 1977
Young visits Linda Ronstadt's home to meet singer Nicolette Larson, who has been recommended to him as a session singer.

APRIL 1977
Young makes an unannounced appearance at the Crosby, Stills and Nash sessions at Criteria Studios in Miami, the first meeting of the CSNY quartet since the collapse of their studio project the previous year. "We never hold any grudges," notes Graham Nash.
Recording: a second shot at 'Everybody's Alone'.

4 APRIL 1977
Linda Ronstadt and Nicolette Larson are invited to join Young for a rehearsal session at his ranch. Unknown to them, the rehearsals are taped, and 'The Old Country Waltz',

'Saddle Up The Palomino', 'Hey Babe', 'Hold Back The Tears' and 'Bite The Bullet' are used on his next album.

3 MAY 1977
Recording: 'Field Of Opportunity', 'It Might Have Been' and a remake of 'Dance, Dance, Dance'.

JUNE 1977
'American Stars And Bars' released in the USA. "I think it would be just about impossible to over-rate Neil Young," raves *Rolling Stone*'s reviewer, Paul Nelson.

AUGUST 1977
'Like A Hurricane' single mix prepared.

12 AUGUST 1977
Crosby, Nash and Young at the Civic Auditorium, Santa Cruz, California. The show begins as a Crosby benefit for the United Farmworkers union, before Nash and Young join him onstage. Young performs 'Human Highway', 'New Mama', 'Only Love Can Break Your Heart' and a closing three-part harmony rendition of 'Sugar Mountain'.

22 AUGUST 1977
Young begins an anonymous set of guest appearances with a band led by former Moby Grape bassist Bob Mosely and guitarist Jeff Blackburn, with a show at the Crossroads, Santa Cruz. The band take on the identity of The Ducks, and amaze the paltry audiences of drinkers with blistering sets of electric rock'n'roll.
The tumultuous instrumental 'Windward Passage' is performed for the first time, alongside Young songs like 'Crying Eyes', 'Mr Soul', 'Comes A Time', 'Sail Away' and 'Are You Ready For The Country', Randy Newman's 'Gone Dead Train', some Fifties rock'n'roll covers, and a bunch of material written by the other members of the band. Bootleg: 'Northern Sky' (5 songs).

24 AUGUST 1977
The Crossroads, Santa Cruz, with The Ducks.

27 AUGUST 1977
The Catalyst, Santa Cruz, with The Ducks.
'American Stars And Bars' peaks at No. 21 on *Billboard*'s US LP chart.

SEPTEMBER 1977
Recording: 'Lost In Space'.

1 SEPTEMBER 1977
Santa Cruz Civic Auditorium, Santa Cruz, California. This is the final Ducks show: Young abruptly ends his bar-room experiment after his secret run of gigs is exposed in the media.

9 SEPTEMBER 1977
'American Stars And Bars' enters the UK LP chart at its peak position of No. 17.

OCTOBER 1977
Young begins a relationship with singer Nicolette Larson.
   Recording: 'Goin' Back' and 'Human Highway' (version 2).
   The three-LP set 'Decade' is finally released, a year after the original test pressings are manufactured. It features several unreleased recordings, with the bonus of Young's handwritten notes explaining (or sometimes not) the genesis of the songs.

31 OCTOBER 1977
Recording: 'Sail Away'.

NOVEMBER 1977
Recording: 'Comes A Time', 'Peace Of Mind', 'Already One' and 'Four Strong Winds'.

19 NOVEMBER 1977
Bicentennial Park, Miami, Florida, for the only performance with the Gone With The Wind Orchestra. The ensemble perform 'Are You Ready For The Country', 'Dance Dance Dance'/'Love Is A Rose', 'Old Man', 'The Losing End', 'Heart Of Gold', 'The Needle And The Damage Done', 'Sugar Mountain', the first known performances of 'Already One' and 'Lady Wingshot' (available on 'Northern Sky' bootleg), 'Four Strong Winds', 'Down By The River', a version of Young's 'Alabama' that segues into Lynyrd Skynyrd's anti-Young tirade 'Sweet Home Alabama' (a tribute to the members of the band killed in an air crash three months earlier), and a closing reprise of 'Are You Ready For The Country'.

21 NOVEMBER 1977
Recording: 'Daughters' (version 2), 'Please Help Me I'm Falling' and 'Motorcycle Mama'.

23 NOVEMBER 1977
Recording: 'We're Having Some Fun'.

17 DECEMBER 1977
'Decade' reaches its peak position on both the US (No. 48) and UK (No. 46) LP charts.

1978

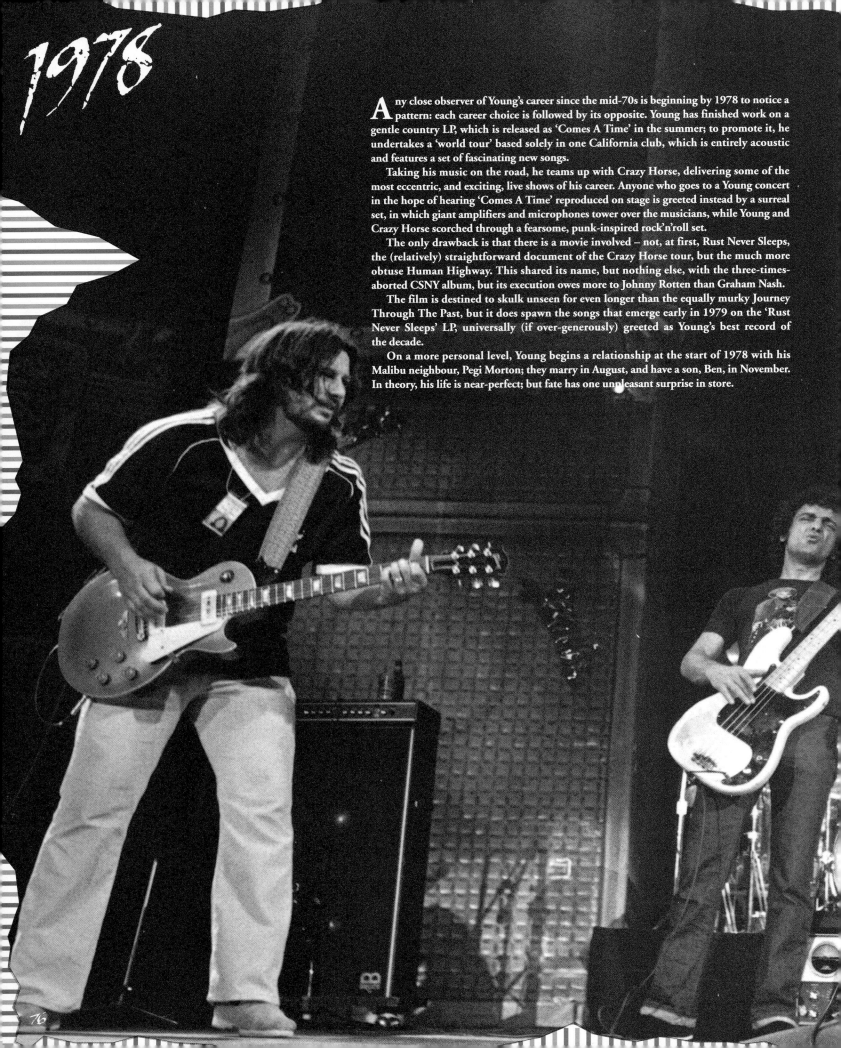

Any close observer of Young's career since the mid-70s is beginning by 1978 to notice a pattern: each career choice is followed by its opposite. Young has finished work on a gentle country LP, which is released as 'Comes A Time' in the summer; to promote it, he undertakes a 'world tour' based solely in one California club, which is entirely acoustic and features a set of fascinating new songs.

Taking his music on the road, he teams up with Crazy Horse, delivering some of the most eccentric, and exciting, live shows of his career. Anyone who goes to a Young concert in the hope of hearing 'Comes A Time' reproduced on stage is greeted instead by a surreal set, in which giant amplifiers and microphones tower over the musicians, while Young and Crazy Horse scorched through a fearsome, punk-inspired rock'n'roll set.

The only drawback is that there is a movie involved – not, at first, Rust Never Sleeps, the (relatively) straightforward document of the Crazy Horse tour, but the much more obtuse Human Highway. This shared its name, but nothing else, with the three-times-aborted CSNY album, but its execution owes more to Johnny Rotten than Graham Nash.

The film is destined to skulk unseen for even longer than the equally murky Journey Through The Past, but it does spawn the songs that emerge early in 1979 on the 'Rust Never Sleeps' LP, universally (if over-generously) greeted as Young's best record of the decade.

On a more personal level, Young begins a relationship at the start of 1978 with his Malibu neighbour, Pegi Morton; they marry in August, and have a son, Ben, in November. In theory, his life is near-perfect; but fate has one unpleasant surprise in store.

The 'Rust Never Sleeps' tour with Crazy Horse in 1978 was Young's last full-scale series of concerts for four years.

JANUARY 1978
Young and Nicolette Larson split up; he begins dating Pegi Morton.

MARCH 1978
Reprise press up test copies of Young's new album, 'Give To The Wind'. The record is also briefly scheduled as 'Gone With The Wind', but eventually appears with the tracks slightly rejigged as 'Comes A Time'.

22 MARCH 1978
At a California press conference, Friends of the Earth announce plans for a charity concert on Memorial Day in Los Angeles, which will star an impressive list of artists – among them a re-formed Beatles line-up, and Neil Young. It transpires during the event that only the very loosest messages of support for the environmental cause have been obtained from the supposed headliners.

MAY 1978
Young confirms that he has begun work on a new movie called *Human Highway*, to be directed and co-written by Dean Stockwell. Devo, Dennis Hopper and Sally Kirkland are confirmed as co-stars in the film, to be shot on Young's ranch, in Taos, New Mexico, and in concert. Its theme, so a spokesman explains, will be "the people who follow Neil around".

Neil also reveals that he has signed another deal with Warner/Reprise, linking him with the label until 1982.

3 MAY 1978
A movie about a fictional radio station, *FM*, is premièred in Los Angeles, with a snippet of Young's 'Southern Man' included on the soundtrack.

24 MAY 1978
First of five nights at the Boarding House, San Francisco, California, which are partly filmed for the *Human Highway* project. The brief run of solo acoustic shows is billed as 'Neil Young's 1978 World Tour'. For the first time, Young utilises portable radio-mikes for these shows, enabling him to wander the stage at will; "I'm wired for sound," he quips, "and that's not all".

Young's first-night set features 'Pocahontas', 'Human Highway', 'Already One', 'Comes A Time', 'Birds', 'My My Hey Hey', 'Shots', 'Cowgirl In The Sand', 'After The Goldrush', 'Thrasher', 'The Ways Of Love', 'I Believe In You', 'Sugar Mountain' and 'Sail Away'. Bootleg: 'World Tour 1978'.

25-28 MAY 1978
Boarding House, San Francisco, California. A rare live performance of Buffalo Springfield's 'Out Of My Mind' is featured on the opening night.

EARLY JUNE 1978
Young stages a private gig with punk band Devo at Mabuhay Gardens in San Francisco, which is filmed for the *Human Highway* movie.

2 AUGUST 1978
Neil Young and Pegi Morton are married at Young's Malibu Beach home.

18 SEPTEMBER 1978
Young and Crazy Horse begin the 'Rust Never Sleeps' tour at the Pine Knob Theater, Clarkston, Michigan.

Young opens proceedings with an acoustic set: 'Sugar Mountain', 'I Am A Child', 'Comes A Time', 'Already One', 'After The Goldrush', 'Thrasher' and 'I Am A Child'. The electric set features 'When You Dance I Can Really Love', 'The Loner', 'Welfare Mothers', 'C'mon Baby Let's Go Downtown', 'The Needle And The Damage Done' (acoustic), 'Lotta Love', 'Sedan Delivery', 'Powderfinger', 'Cortez The Killer', 'Cinnamon Girl', 'Like A Hurricane', 'Hey Hey My My' and an encore of 'Tonight's The Night'.

For this tour, Young designs an outlandish stage set, featuring drastically oversized amplifiers and equipment; he dresses the 'Road-Eyes' as Star Wars extras, clad in monkish gowns with their faces hooded. The shows incorporate sections of the *Woodstock* film soundtrack and dialogue; Young emerges at the start of each performance from on top of one of the giant speakers, like a child awoken from a dream.

19 SEPTEMBER 1978
Pine Knob Theater, Clarkston, Michigan. First known performance of 'The Price That You Pay'.

21 SEPTEMBER 1978
Capitol Center, Largo, Maryland.

22 SEPTEMBER 1978
Richfield Coliseum, Cleveland, Ohio.

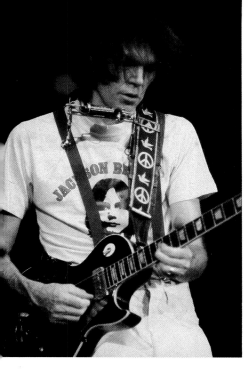

23 SEPTEMBER 1978
The Spectrum, Philadelphia, Pennsylvania.

25 SEPTEMBER 1978
Civic Auditorium, Providence, Rhode Island.

27/28 SEPTEMBER 1978
Madison Square Garden, New York, New York.

29 SEPTEMBER 1978
Nassau Coliseum, Hampstead, Long Island.

OCTOBER 1978
'Comes A Time' is released.
  Motown Records toy with the idea of releasing an album of Young's 1965 recordings with The Mynah Birds, but eventually conclude that there is insufficient material to justify the release.

1 OCTOBER 1978
Maple Leaf Gardens, Toronto, Canada.

4 OCTOBER 1978
Boston Garden, Boston, Massachusetts.

5 OCTOBER 1978
War Memorial, Rochester, New York.

7 OCTOBER 1978
William & Mary College, Williamsberg.

8 OCTOBER 1978
Coliseum, Charlotte, Virginia.

10 OCTOBER 1978
Omni Auditorium, Atlanta, Georgia.

11 OCTOBER 1978
Nashville, Tennessee.

12 OCTOBER 1978
Rupp Arena, Lexington, Kentucky.

14 OCTOBER 1978
Chicago Stadium, Chicago, Illinois. 'The Loner' and 'Like A Hurricane' from this show appear on 'Live Rust'

15 OCTOBER 1978
St. Paul Arena, St. Paul, Minneapolis. 'The Needle And The Damage Done', 'Lotta Love', 'Cortez The Killer' and 'Tonight's The Night' all end up on 'Live Rust'.

16 OCTOBER 1978
Dane County Coliseum, Madison.

17 OCTOBER 1978
Kemper Arena, Kansas City.

19 OCTOBER 1978
McNicholls Arena, Denver, Colorado. 'Cinnamon Girl' is retrieved for the 'Live Rust' album.

22 OCTOBER 1978
Cow Palace, San Francisco, California. A whole slew of songs are included on 'Live Rust': 'Sugar Mountain', 'I Am A Child', 'Comes A Time', 'After The Goldrush', 'My, My, Hey, Hey (Out Of The Blue)', 'When You Dance I Can Really Love', 'Sedan Delivery', 'Powderfinger' and 'Hey, Hey, My, My (Into The Black)'. This show is filmed, and subsequently released as *Rust Never Sleeps*, directed by Young under the pseudonym 'Bernard Shakey'.
  Young: "This is better than the concert, especially for all my friends who could never handle a concert scene, anyway. If you're into my music, you'll enjoy it, probably."

23/24 OCTOBER 1978
The Forum, Los Angeles, California. Bootlegs: 'Rust Never Sleeps'/'American Tour'. During the first show, Young's Zuma Beach house, once owned by F. Scott Fitzgerald, is destroyed by a bush fire on what comes to be known locally as Black Monday. Bootleg (24th): 'Rust Never Sleeps'/'Spring-field Slaughter'.

NOVEMBER 1978
Neil and Pegi Young's son Ben is born. Within a few months, he is diagnosed – like Young's first son, Zeke – as suffering from cerebral palsy.

4 NOVEMBER 1978
Former CSNY bassist Greg Reeves sues the four leaders of the band for $1million of alleged unpaid royalties.

9 DECEMBER 1978
'Comes A Time' reaches its peak position of No. 7 on the *Billboard* US LP chart.

In 1979, Young releases 'Rust Never Sleeps', a concert movie of the same name, and a tie-in (some thought cash-in) double-live album, 'Live Rust' – which may have been predictable, but still remains the ultimate testament to the sonic force of the Young/Crazy Horse combination. He also prepares an eccentric soundtrack for the movie *Where The Buffalo Roams*, which was premièred in 1980.

But the most important, and sickening, event of 1979 is the discovery that Neil and Pegi's son, Ben, is suffering from the same condition as his first child, Zeke: cerebral palsy. It was a one-in-a-million chance, there being no genetic reason why two children of the same parent should share the condition. But it leaves them reeling, and undoubtedly contributes to Neil's creative pause during this year – when he concentrates what energies he had on the *Human Highway* movie project.

FEBRUARY 1979
Crazy Horse release their 'Crazy Moon' album, several tracks of which have Young as co-producer and guest guitarist.

8 FEBRUARY 1979
Cameron Crowe's latest interview with Neil Young appears as the *Rolling Stone* cover story, under the title, 'The Last American Hero'.

29 JUNE 1979
Former Young cohort Jack Nitzsche is arrested on rape charges after an incident at the home of Young's former partner, actress Carrie Snodgrass.

EARLY JULY 1979
Accompanied by Nicolette Larson, Young attends a pre-release party for the 'Rust Never Sleeps' LP at Bundy Rent-A-Wreck, outside Los Angeles. When the album is released a few days later, *Rolling Stone*'s Paul Nelson raves: "Neil Young has made a record that defines the territory. Defines it, expands it, explodes it. Burns it to the ground... Neil

Young can outwrite, outsing, outplay, outthink, outfeel and outlast anybody in rock today."

Young: "I can relate to 'Rust Never Sleeps'. It relates to my career: the longer I keep going, the more I have to fight this corrosion."

11 JULY 1979
Rust Never Sleeps is premièred simultaneously at the Village Theater, Westwood, California, and the New Chinese Theater, Hollywood, California.

18 JULY 1979
Rust Never Sleeps opens in New York at the Palladium Theater.

3 SEPTEMBER 1979
Young is interviewed by Mary Turner for a promo LP.

22 OCTOBER 1979
In a preliminary court hearing, Carrie Snodgrass denies having accused Jack Nitzsche of rape, but the producer still faces charges of assault with a deadly weapon, and assault with intent to murder.

NOVEMBER 1979
The double-LP 'Live Rust', taken from the late 1978 tour, is released.

Young: "The first album that came out was all new songs, which was to give people an even break if they didn't want to buy the soundtrack album. If they don't want to hear the old songs again, they don't have to buy this one."

The Rust Never Sleeps movie documented the '78 tour, with its oversized stage sets and cameo appearances from the hooded 'Roadeyes'.

If Ben's sickness wasn't enough to bear, Young's wife Pegi is diagnosed as suffering from a potentially fatal brain condition early in 1980; for two months, she is given only a 50/50 chance of survival. It's not surprising that when she comes through surgery intact, Young celebrates the fact in a song called 'Stayin' Power'.

Young cuts that tune, and several more blue-collar country songs, in the early summer, and then sets out on a two-month family cruise. When he returns, he compiles a new record called 'Hawks & Doves', adding several vintage acoustic songs to the recent recordings, and then joins Pegi in abandoning their daily lives to the demands of The Program. This sinister-sounding schedule is designed to provide full-time stimulus and therapy for children suffering from cerebral palsy, and it rules out any question of Young simultaneously carrying on his usual round of recording and touring. Having a home studio does allow him to begin work on a new Crazy Horse LP at the end of the year, but the music they produce sounds as much like self-therapy as it does art.

2 FEBRUARY 1980
'Live Rust' attains its peak position of No. 15 in *Billboard*'s US LP chart.

MARCH 1980
Pegi Young is diagnosed as suffering from a brain tumour.

MCA release 'Where The Buffalo Roam', the soundtrack LP to a film based on the life and work of writer Hunter S. Thompson. Young is responsible for compiling the music, which includes several brief versions of the vintage cowboy song 'Home On The Range', performed in a variety of arrangements and retitled 'Buffalo Stomp' and 'Ode To Wild Bill'. The LP also features tracks by Jimi Hendrix, Bill Murray (the film's star), The Temptations, Bob Dylan, The Four Tops, and Creedence Clearwater Revival – a reflection of Young's own musical tastes.

APRIL 1980
Young attends The Eagles show at the L.A. Forum.

8 MAY 1980
Pegi Young successfully undergoes brain surgery.

late JUNE 1980
Recording: 'Stayin' Power', 'Coastline', 'Union Man', 'Comin' Apart At Every Nail' and 'Hawks & Doves'.

AUGUST/SEPTEMBER 1980
To celebrate Pegi Young's return to health, the family holiday for several weeks, sailing to the islands around Tahiti.

3 OCTOBER 1980
Young appears with The Hawks & Doves Band at the Bread & Roses Festival at the Greek Theater in Los Angeles, California, performing 'Turbine' for the only time in his career. Also performed are 'Are You Ready For The Country', 'Coastline', 'Staying Power', 'Motor City', 'Union Man', 'Comin' Apart At Every Nail', 'Hawks And Doves', 'Homegrown', 'Four Strong Winds' and a reprise of 'Are You Ready For The Country'.

9 OCTOBER 1980
Recording: 'Turbine' and 'Motor City'.

MID-OCTOBER 1980
The Youngs decide that radical therapy is required to alleviate their son Ben's condition: they decide to enrol in 'The Program', a rigid, demanding daily routine of treatment and education, propagated by the Institute for the Awareness of Human Potential. Young's commitment to the course entails his effective retirement from public life, with only brief periods in his home recording studio being devoted to his career over the next two years.

6 DECEMBER 1980
Recording: 'Get Back On It'.

7 DECEMBER 1980
Recording: 'Southern Pacific'.

8 DECEMBER 1980
Recording: 'Opera Star'.

9 DECEMBER 1980
Recording: 'Are There Any More Real Cowboys'.

27 DECEMBER 1980
Young is interviewed on the *Great American Radio Show*.

1981

The Program dominates the Youngs' life in 1981: he finishes work on the 'Re-Ac-Tor' LP with Crazy Horse, but makes little attempt to promote it. He plays no live gigs bar an unscheduled guest appearance at a tribute to bluesman Mike Bloomfield. Instead, he buys a vocal synthesiser, partly as a musical toy, and partly because he realises that it might help him to communicate with Ben.

10 JANUARY 1981
'Hawks & Doves' peaks at No. 30 on the *Billboard* US LP chart.

14 JANUARY 1981
Recording: 'Get Up Now'.

16 JANUARY 1981
Recording: 'Rapid Transit'.

MARCH 1981
Young appears onstage during the impromptu Mike Bloomfield Tribute at the Ritz Club in New York, playing a series of blues and rock'n'roll standards with the Danny Shea Band.

17 JUNE 1981
Recording: 'Surfer Joe And Moe The Sleaze', 'Shots' and 'To Me, To Me'.

20 JULY 1981
Recording: 'T-Bone'.

AUGUST 1981
Young buys himself a vocoder, which enables him to synthesise the human voice, and inspires him to write a batch of new songs.

23 NOVEMBER 1981
Young appears on the phone-in radio show *Rockline*.

DECEMBER 1981
The 'Re-Ac-Tor' album is released.

Movement and progress aren't always the same thing. Between 1982 and 1989, Neil Young shifts record labels twice, and musical direction many more times than that. It looks and probably feels like eclecticism, but only in retrospect is it as obvious to Young as it becomes to his fans that his diversity is a rambling effort to avoid committing himself artistically, at a stage of his life when his emotional reserves are being drained by personal and political traumas.

Two major shifts occur early in 1982, as Young quit Reprise Records, his contractual home since 1968, and then pulls his son Ben out of The Program. The latter decision frees Neil to resume his musical career; in theory, the former choice, which saw him sign with Geffen Records, the label owned by former CSNY manager David Geffen, should help him capitalise on that move.

No sooner has Young moved labels than he is almost enticed into a journey through the past, via a Buffalo Springfield reunion. Instead, he picks up Springfield bassist Bruce Palmer, unrecognisable as Young's skinny mid-60s sidekick, and transports him into the Trans Band, who tour Europe offering a mix of Young standards and vocoder music.

'Trans' is also the name of the album Young prepares during 1982 – but only after Geffen has refused his initial offering, deciding it is too close to his acoustic hippie past. Within a year or two, Geffen would be clutching desperately for anything that sounded remotely like a Neil Young record from the past. For the moment, they – and Young – enter into the new electronic age with enthusiasm.

Young's fans are less certain. He neglects to inform them at the time that the new vocoder songs are inspired by Ben; diehards simply see 'Trans' as another left-field meander, in the wake of 'Hawks & Doves' and 'Re-Ac-Tor'. And to some extent, they are right.

1982
Young's brother Bob is arrested for arranging a ring for selling 136 kilograms of hashish, valued at $5 million. He receives a seven-year jail sentence, though the conviction is subsequently overturned.

14 FEBRUARY 1982
The Youngs decide to withdrawn Ben from the strict confines of The Program, and work with him in a more flexible daily routine. Their decision frees Neil to resume his musical career.

MARCH 1982
Young is reported to be leaving Reprise Records for RCA. In fact, he signs with Geffen, the label owned by former CSNY co-manager David Geffen, and offers them an album called 'Island In The Sun'. They reject it, inaugurating a sorry interlude in Young's recording career.

Young: "That album will probably never be heard. The three acoustic songs from 'Trans' were on it. It didn't really register to me that I was being manipulated."

APRIL 1982
At the Canadian Music Awards, the Juno's, in Toronto, Neil Young is inducted into the Canadian Music Hall of Fame.

Simultaneously, Bruce Palmer schedules a reunion of the original Buffalo Springfield line-up, including Young, in California, but the meeting never takes place, because of Young's commitment to the Juno Awards ceremony. Instead, Young requests Palmer's presence on the sessions for 'Trans'.

Young: "We were thinking about getting the Springfield back together, and as a joke, I made an audition tape so that they'd know I was still kicking. I made 'Mr Soul' at home with the drum machine, but I never did play it for them."

MAY 1982
Young begins rehearsals with The Trans Band.

JUNE 1982
Young completes work on the *Human Highway* movie. "We tried to get the 'big bucks' people to distribute it," he explains in 1986. "Nobody put it out because it was too weird."

13 JULY 1982
The first night of The Trans tour warm-up shows, at Catalyst, Santa Cruz, California. The Trans band comprises Ralph Molina (drums), Ben Keith (steel guitar), Joe Lala (percussion), Nils Lofgren (guitar/keyboards/vocals) and Bruce Palmer on bass.

This show features 15 songs: 'On The Way Home', 'Don't Cry No Tears', 'Everybody Knows This Is Nowhere', 'Cowgirl In The Sand', the first ever live performance of 'If You Got Love', 'Helpless', 'Are You Ready For The Country', 'Southern Man', the only version of 'Only Love Can Break Your Heart' played by the Trans band, 'Little Thing Called Love', 'Old Man', 'Like An Inca', 'Hey Hey My My', 'Like A Hurricane' and a reprise of The Buffalo Springfield chestnut, 'On The Way Home'.

MID-JULY 1982
Bruce Palmer is fired from The Trans Band because of his drinking problem.

AUGUST 1982

Rolling Stone reports that Stephen Stills is "waiting for Neil Young to join" the summer Crosby, Stills and Nash tour so that they can re-form Buffalo Springfield. Stills rebuts the rumours: "A while back, Neil, me, Dewey, the original guys in the Springfield, got together in a hotel room and talked about maybe getting something together, but then Neil had to split to get some award in Canada and I had to get back to CSN."

3 AUGUST 1982

Keystone Club, Palo Alto, California. Bob Mosley replaces Bruce Palmer on bass for the Palo Alto shows, during which Nils Lofgren performs his own 'Destined To Love' for the only time on The Trans tour. Other additions to the set are 'Comes A Time', 'Cinnamon Girl', 'Sample And Hold' and 'Mr Soul'.

4 AUGUST 1982

Keystone Club, Palo Alto, California.

c 8 AUGUST 1982

Bruce Palmer is reinstated in The Trans Band, on condition he controls his drinking.

11 AUGUST 1982

Sherwood Hall, Salinas, California. The set includes the first ever live performance of 'Soul Of A Woman', while 'The Needle And The Damage Done' is also added to the repertoire.

12 AUGUST 1982

Sherwood Hall, Salinas, California.

13/14 AUGUST 1982

Catalyst, Santa Cruz, California. 'Cortez The Killer' replaces 'Cowgirl In The Sand' in the set on the 13th. 'Computer Age' is added to the set-list on the 14th.

LATE AUGUST 1982

Young tells reporter David Gans, "Neil Young from the Sixties and early Seventies is like Perry Como. If I was still taking that seriously, I'd be where Crosby, Stills and Nash are today."

31 AUGUST 1982

Parc De Sports, Annecy, France. The set-list for the first show of the main Trans tour comprises 'On The Way Home', 'Don't Cry No Tears', 'Everybody Knows This Is Nowhere', 'Cortez The Killer', 'If You Got Love', 'Soul Of A Woman', 'Are You Ready For The Country', 'Southern Man', 'Little Thing Called Love', 'Old Man', 'The Needle And The Damage Done', 'Comes A Time', 'Birds', Nils Lofgren's 'Beggars' Day', 'Like An Inca', 'Hey Hey My My', 'Cinnamon Girl', 'Like A Hurricane', 'Sample And Hold' and 'Mr Soul'.

SEPTEMBER 1982

CSNY's studio-enhanced live recording of 'Pushed It Over The End', based on a concert performance from Chicago in 1974, receives its only official release, as part of an Italian boxed set of Young's work.

1 SEPTEMBER 1982

Les Arènes, Fréjus, France. The show takes place during a violent thunderstorm.

4 SEPTEMBER 1982

Rheinweissen, Wiesbaden, W. Germany.

5 SEPTEMBER 1982

Zeppelinfield, Nuremburg, W. Germany. 'I Am A Child' makes its tour début. Bootleg: 'Hurricane Over Nuremberg'/'Wild Bunch'.

7 SEPTEMBER 1982

Arena di Verona, Verona, Italy.

8-10 SEPTEMBER 1982

Concerts in Verona (8th) and Milan (9th/10th) are cancelled.

11 SEPTEMBER 1982

Stadio dei Pini, Viareggio, Italy. Bootleg: 'Ippodromo Le Capannelle, Roma' (sic)/'Live'/'The Best Of Neil Young'/'Live In Italy'.

12 SEPTEMBER 1982

Ippodromo de Capanelle, Rome, Italy. Young stages a press conference at the Hilton Hotel before the show. 'Sugar Mountain' features for the first time on the *Trans* tour. Bootleg: 'Neil Young'.

Young: "Sometimes I was scared because people were throwing things, and glass was exploding on the stage, but mostly it was a good experience."

14 SEPTEMBER 1982

Sportshalle, Basle, Switzerland.

15 SEPTEMBER 1982

Parc Des Expositions, Dijon, France.

16 SEPTEMBER 1982

Isle St. Germain, Paris, France. The following night's show in Nantes is cancelled.

18 SEPTEMBER 1982

Stade Municipale, Quimper, France.

20/21 SEPTEMBER 1982

Ahoy Hall, Rotterdam, Holland. 'Computer Age' joins the regular tour set on the 20th.

22 SEPTEMBER 1982

French TV broadcast a Young interview from August, plus a live performance of 'Computer Cowboy'.

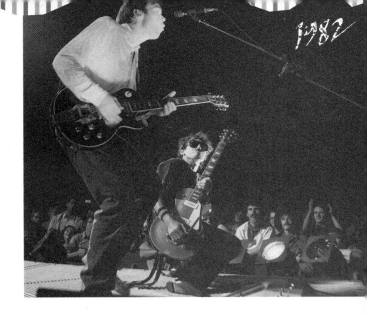

24 SEPTEMBER 1982
NEC, Birmingham. A show scheduled for the previous night is announced and then cancelled.

First and only live performance of 'Love Hotel', which Young had previously débuted during the soundcheck in an entirely different arrangement. 'Transformer Man' is also performed for the first time this tour. Guitar technician Joel Bernstein joins the band on vocoder for the remainder of the European shows.

26-28 SEPTEMBER 1982
Wembley Arena, London. Bootleg (26th): 'Wembley 83'. Nils Lofgren's mini-set is doubled by the inclusion of 'I Don't Want To Talk About It' on the 28th.

29 SEPTEMBER 1982
Young is interviewed for BBC Radio's *Rock On*.

30 SEPTEMBER 1982
Voorst National Stadium, Brussels, Belgium.

1 OCTOBER 1982
Parc Des Expositions, Lille, France.

3 OCTOBER 1982
Parc Des Expositions, Bordeaux, France.

5 OCTOBER 1982
Sportshalle, Cologne, West Germany. 'The Old Laughing Lady' and 'After The Goldrush' join the set-list, which is rejigged with 'On The Way Home', 'Don't Cry No Tears', 'Cortez The Killer', 'Birds', 'Like An Inca', 'I Am A Child' and 'I Don't Want To Talk About It' being dropped from this point on the tour, and 'Sugar Mountain', 'If You Got Love' and 'Soul Of A Woman' returning as regulars.

7 OCTOBER 1982
Drammenshalle, Oslo, Norway.

8 OCTOBER 1982
Scandinavium, Gothenburg, Sweden. Bootlegs: 'Transworld Tour'/'Forever Young'/'Like A Hurricane'/'Rock'n'Roll Can Never Die'/'Göteborg'.

9 OCTOBER 1982
Isstadion, Stockholm, Sweden. 'Helpless' is performed for the first time since the début warm-up show in Santa Cruz. Bootlegs: 'Criticism'/'My My Hey Hey'.

10 OCTOBER 1982
Broenbyhallen, Copenhagen, Denmark.

11 OCTOBER 1982
Westfallenhalle, Dortmund, W. Germany.

Young performs an unscheduled second encore of 'I Am A Child'. Bootleg: 'Computer Age'.

12 OCTOBER 1982
Olympiahalle, Munich, W. Germany.

14 OCTOBER 1982
Killesberghalle, Stuttgart, W. Germany. The venue for this show is switched from Dortmund after poor ticket sales.

15 OCTOBER 1982
Rhein-Necker-Halle, Heidelberg, W. Germany.

18 OCTOBER 1982
Deutschlandhalle, Berlin, W. Germany.

19 OCTOBER 1982
Deutschlandhalle, Berlin, W. Germany. Both the Berlin shows are videotaped by Young; this performance is subsequently used for the home-video, *Berlin Live*. Despite the line in the film credits stating 'Soundtrack available on Geffen Records', no live album was issued from this show, or tour.

First and only live performance of 'After Berlin'. 'Roll Another Number' played for the only time on this tour. What would have been the final night of the tour, at Berlin on the 20th, is cancelled.

NOVEMBER 1982
CBS International in Europe press up a limited number of test pressings of the 'Trans' LP, featuring one track omitted from the finished album ('If You Got Love') and a different mix of 'Like An Inca'. The change occurs too late to prevent early US copies of the album being distributed with 'If You Got Love' still listed on the back cover.

DECEMBER 1982
'Trans' is released, outraging many of Young's more conservative supporters, but winning praise from many reviewers for its radical blend of modernist and traditional styles.

Young: "The vocoders on 'Trans' are me trying to communicate with my younger son, Ben, who is unable to talk. He can understand what people are saying to him but can't reply. The more I am able to communicate with Ben, the less of a heavy thing it is."

For the Trans tour, Young adopted the persona of a techno-buff, using a vocoder to force his voice into an electronic whine; (top) with Nils Lofgren.

'Motorcity' and 'Revolution Blues' as his typical opening flurry, and introducing 'Heart Of Gold', 'Don't Be Denied' (on which he is accompanied by synth-drums) and 'Computer Age' later in the proceedings.

11 JANUARY 1983
Lloyd Noble Center Arena, Norman, Oklahoma.

13 JANUARY 1983
Music Hall, Houston, Texas. Young performs 'Are You Ready For The Country' for the only time on this US tour – on piano.

14 JANUARY 1983
Palmer Auditorium, Austin, Texas. 'Soul Of A Woman' and 'Helpless' join the regular set-list.

16 JANUARY 1983
McNicholls Arena, Denver, Colorado.

18 JANUARY 1983
ASU Activity Center, Tempe, Arizona.

19 JANUARY 1983
University Events Center, Santa Barbara, California.

20 JANUARY 1983
Golden Hall, San Diego, California.

22-24 JANUARY 1983
Universal Amphitheater, Los Angeles, California.

25 JANUARY 1983
Cow Palace, San Francisco, California. Bootlegs: 'Acoustic Tales Of Cowboys And Ladies'/'The Loner'.

26 JANUARY 1983
Young begins a set of sessions with his country band, cutting 'Depression Blues' and 'Winter Winds'.

27 JANUARY 1983
'Silver & Gold' recorded at House Of David Studios, Nashville.

28 JANUARY 1983
'Dance, Dance, Dance' recorded at House Of David Studios, Nashville.

29 JANUARY 1983
'Soul Of A Woman' recorded at House Of David Studios, Nashville.

30 JANUARY 1983
Keil Auditorium, St. Louis, Missouri.

31 JANUARY 1983
UICC Pavilion, Chicago, Illinois.

To celebrate the release of 'Trans', Young sets out on a solo US tour, mixing his past and present personas in carefree style. As if to confirm the forced eclecticism of this period, Young interrupts his tour only to start work on a country album, finished by early summer and presented to Geffen as 'Old Ways'. They reject it, and instead Young delivers the disastrously short and lacklustre 'Everybody's Rockin'', part of a rockabilly venture for which he enlists the help of The Shocking Pinks. Their live sets form an amusing climax to a second US tour, which is once again dominated by solo performances; but what was whimsical, sometimes even exciting on stage, is distressingly weak on record.

In the midst of The Shocking Pinks tour, Young comes under assault from an unexpected quarter: apparently not caring that Neil and Pegi are devoting themselves to helping Ben, Carrie Snodgrass chooses an interview with *People* magazine to call Neil's abilities as a father into question.

5 JANUARY 1983
Young opens his solo US tour, billed as 'A Very Special Evening With Neil Young', at the Civic Auditorium, Santa Cruz, California. The basic structure of the shows features an acoustic set, supported by eclectic video footage; an intermission, in which video MC 'Dan Clear' (played by actor Newell Alexander) entertains the audience; and a second set which incorporates some of the technology Young utilised on 'Trans'.

The opening night set-list is quite different from later concerts, as Young begins by playing 'Comes A Time', 'Country Home', 'Goin' Back', 'Coastline', 'Don't Let It Bring You Down', 'Cowgirl In The Sand', 'Don't Say You Win, Don't Say You Lose' and 'California Sunset'.

The second stage of the set remains virtually unchanged throughout the tour, and features 'Are There Any More Real Cowboys', 'Dance Dance Dance', 'My Boy', 'Pocahontas', 'Sail Away', 'Powderfinger', 'Ohio', 'Human Highway', 'After The Goldrush', 'Transformer Man', 'My, My, Hey, Hey', 'Mr Soul' and 'I Am A Child', before Young closes the first show with 'Sugar Mountain'.

10 JANUARY 1983
Fair Park Music Hall, Dallas, Texas. Young totally revamps the beginning of his set, adding 'The Old Laughing Lady',

FEBRUARY 1983
Young is reported to have recorded at least nine songs for a forthcoming country album – working in the studio "only when there's a full moon".

1 FEBRUARY 1983
Assembly Hall, Champaign, Illinois.

3 FEBRUARY 1983
University Of Georgia Coliseum, Athens, Georgia.

4 FEBRUARY 1983
Sundome, Tampa, Florida.

5 FEBRUARY 1983
James L. Knight Center, Miami, Florida. Another revamp for the Miami shows: 'Everybody Knows This Is Nowhere', 'Down By The River', 'Only Love Can Break Your Heart', 'Southern Man', 'The Losin' End' and 'Cortez The Killer' make their tour début.

6 FEBRUARY 1983
James L. Knight Center, Miami, Florida.

8 FEBRUARY 1983
Carmichael Auditorium, Chapel Hill, North Carolina.

10 FEBRUARY 1983
Civic Center, Hartford, Connecticut.

13 FEBRUARY 1983
Centrum, Worcester, Massachusetts.

14 FEBRUARY 1983
Coliseum, New Haven.

15 FEBRUARY 1983
Civic Center, Providence, Massachusetts. Young returns to 'Cortez The Killer' for another unusual acoustic performance, and plays 'Love Is A Rose' for the only time this tour – followed immediately by the melodically identical 'Dance Dance Dance'.

17 FEBRUARY 1983
War Memorial Auditorium, Buffalo, New York.

19 FEBRUARY 1983
Cobo Hall, Detroit, Michigan.

21 FEBRUARY 1983
Richfield Coliseum, Cleveland, Ohio.

22 FEBRUARY 1983
Civic Center, Baltimore, Maryland.

23 FEBRUARY 1983
Nassau Coliseum, Hampstead, Long Island.

24 FEBRUARY 1983
Madison Square Garden, New York, New York.

1 MARCH 1983
Market Square Arena, Indianapolis, Indiana.

2 MARCH 1983
Riverfront Coliseum, Cincinnati, Ohio.

3 MARCH 1983
Athens, Georgia.

4 MARCH 1983
The *Trans* tour is cancelled when Young collapses 45 minutes into his show in Louisville, Kentucky; doctors say he is suffering from flu and exhaustion.

MID-MARCH 1983
Young is reported to be considering a summer stadium tour, on a bill with The Stray Cats and The Cars.

Young has two completed albums ready for release, 'Everybody's Rockin' ' and 'Old Ways': he is told by Geffen to shelve the latter.

Young: "Geffen rejected the original 'Old Ways'. They said, 'Frankly, Neil, this record scares us a lot. We don't think this is the right direction for you to be going in.' It was like 'Harvest II', a combination of the musicians from 'Harvest' and 'Comes A Time'. It was much more of a Neil Young record than 'Old Way II'. "

JUNE 1983
Young's manager Elliott Roberts, announces that the performer is not interested in obtaining corporate sponsorship for his tours. "You couldn't believe a word Neil Young said if he did that," Roberts notes.

21 JUNE 1983
The Shocking Pinks tour is scheduled to begin at the Blossom Music Center in Cleveland, Ohio, but the date is cancelled.

1 JULY 1983
The Shocking Pinks tour begins belatedly at the Kansas Coliseum, Wichita. The concerts are designed to showcase Young's acoustic music at venues where he didn't play on the Trans tour; after a lengthy solo performance, he is joined for the brief second set by his rockabilly combo, The Shocking Pinks (Larry Byrom, Anthony Crawford, Rick Palombi and Larry Cragg).

Young's acoustic set ranges across his entire career: throughout the first half of the tour (up to the end of July), it remains effectively unchanged, featuring the following songs: 'Comes A Time', 'Motor City', 'Down By The River', 'Soul Of A Woman', 'Old Ways',

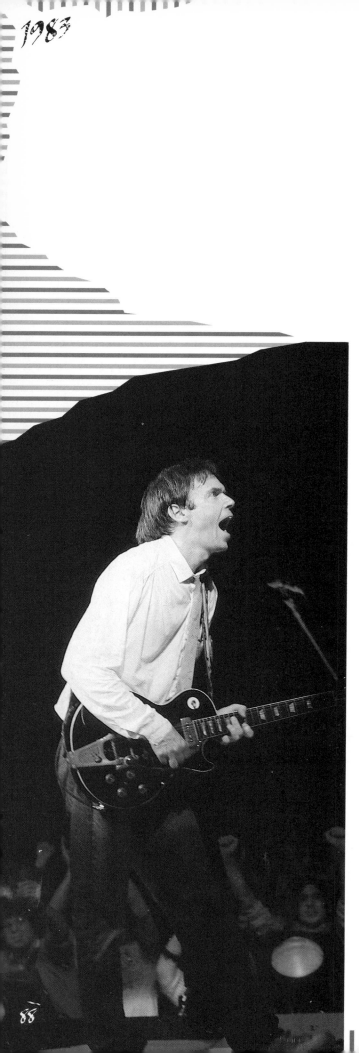

'Old Man', 'Helpless', 'Dance Dance Dance', 'Heart Of Gold', 'Don't Be Denied', 'Sail Away', 'Powderfinger', 'Ohio', 'After The Goldrush', 'Transformer Man', 'My, My, Hey, Hey', 'Mr. Soul' and 'Sugar Mountain'. The Shocking Pinks' set is slightly more flexible, though it is based around a standard group of songs: 'Jelly Roll Man', 'It's All Right', 'Kinda Fonda Wanda', 'Bright Lights, Big City', 'Wonderin'' and 'Everybody's Rockin''.

2 JULY 1983
Kemper Arena, Kansas City, Oklahoma. In honour of the venue, The Shocking Pinks' perform the Leiber/Stoller R&B chestnut, 'Kansas City'.

4 JULY 1983
Civic Auditorium, Omaha, Nebraska. 'Cry Cry Cry' makes its sole appearance in a Shocking Pinks set.

7 JULY 1983
Metro Center, Minneapolis, Minnesota. 'Do You Wanna Dance' enters The Shocking Pinks' repertoire, becoming a staple by the end of the tour.

9 JULY 1983
Alpine Valley Music Theater, East Troy, Wisconsin.

10 JULY 1983
Civic Center, Peoria, Illinois.

12 JULY 1983
Mid-South Coliseum, Memphis, Tennessee.

15 JULY 1983
Reunion Arena, Dallas, Texas.

16 JULY 1983
The Summit, Houston, Texas. The final performance of 'Betty Lou's Got A New Pair Of Shoes', which has featured in most of The Shocking Pinks' sets to this point.

18 JULY 1983
Convention Center, San Antonio, Texas. 'Get Gone' replaces 'Betty Lou...' in the set-list.

20 JULY 1983
Pan American Center, Las Cruces, New Mexico.

23/24 JULY 1983
Irvine Meadows, Laguna Hills, California. Graham Nash guests on 'Ohio' both nights.

26 JULY 1983
California Expo, Sacramento, California.

27 JULY 1983
Coliseum, Portland, Oregon.

28 JULY 1983
Coliseum, Seattle, Washington.

30 JULY 1983
Coliseum, Vancouver, Canada.

AUGUST 1983
Release date of 'Everybody's Rockin'' LP in US.

Carrie Snodgrass makes disparaging remarks about Young's performance as a father during an interview with *People* magazine. She is explaining her decision to sue Neil for $10,000 child support/ maintenance per month; the story fails to mention that Neil is already paying Carrie and Zeke more than $6,000 per month. The court eventually fixes maintenance at less than Neil is already paying.

27 AUGUST 1983
Coliseum, Hampton, Virginia. Young revises the acoustic set for the second leg of the tour, dropping 'Motorcity', 'Soul Of A Woman', 'Old Ways', 'Powderfinger' and 'After The Goldrush', and replacing them with 'Love Is A Rose', 'Only Love Can Break Your Heart', 'The Needle And The Damage Done', 'Field Of Opportunity', 'I Got A Problem' and 'Computer Age'. With minor revisions, this repertoire remains intact for the rest of the tour. Meanwhile, The Shocking Pinks' set-list is identical to the previous show in Vancouver.

28/29 AUGUST 1983
The Spectrum, Philadelphia, Pennsylvania.

30 AUGUST 1983
State Fair, Syracuse, New York. Young drops 'It's All Right', 'Kinda Fonda Wanda' and 'Bright Lights, Big City' from the increasingly static Shocking Pinks' set, and introduces 'Payola Blues' and 'Don't Take Your Love'.

1 SEPTEMBER 1983
Brendan Byrne Arena, East Rutherford, New Jersey. Young performs 'Don't Let It Bring You Down' for the only time during this tour.

2 SEPTEMBER 1983
Tanglewood Music Center, Boston, Massachusetts.

4 SEPTEMBER 1983
Performing Arts Center, Saratoga Springs, New York.

6 SEPTEMBER 1983
Blossom Music Center, Cuyahoga Falls, Ohio.

7 SEPTEMBER 1983
Civic Center, Pittsburgh, Pennsylvania.

10 SEPTEMBER 1983
University Coliseum, Morgantown.

12 SEPTEMBER 1983
Pine Knob Theater, Clarkstown, Michigan. After Young's solo set (which includes two additions, 'Too Far Gone' and the sole tour performance of 'I Am A Child') is poorly received, he scraps The Shocking Pinks' portion of the performance. "That crowd just didn't deserve The Shocking Pinks," he explains after the show. "I guess I'll get criticised, but you don't put your best horse out on a gravel track, do you?"

13 SEPTEMBER 1983
Civic Center, Lansing, Michigan. The Shocking Pinks return, with a previously unheard song, 'Johnny Ride On', while 'Soul Of A Woman' reappears in the acoustic set.

15 SEPTEMBER 1983
Poplar Creek Music Center, Hoffman Estates, Illinois. Young opens the show with 'The Old Laughing Lady' in place of 'Comes A Time'.

16 SEPTEMBER 1983
Assembly Hall, Bloomington, Indiana.

18 SEPTEMBER 1983
Hal Ashby films a 90-minute documentary of The Shocking Pinks' show at the Hara Arena, in Dayton, Ohio: 30 minutes of interview, 60 of music. Young: "I know I finished it, and I gave it to somebody. I don't know what happened to it."

'Get Gone' and 'Don't Take Your Love Away From Me' from this show are eventually issued on the 1993 compilation 'Lucky Thirteen'.

19 SEPTEMBER 1983
Reed Fieldhouse, Kalamazoo, Michigan.

21 SEPTEMBER 1983
Dane County Coliseum, Madison.

24 SEPTEMBER 1983
Evansville, Indiana.

26 SEPTEMBER 1983
Grand Ole Opry, Nashville, Tennessee. Suitably enough, Young includes 'Are There Any More Real Cowboys?' in this show in the heart of the country music industry.

27 SEPTEMBER 1983
Civic Center, Atlanta, Georgia.

28 SEPTEMBER 1983
Cameron Stadium, Durham, North Carolina.

30 SEPTEMBER 1983
James Madison University, Harrisburg, Virginia.

1 OCTOBER 1983
Beacon Theater, New York, New York; the final date of The Pinks' tour.

EARLY OCTOBER 1983
Pegi and Neil Young are named Parents Of The Year by the National Academy of Child Development.

10 OCTOBER 1983
Young makes another appearance on the phone-in radio show, *Rockline*. Asked about the possibility of CSNY ever re-forming, he comments: "The building's still standing. It didn't burn down or anything. I've told David Crosby that if he straightens up, I'll join the group again, and we'll do something. And that's all I can do."

AUTUMN 1983
Young's father, Scott Young, publishes his autobiographical memoir, *Neil And Me*, which gives a unique personal insight into his son's life and career.

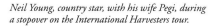

Neil Young, country star, with his wife Pegi, during a stopover on the International Harvesters tour.

Young was a techno freak in 1982, and a country balladeer and a rockabilly cat in 1983. He begins 1984 in more familiar mould, leading Crazy Horse through some hard rock shows in Santa Cruz. But album sessions featuring the same material soon collapse, and instead Young lurches back towards country, forming a new combo called The International Harvesters.

This top-flight band maintains his interest for the next 12 months, allowing him to record and sometimes perform live a slew of fresh material – including one song, 'Amber Jean', celebrating the birth of his daughter, who is mercifully free from any sign of cerebral palsy.

Along with the trappings of country music, Young begins to take on the mind-set of the Deep South. In a confusing series of political statements in US election year, the Canadian singer seems to align himself firmly behind Republican incumbent Ronald Reagan, to the disgust of the remnants of the international counter-culture. In retrospect, part of Young's attitude can be written off as sheer wilfulness, a refusal to be understood too quickly. Part, though, comes from his conviction that it is nothing short of naïve to write off every one of Reagan's policies as reactionary bunkum. The man who once railed against Nixon's heavy-handed policies now relishes the smack of firm government in his adopted country.

Nothing in Young's career damages his reputation in Europe as much as his partial defence of President Reagan. Five years after he was greeted as the only surviving icon of the hippie era, he is ridiculed and dismissed in the British rock press and beyond – held up as an example of everything that is corrupt and tired about the Sixties rock establishment. The fact that he cancels a European tour at short notice, apparently in fear of terrorist attack, simply increases the media attacks.

Young has brought that trouble upon himself, but his other conflict of 1984 comes from a less expected quarter. Even before he has completed work on the revised version of his 'Old Ways' country album, it emerges that Young is being sued by Geffen Records for delivering "unrepresentative" product. After the meagre sales of 'Trans' and 'Everybody's Rockin' ', David Geffen is now demanding exactly the kind of Young LP that he'd rejected back in 1982. Stubborn to a fault, Young is prepared to play country music for the rest of his life, rather than back down.

6/7 FEBRUARY 1984

Catalyst, Santa Cruz, with Crazy Horse. (2 shows) The explosive first night electric set features the first known performances of several songs (marked with an *): 'Rock Forever*', 'So Tired*', 'The Violent Side*', 'I Got A Problem*', 'Stand By Me (sung by Billy Talbot)*', 'Your Love*', 'Powderfinger', 'Barstool Blues', 'Welfare Mothers', 'Touch The Night*', 'Tonight's The Night' and 'Hey Hey My My'. The last song isn't played in the second set, where it's replaced by 'Cinnamon Girl' and 'Homegrown'. Bootlegs: 'Stand By Me'/'Touch The Night'/'The Violent Side'.

The second nights two sets duplicate the previous night's performances, except that 'Cortez The Killer' replaces 'Homegrown' in the second set. Bootlegs: 'Touch The Night'/'The Violent Side'/'Catalytic Reaction'/'Stand By Me'.

FEBRUARY/MARCH

Young attempts to record a new album with Crazy Horse, but the sessions are eventually aborted, and Young ends up taping some solo tracks with a synclavier.

Billy Talbot (Crazy Horse): "It just wasn't the right time. Everything was wrong. It was a very bad experience. We tried 'Touch The Night' and 'Violent Side', but it didn't work."

David Briggs (producer): "They played like monkeys."

MAY 1984

Young assembles a new band, The International Harvesters: Tim Drummond (bass), Karl Himmel (drums), Rufus Thibodeaux (fiddle), Spooner Oldham (keyboards), Ben Keith (steel guitar) and Anthony Crawford (rhythm guitar). Crawford excepted, the entire band have previous experience of Young's flirtations with country music — which remains the focus of the Harvesters' year-long career.

15 MAY 1984

Amber Jean Young, Pegi and Neil's daughter, is born.

6 JUNE 1984

Two shows with International Harvesters at the Saddle Rock Club, San Jose, California. The set list for the opening show comprises 'Are You Ready For The Country', 'Motor City', 'Comes A Time', 'Hawks And Doves', 'Saddle Up The Palomino', 'Old Man', the first known performance of 'Amber Jean', 'Roll Another Number', 'The Ways Of Love', 'Southern Pacific', 'It Might Have Been', 'Heart Of Gold', the first-ever 'California Sunset' and a première of 'Get Back To The Country'.

For the second set, Young reprises 'Are You Ready For The Country' at the close, and adds 'Flying On The Ground Is Wrong' and 'Bite The Bullet'.

18 JUNE 1984
Two shows with The International Harvesters at the Country Club, Los Angeles.

19 JUNE 1984
Two shows with The International Harvesters at the Palomino Club, Los Angeles. 'Comes A Time' is performed twice during the first set, which also features 'Too Far Gone' and 'Field Of Opportunity'. In the second set, Young adds three more songs to the Harvesters' repertoire, 'Hold Back The Tears', the first known performance of 'Razor Love' and 'Dance Dance Dance'.

22 JUNE 1984
Austin Opry House, with The International Harvesters. At the Austin shows, Young closes both the main set and the encores with 'Get Back To The Country'. Making their Harvesters début are 'Are There Any More Real Cowboys', 'Soul Of A Woman' and 'Love Is A Rose', which replaces the almost identical 'Dance Dance Dance'.

23 JUNE 1984
Austin Opry House, with The International Harvesters.

26 JULY 1984
'Overnight' & 'Higher Than Anyone Can Count' recorded at Right Track Studios, New York.

27 JULY 1984
'Up Jumped Love' recorded at Right Track.

10 AUGUST 1984
Proposed date for start of cancelled European tour – called off, according to rumours in the UK press, because Young is afraid to travel across the Atlantic in case of a Libyan terrorist attack on his aircraft. American sources, meanwhile, stress that commercial advice from the promoters is the reason for the cancellation.

23 AUGUST 1984
The International Harvesters launch a North American arena tour with Waylon Jennings and his wife Jessi Colter as support act, in Ottawa, Ontario, Canada. The sets on this tour are made up of the songs played at the Los Angeles and Austin shows in June.

24 AUGUST 1984
The Forum, Montreal, Canada.

25 AUGUST 1984
Civic Center, Cornwall, Ontario, Canada.

27 AUGUST 1984
Metro Center, Halifax, Canada.

28 AUGUST 1984
Monckton, Canada.

29 AUGUST 1984
Fredericton, New Brunswick, Canada.

SEPTEMBER 1984
Young is reported to be involved in litigation with his label, Geffen Records, with the company accusing him of having delivered "unrepresentative" material on his albums.
  Young: "Eventually they dropped that lawsuit after a year and a half of harassing me, because I told them the longer you sue me for playing country music, the longer I'm going to play country music. Either you back off or I'm going to play country music forever. And then you won't be able to sue me because country music will be what I always do, so it won't be uncharacteristic anymore."

1 SEPTEMBER 1984
CNE Grandstand, Toronto, Canada. Supported by The Good Brothers. The night's performance of 'Helpless' is dedicated to "the people of Omemee". Bootleg: 'Depression Blues' (1 song).

3 SEPTEMBER 1984
Popular Creek Outdoor Theater, Hoffman Estates, Chicago, Illinois. This concert was originally booked as a Waylon Jennings show, but Young was added to the bill after two weeks.

4 SEPTEMBER 1984
Meadowbrook Center, Rochester, New York.

5 SEPTEMBER 1984
Pittsburg Civic Arena, Philadelphia.

7 SEPTEMBER 1984
Cumberland County Civic Center, Portland, Maine.

8 SEPTEMBER 1984
Sullivan Stadium, Foxboro', Massachusetts.

9 SEPTEMBER 1984
Jones Beach Theater, Wantaugh, New York. Nils Lofgren joins The International Harvesters for this show, his night off from playing on the Bruce Springsteen tour. Support acts were Waylon Jennings and Jessi Colter.

11 SEPTEMBER 1984
The Newport Music Hall, Columbus, Ohio.

12 SEPTEMBER 1984
The Newport Music Hall, Columbus, Ohio.

First known performance of 'Good Phone', while 'Razor Love' disappears from Young's repertoire after this show.

14 SEPTEMBER 1984
Blossom Music Center, Cuyahoga Falls, Ohio.

15 SEPTEMBER 1984
Charlie Starr's, Springfield, Ohio. 'Hold Back The Tears' and 'Long May You Run' make rare appearances.

16 SEPTEMBER 1984
Emins Auditorium, Muncie, Indiana.

18 SEPTEMBER 1984
Grand Ole Opry, Nashville, Tennessee.

20 SEPTEMBER 1984
Nashville Now TV taping, TNN Studios, Nashville, Tennessee. Young performs 'Field Of Opportunity', 'Amber Jean' and 'Are You Ready For The Country' (with Waylon Jennings), and is interviewed by host Ralph Emery.

21 SEPTEMBER 1984
Riverbend Music Center, Cincinnatti, Ohio.

22 SEPTEMBER 1984
Rupp Arena, Lexington, Kentucky.

23 SEPTEMBER 1984
Omni Auditorium, Atlanta, Georgia.

25 SEPTEMBER 1984
Austin City Limits KLRU TV taping at University Of Texas, Austin, Texas. The show is screened on 27 January 1985, though from a two-hour show, only 14 songs are broadcast: 'Are You Ready For The Country', 'Field Of Opportunity', 'Are There Any More Real Cowboys', 'Good Phone', 'Heart Of Gold', 'Amber Jean', 'Roll Another Number', 'Comes A Time', 'The Needle And The Damage Done', 'Helpless', 'California Sunset' (a performance included on the 1985 LP 'Old Ways'), 'Old Man', 'Get Back To The Country' and 'Down By The River'. The show is subsequently re-edited twice – once with 'Powderfinger' added to the line-up, the other with the set reduced to 25 minutes of highlights. Bootleg: 'Austin City Limits'/'Live In Austin, Texas, '84'.

26 SEPTEMBER 1984
Municipal Auditorium Shreveport, Louisiana.

27 SEPTEMBER 1984
World's Fair, International Amphitheater, New Orleans, Louisiana. Bootlegs: 'Down By The River'/'Love Art Blues' (2 tracks).

29 SEPTEMBER 1984
Gilley's Rodeo Arena, Pasadena, Texas.

30 SEPTEMBER 1984
Billy Bob's, Fort Worth, Texas.

2 OCTOBER 1984
Canes Ballroom, Tulsa, Oklahoma.

3 OCTOBER 1984
Norman, Oklahoma.

9 OCTOBER 1984
Winnipeg, Canada.

11 OCTOBER 1984
Regina, Saskatchewan, Canada

13 OCTOBER 1984
Edmonton, Canada.

14 OCTOBER 1984
Olympic Saddledrome, Calgary, Canada.

16 OCTOBER 1984
Kamloops, Canada.

17 OCTOBER 1984
Pacific National Exhibition Coliseum, Vancouver, Canada. First known performance of 'Silver And Gold', while 'The Losing End' also makes a rare appearance.

18 OCTOBER 1984
Portland, Oregon.

20 OCTOBER 1984
Reno, Nevada.

22 OCTOBER 1984
Universal Amphitheater, Los Angeles, California. First known performance of 'Thank God I'm On The Road Tonight'.

23 OCTOBER 1984
'Mystery Man' recorded at Amigo Studio, North Hollywood.
Universal Amphitheater, Los Angeles, California.

24 OCTOBER 1984
Pacific Amphitheater, Costa Mesa, California.

26 OCTOBER 1984
Greek Theater, Berkeley, California.

5 NOVEMBER 1984
'Someone Who Cares For Me' recorded at Power Station, New York.

7 DECEMBER 1984
'Don't Make Me Wait' recorded at Shakedown Studio, New York.

One of the lowpoints of Live Aid was the disgracefully ragged CSNY reunion. "Man, you should have heard us in the trailer before the show," Crosby said later. "We sounded great!"

Young's "unrepresentative" work as a country singer continues throughout 1985, even though he has to involve Crazy Horse in his Australasian tour early in the year when he isn't able to take the full International Harvesters line-up on the road. The band resume their touring in the summer, however, promoting Young's finally-completed 'Old Ways' album, which shows how close he's become to country veterans like Willie Nelson and Waylon Jennings.

One of the shows The International Harvesters performed was Live Aid, which is where Bob Dylan makes his fateful, throwaway comment from the stage about diverting some of the money away from African famine victims and towards American farmers. Heavily criticised in the press, Dylan's remark leads directly to the founding of a new charity: Farm Aid. Young is one of the leading lights in the movement, recruiting rock musicians (including Dylan) for the first Farm Aid concert, and performing there himself with the Harvesters. Benefiting farmers who have been deserted by the major American financial institutions is firmly in keeping with Young's country persona, and this effort, at least, proves to be more lasting than any of his musical ventures in the 80s: nearly a decade on, he is still a vocal supporter of the Farm Aid cause.

Live Aid also proves strong enough to provoke a CSNY reunion, made into a shambles by a combination of adverse sound and David Crosby's deep drug sickness. By the end of the year, Crosby has finally given up running from the law and himself, and is committed to jail, and a forcible detox. Young promises that if Crosby can keep off the freebase cocaine, his reward will be a full CSNY regrouping.

27 JANUARY 1985
Young's performance with The International Harvesters is broadcast on *Austin City Limits*.

10 FEBRUARY 1985
Young takes part in the recording of a charity single in Toronto. The all-star Canadian group, Northern Lights, is the local equivalent of USA For Africa and Band Aid, and proceeds from the sale of their single, 'Tears Are Not Enough', go to the Ethiopian famine relief fund. The song is written by David Foster, Bryan Adams and Jim Vallance, and besides Adams and Young, the single also features Joni Mitchell, Gordon Lightfoot and Anne Murray.

After Young records his solo line of the song, producer David Foster comments: "That was good, Neil, but the word 'innocent' was flat." "Hey, man," Neil retorts, "that's my style."

24 FEBRUARY 1985
Athletic Park, Wellington, New Zealand.

26 FEBRUARY 1985
Addington Showgrounds, Christchurch, New Zealand. Before the show, Young is interviewed for New Zealand TV.

1/2 MARCH 1985
Entertainment Center, Perth, Australia.

5 MARCH 1985
Memorial Park Drive, Adelaide, Australia.

7-12 MARCH 1985
Festival Hall, Melbourne, Australia. 'Homegrown' appears in the country set on the 8th, while Young performs solo renditions of 'Birds' and 'Sugar Mountain'. The set on the 9th includes 'Cowgirl In The Sand'. There's a rare performance of 'Midnight On The Bay' and 'Once An Angel' on the 11th.

14-16 & 18 MARCH 1985
Entertainment Center, Sydney, Australia. The show on the 16th is an extra concert added as a benefit to aid a charity for spastic children.

20 MARCH 1985
Chandler Velodrome, Brisbane, Australia.

22 MARCH 1985
Nils Lofgren performs two songs with Young during his final Australian show, back at the Entertainment Centre, Sydney. Bruce Springsteen joins Young for the encore.

20 APRIL 1985
'Hillbilly Band' recorded at The Castle, Nashville.

21 APRIL 1985
'Let Your Fingers Do The Walking' recorded at The Castle, Nashville.

22 APRIL 1985
'Silver & Gold', 'Ways Of Love', 'One More Sign' and 'Try' recorded at The Castle, Nashville.

26 APRIL 1985
'Your Love Again' recorded at The Castle, Nashville.

1 MAY 1985
'Amber Jean' recorded at The Castle, Nashville.

25 MAY 1985
Young appears on the US TV show *Entertainment This Week*.

Outlaw superstar Waylon Jennings (right) welcomes Neil Young into the 'rebels' compound of the country music industry.

22 FEBRUARY 1985
The first date of Young's Australasian tour with Crazy Horse, at the Western Springs Stadium, Auckland, New Zealand. The tour was originally supposed to be an International Harvesters jaunt, but Tim Drummond's impending fatherhood forces him to withdraw, and rather than rejig the band, Young reverts to his trusty rock'n'roll standbys. The shows are divided into three sets: a country segment, a brief solo set, and then a full-bore electric romp with Crazy Horse. Among the songs played on this tour is 'Southern Dakota', a revamped version of what is released on 'Old Ways' as 'Misfits'.

Set-list: 'Are You Ready For The Country', 'Motor City', 'Comes A Time', 'Good Phone', 'Too Far Gone', 'Roll Another Number', 'Southern Pacific', 'The Needle And The Damage Done', 'Tell Me Why', 'My My Hey Hey', 'After The Goldrush', 'Amber Jean', 'Helpless', 'California Sunset', 'Are There Any More Real Cowboys', 'Heart Of Gold', 'Old Man', 'Get Back To The Country', 'Cinnamon Girl', 'Cortez The Killer', 'Touch The Night', 'Everybody Knows This Is Nowhere', 'Southern Dakota', 'Hey Hey My My', 'Tonight's The Night', 'Like A Hurricane' and 'Powderfinger'.

30 JUNE 1985
'Beautiful Bluebird', 'Nothing Is Perfect' and 'Leavin' The Top 40 Behind' recorded at The Castle, Nashville.

1 JULY 1985
'Time Off For Good Behaviour' recorded at Bennett House, Franklin, Nashville.

4 JULY 1985
Willie Nelson's 4th July Picnic, in a giant field at South Park Meadows, Austin, Texas. Young performs 'This Land Is Your Land' with Jerry Jeff Walker, then plays a set with The International Harvesters that includes 'Are You Ready For The Country', 'Hawks And Doves', 'Are There Any More Real Cowboys' (with Willie Nelson), 'Heart Of Gold', 'Bound For Glory', 'Southern Pacific', 'The Needle And The Damage Done', 'California Sunset', 'Once An Angel', 'Soul Of A Woman', 'It Might Have Been', 'Field Of Opportunity', 'Old Man', 'Powderfinger' and 'Get Back To The Country'.

13 JULY 1985
Live Aid, JFK Stadium, Philadelphia. At the most prestigious rock concert since Woodstock, televised live around the globe, Young performs 'Sugar Mountain' and 'The Needle And The Damage Done' solo, then 'Helpless', the first known performance of 'Nothing Is Perfect' and 'Powderfinger' with The International Harvesters. His appearance is a striking artistic success, in contrast with his earlier performance alongside Crosby, Stills and Nash for the first CSNY reunion on stage since 1974. Plagued by monitor problems, CSNY play shambolic versions of 'Only Love Can Break Your Heart' and 'Daylight Again/Find The Cost Of Freedom'. Bootlegs: 'Live Aid – A Short Shame Story'/'Solidarity With A Stringman'.
   Young: "The CSNY reunion was terrible, the worst thing I've ever seen. It was totally untogether. We sounded much better in the trailer when we were rehearsing. I'm glad we did it, but we didn't do it very well."

MID-JULY 1985
Young and Willie Nelson record a video for 'Are There Any More Real Cowboys', during the making of which they discuss the possibility of staging a concert to benefit American farmers.

9 AUGUST 1985
Young and The International Harvesters begin another US tour at the State Fair, Milwaukee, Wisconsin. The set-list includes 'Lookin' For A Love', 'Once An Angel', 'Nothing Is Perfect' and the first known performance of 'Grey Riders', alongside the regular Harvesters' repertoire.

10 AUGUST 1985
Pavilion, University Of Illinois, Chicago, Illinois. 'Barstool Blues' and 'Country Home' are performed.

12 AUGUST 1985
Illinois State Fair, Springfield, Illinois. Set includes 'This Old House'.

14 AUGUST 1985
Community War Memorial Auditorium, Rochester, New York.

15 AUGUST 1985
Fieldhouse Institute, Albany, New York.

17 AUGUST 1985
CNE Exhibition Center, Toronto, Ontario, Canada.

18 AUGUST 1985
Riverbend Music Center, Cincinnati, Ohio.

19 AUGUST 1985
The Coliseum, Indianapolis, Indiana. Country singer David Allan Coe duets with Young on 'Southern Man'.

21 AUGUST 1985
Richfield Coliseum, Cleveland, Ohio.

23 AUGUST 1985
Oklahoma City Zoo Amphitheater, Oklahoma City, Oklahoma.

24 AUGUST 1985
Sandstone Amphitheater, Kansas City, Missouri. Young duets with Willie Nelson on 'Are There Any More Real Cowboys'.

25 AUGUST 1985
Red Rocks Amphitheater, Denver, Colorado.

27 AUGUST 1985
Fox Theater, St. Louis, Missouri.

28 AUGUST 1985
Frontier Days Park, Cheyenne, Wyoming, benefit show. "When the National Guard flies me into Wyoming for a benefit," Young notes, "we've come a long way."

30 AUGUST 1985
Cactus Corral, Perham, Minneapolis.

31 AUGUST 1985
State Fairground, Seymour, Wisconsin.

1 SEPTEMBER 1985
Minnesota State Fair, St. Paul, Minneapolis.

3 SEPTEMBER 1985
War Memorial Auditorium, Buffalo, New York.

5 SEPTEMBER 1985
Meadowbrook Center, Rochester, Michigan.

6 SEPTEMBER 1985
Hershey Arena, Hershey, Pennsylvania.

7 SEPTEMBER 1985
Mann Music Center, Philadelphia, Pennsylvania. First known performance of 'Interstate'.
   NY interviewed by BBC for *Whistle Test* (broadcast 15 October).

9 SEPTEMBER 1985
Garden State Performing Arts Center, Holmdel, New Jersey.

10 SEPTEMBER 1985
Pier 84, New York, New York. Young dedicates 'Helpless' to David Crosby. Bootleg: 'Live On The River'.

11 SEPTEMBER 1985
Young makes a brief appearance on ABC-TV's *Good Morning America*, talking about Farm Aid. He then flies to Washington to lobby senators for support of the Farm Policy Reform Act being introduced by Iowa Senator Tom Harkin.
   Interviewed by the *Washington Post*, Young comments: "CSNY can get back together very easily. All it will take is for David Crosby to clean up his act. If he does that, I'll join them. I don't want my kids or anyone else's kids watching us on TV saying, 'I heard about this guy – he's been in jail a couple of times and he doesn't have any respect for the law. He keeps doing this thing to himself and it's hurting him and look at the way he looks. Yet he's still a big success and he's on television and people are saying these guys are great.' I just won't let that happen."

12 SEPTEMBER 1985
Hampton Roads Coliseum, Hampton, Virginia.

13 SEPTEMBER 1985
Chastain Memorial Park, Atlanta, Georgia.

15 SEPTEMBER 1985
James L. Knight Center, Miami, Florida.

16 SEPTEMBER 1985
O'Connell Center, Gainesville, Florida.

17 SEPTEMBER 1985
Bayfront Center, St. Petersburg, Florida.

20 SEPTEMBER 1985
Southern Star Amphitheater, Houston, Texas.

21 SEPTEMBER 1985
Memorial Arena, Dallas, Texas.

22 SEPTEMBER 1985
Farm Aid 1: Memorial Stadium, University of Illinois, Champaign, Illinois. (see BA 21/22-3) Young opens up the show by performing 'Are There Any More Real Cowboys' with Willie Nelson; their studio performance of this song is issued simultaneously as a single, and also appears on Nelson's 'Half Nelson' album. His own brief set comprises 'My My Hey Hey', 'Heart Of Gold', 'This Old House' and 'Get Back To The Country'.
   Young has been responsible for recruiting many of the rock acts appearing on this vast benefit show, which raises around $9 million to help alleviate the financial problems of American farmers.

12 DECEMBER 1985
After being on the run since 25 November, when he was due to appear at a drugs and firearms hearing in Dallas, David Crosby gives himself up to FBI officials in West Palm Beach, Florida. He is subsequently incarcerated in Texas State Penitentiary.

97

Neil Young

Neil Young

*For his 1993 tour, Young recruited the legendary
Memphis R&B band, Booker T & The MGs.*

Neil Young

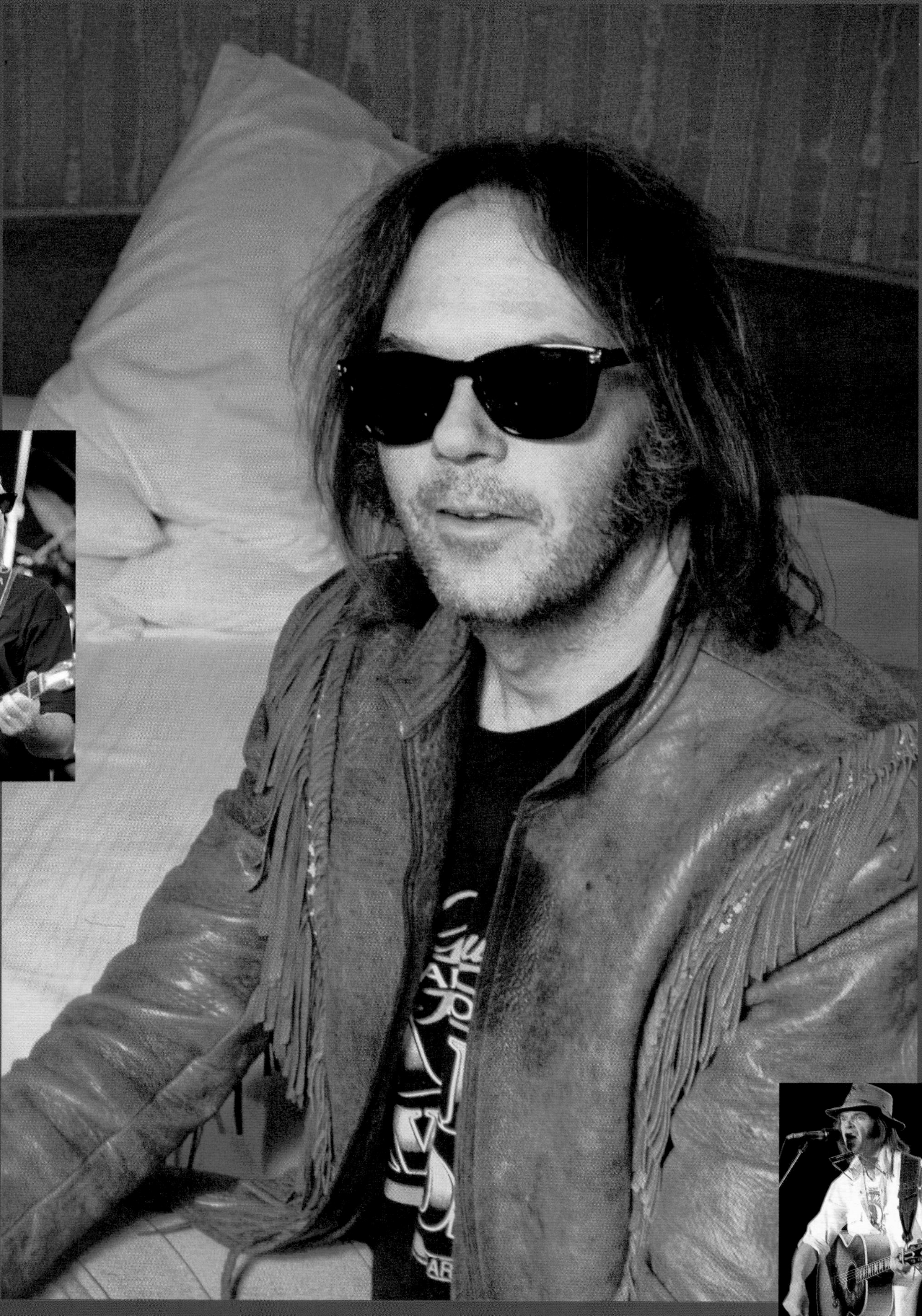

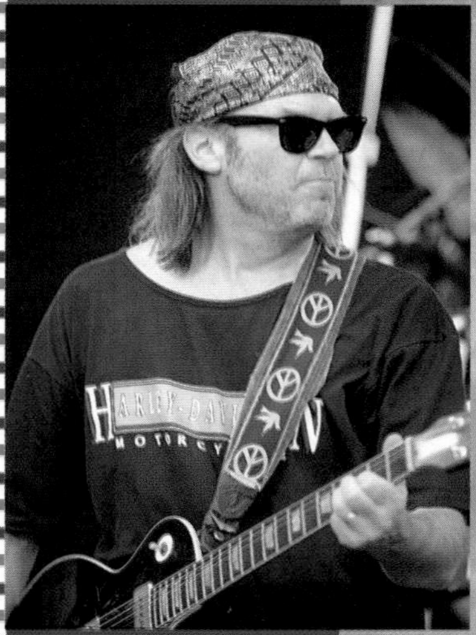

Neil Young

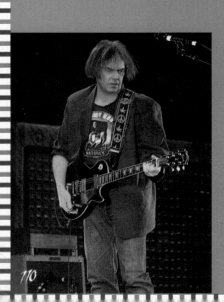

Even charity isn't enough to counter Geffen Records' opposition to Young's career as a country musician; the label blocks an EP which would have raised funds for Farm Aid. By then, Young is already deep into another project, retrieving the songs he'd tried to record with Crazy Horse two years earlier, and emerging with the computerised rock/dance sound of 'Landing On Water' – another flop for Geffen to promote. They must have been furious when Young admits that the album was a dud just a matter of months after it was released.

For the second time in little more than two years, he announces, then cancels, a European tour; when fans hear 'Landing On Water', they may be secretly relieved. But when he reunites with Crazy Horse for the 'Rusted-Out Garage Tour', it is as if the eight years since the 'Rust Never Sleeps' concerts have passed in a day. On display again are the bizarrely child-like sets, and full-bore, metallic rock'n'roll. And as he did in 1978, Young tapes the shows, preparing to create a 'studio' album by overdubbing a set of live recordings.

Even closer to Young's heart is another charity venture – the first benefit concert to raise funds for The Bridge School, an educational establishment for children suffering from conditions like cerebral palsy. Neil and Pegi have been long-term supporters of the school, and his fame allows him to stage a series of annual shows in aid of this very deserving cause which continue to this day. With David Crosby now out of prison and off drugs, the first Bridge Benefit proves to be the ideal venue for a CSNY reunion that lives up to the band's weighty past.

JANUARY 1986
Geffen refuse to release Young's planned 5-song EP to benefit Farm Aid, which would have included 'Depression Blues' and 'Interstate'.

23 JANUARY 1986
At the first Rock & Roll Hall of Fame dinner in New York (at the Waldorf Astoria Hotel), Young is invited to make an induction speech on behalf of The Everly Brothers. He notes that Buffalo Springfield took their harmony blend from the duo, but that "we didn't get it right". He later joins John Fogerty, Keith Richards, Jerry Lee Lewis, Chuck Berry and many others in a closing jam session.

24 FEBRUARY 1986
Young takes part in a Vietnam Veterans' Benefit in Inglewood, California, titled 'Welcome Home', He performs 'Powderfinger' and 'Heart Of Gold' solo, joins Nils Lofgren for one song, and plays 'Ohio' and 'Teach Your Children' with Graham Nash.

31 MARCH 1986
Young attends a dinner staged by the American Society of Composers, Authors and Publishers as a tribute to Bob Dylan.

5 APRIL 1986
Young, Graham Nash and Jackson Browne appear at a Greenpeace International benefit concert in Auckland, New Zealand.

25 MAY 1986
The European Young/Crazy Horse tour, due to begin on this date in Copenhagen and stretch through to mid-July, is cancelled in early May, after Young apparently injures his shoulder in an accident – described by his father, Scott, as being "of no consequence".

4 JULY 1986
Farm Aid II, Austin, Texas. Young performs 'Are You Ready For The Country', 'Comes A Time' and 'Homegrown' with The International Harvesters. The fundraising event is a comparative failure, garnering less than $2 million for the farmers' cause, as against more than $9 million raised by the first Farm Aid show.
   Young: "Why did Farm Aid II not do as well as Farm Aid I? It was done on July 4, and people are out on July 4, generally. I think that had something to do with it. But I don't consider it a failure in any way."

28 JULY 1986
Release date for 'Landing On Water'. Amidst a shoal of bad reviews, *Rolling Stone* breaks the trend, describing it as "his most consistent LP of the Eighties... a healthy new shot of neurosis".

8 AUGUST 1986
David Crosby is released from the Texas Department of Corrections, free of his long addiction to freebase cocaine. His manager, Bill Siddons, reveals: "David wrote to Stephen Stills, Graham Nash and Neil Young about getting back as a group. The response has been favourable."

18 AUGUST 1986
Young is interviewed for the syndicated radio service, *Rockline*. He reveals that Buffalo Springfield are having regular meetings to try out a reunion, and comments on David Crosby's release: "He's in great shape. I think he's going to make it. He's a great guy, a great human being, a wonderful soul, and he's the core of CSNY. There's no point in him playing in that band without being in great shape. He's always been the catalyst, keeping it together."

28 AUGUST 1986
NY appears at Long Beach Arena, Long Beach, California, as part of the charity bill for Get Tough On Toxics & Citizens For A Livable Los Angeles, alongside Lindsey Buckingham, Jimmy Buffett, Glenn Frey, Don Henley, Joni Mitchell & Stevie Nicks. Young performs five acoustic songs: 'Heart Of Gold', 'Highway Patrol', 'Mid-East Vacation', 'If You Got Love' (its only performance in acoustic form) and 'After The Goldrush'.

15 SEPTEMBER 1986
Young and Crazy Horse – billing themselves as the '3rd Best Garage Band In The World' – open the Rusted-Out Garage tour at the War Memorial Arena, Rochester, New York.

Neil was instrumental in staging the Farm Aid stadium shows, to raise funds for American farmers under threat from US banks.

Young returned to Crazy Horse, and the persona of a crazed electric rocker, for the Rusted-Out Garage tour in 1986.

The basic set for the tour comprises 'Mr Soul', 'Cinnamon Girl', 'When You Dance I Can Really Love', 'Touch The Night', 'Bad News Beat', 'Heart Of Gold', 'Too Lonely', 'Inca Queen', 'After The Goldrush', 'Sample And Hold', 'Down By The River', 'Cortez The Killer', 'Drive Back', 'Opera Star', 'The Needle And The Damage Done', 'Computer Age', 'Mideast Vacation', 'Long Walk Home', 'Like A Hurricane', 'My My Hey Hey', 'Hippie Dream', 'Eldorado' (still known then as 'Road Of Plenty'), 'Violent Side' and 'Prisoners Of Rock'n'Roll'.

The US shows on the Rusted-Out Garage tour take place, appropriately enough, in a 'garage' set, complete with squeaking mice, a radio-controlled beetle, and phone calls from an irate neighbour who wants the music to be turned down.

17 SEPTEMBER 1986
The Spectrum, Philadelphia, Pennsylvania. Before the show, Young is interviewed for TV's *Rock'n'Roll Evening News*.

18 SEPTEMBER 1986
Stabler Arena, Allentown, Pennsylvania.

20 SEPTEMBER 1986
Great Woods Music Center, Mansfield, Massachusetts. Before the show, which climaxes with 'The Loner', Young is interviewed for MTV.

21 SEPTEMBER 1986
Great Woods Music Center, Mansfield, Massachusetts. Bootleg: 'Old Nightmares' (1 song)/'Mansfield '86'.

23 SEPTEMBER 1986
Civic Center, Hartford, Connecticut.

24 SEPTEMBER 1986
RPI Fieldhouse, Troy, New York.

26 SEPTEMBER 1986
GMU Patriots' Center, Fairfax, Virginia.

27 SEPTEMBER 1986
David Crosby and Graham Nash join NY & Crazy Horse onstage at Brendan Byrne Arena, East Rutherford, New Jersey, for 'Only Love Can Break Your Heart' and 'Ohio'.

28 SEPTEMBER 1986
Civic Arena, Pittsburgh, Pennsylvania.

30 SEPTEMBER 1986
Montreal Forum, Montreal, Canada.

OCTOBER 1986
Graham Nash reveals that he is producing the soundtrack for *Eight Miles High*, a documentary film about David Crosby's life, and that he has solicited new material from Neil Young and Joni Mitchell.

Young's friend and guitar technician, Joel Bernstein, announces the imminent release of

his book about Young's career, co-written with *Rolling Stone* journalist Cameron Crowe, and with contributions from Young's mother, Rassy. To date, the book remains unpublished.

2 OCTOBER 1986
Civic Center, Ottawa, Canada.

3 OCTOBER 1986
Maple Leaf Gardens, Toronto, Canada. A rare performance of 'Rock Forever'. Young is interviewed by City TV, for a show broadcast on 6 October, and by *New Music*, broadcast on 11 October.

4 OCTOBER 1986
Memorial Auditorium, Buffalo, New York.

7 OCTOBER 1986
Madison Square Garden, New York, New York. Once again, David Crosby and Graham Nash appear as guests during the show, to perform 'Only Love Can Break Your Heart' and 'Ohio'.

8 OCTOBER 1986
Baltimore Arena, Baltimore, Maryland.

10 OCTOBER 1986
Richfield Coliseum, Richfield, Ohio.

11 OCTOBER 1986
Cobo Arena, Detroit, Michigan.

12 OCTOBER 1986
Mecca Arena, Milwaukee, Wisconsin.

13 OCTOBER 1986
First Bridge Benefit show, at Shoreline Amphitheater, Mountain View, California; NY headlines a spectacular acoustic show at which CSNY re-form, plus Bruce Springsteen, Don Henley, Nils Lofgren, Tom Petty, Robin Williams.

The event is organised by Young's wife, Pegi, to raise fund for the San Francisco-based Bridge School, which caters for severely handicapped children. Young opens the show with acoustic renditions of 'Comes A Time' and 'Heart Of Gold', before being joined by Bruce Springsteen and Nils Lofgren for 'Helpless'. After 'I Am A Child', Young brings Crosby, Stills and Nash onstage, and the quartet perform 'Only Love Can Break Your Heart', 'Change Partners', 'Daylight Again' and an emotionally-charged 'Ohio'.

Sets follow from Nils Lofgren, Don Henley, Tom Petty and Bruce Springsteen, who closes his set with 'Hungry Heart', augmented by CSNY. The all-star finale is Graham Nash's 'Teach Your Children'.

14 OCTOBER 1986
After the Bridge Benefit show, Young is interviewed by Mary Turner for her syndicated *Off The Record* show.

16 OCTOBER 1986
Kemper Arena, Kansas City, Missouri.

17 OCTOBER 1986
Metropolitan Center, Minneapolis, Minnesota. Bootlegs: 'Powderfinger' (Parts 1 & 2).

18 OCTOBER 1986
Horizon Center, Chicago, Illinois.

20 OCTOBER 1986
Ohio Center, Columbus, Ohio.

21 OCTOBER 1986
Riverfront Center, Cincinnati, Ohio.

22 OCTOBER 1986
Fox Theater, St. Louis, Missouri.

23 OCTOBER 1986
Market Square Arena, Indianapolis, Indiana.

25 OCTOBER 1986
Omni Auditorium, Atlanta, Georgia.

26 OCTOBER 1986
Charlotte Coliseum, Charlotte, North Carolina.

28 OCTOBER 1986
James L. Knight Center, Miami, Florida.

29 OCTOBER 1986
James L. Knight Center, Miami, Florida. A rare performance of 'We Never Danced'.

31 OCTOBER 1986
Ocean Center, Dayton Beach, Florida.

1 NOVEMBER 1986
Sundome, Tampa, Florida.

3 NOVEMBER 1986
Grand Ole Opry, Nashville, Tennessee.

4 NOVEMBER 1986
Bautwell, Birmingham, Alabama.

5 NOVEMBER 1986
Ocean Center, Daytona Beach.

7 NOVEMBER 1986
The Summit, Houston, Texas. First known performance of 'Around The World'.

8 NOVEMBER 1986
Reunion Arena, Austin, Texas. Bootleg: 'Damage Done', which documents one of the tour's performances of 'Helpless', but not the first playing of 'When Your Lonely Heart Breaks'.

9 NOVEMBER 1986
Lloyd Noble Arena, Norman, Oklahoma.

11 NOVEMBER 1986
McNicholls Arena, Denver, Colorado. 'Sugar Mountain' is broadcast by Westwood One as part of their *Superstars In Concert* programme.

12 NOVEMBER 1986
Governer Ed Herschler of Wyoming proclaims Neil Young Day across the state, at a ceremony in Cheyenne. The honour was in recognition of Young's appearance at the 1985 Silver Lining Benefit show in aid of flood victims.

13 NOVEMBER 1986
Community Center, Tucson, Arizona.

14 NOVEMBER 1986
ASU Activity Center, Phoenix, Arizona. 'Heart Of Gold' is broadcast by Westwood One as part of their *Superstars In Concert* programme.

15 NOVEMBER 1986
Pacific Amphitheater, Costa Mesa, California. (with Crazy Horse). 'Like A Hurricane' is broadcast by Westwood One as part of their *Superstars In Concert* programme.

17 NOVEMBER 1986
Universal Amphitheater, Los Angeles, California.

18 NOVEMBER 1986
Universal Amphitheater, Los Angeles, California. 'Down By The River' is broadcast by Westwood One as part of their *Superstars In Concert* programme, while 'Around The World' and 'Mideast Vacation' from this show are overdubbed for release on the 'Life' album.

21 NOVEMBER 1986
Show at the Cow Palace, San Francisco, California is broadcast live on TV on cable to USA and CanadaThe Shocking Pinks' and Trans Solo videos), and the 'Pressure' video during the intermission. Bootleg: 'Prisoners Of Rock'n'Roll'. The broadcast documents 'When Your Lonely Heart Breaks' and 'Around The World', added to the set during the tour.

1987

Crosby, Stills, Nash and Young have not been a viable entity since 1976; but in 1987, the quartet confirm that they will be re-forming for an album, and a subsequent tour. They began the year by playing some acclaimed charity concerts, but the studio reunion is continually postponed, leading by the autumn to speculation that it will never happen.

To compensate for the 1984 and 1986 cancellations, Young and Crazy Horse finally tour Europe – only to discover that they are unable to attract anything like sell-out audiences. Several shows have to be cancelled as a result; one ends in a riot; and many fans leave before the end at the concerts that do take place, protesting at the excessive volume of Young's performances. Those that survive with their eardrums intact witness consummate proof that Crazy Horse can still provoke Young into making magnificent hard rock music – something nearly, but in the end not quite, captured on his latest album, 'Life'.

The record goes almost unpromoted, as Geffen have finally elected to set Young free from his contract with the label – another factor which is threatening the CSNY reunion. Neil promptly returns to the safer haven of Reprise, who are quite willing to issue any album he delivers, and also to let him record with Crosby, Stills and Nash for their sister label, Atlantic.

First, though, Young has an American tour to complete. Rather than repeat the format of the '86 shows, Young splits his US sets into three sections – separating the solo and Crazy Horse songs with a brief blues excursion. These two- or three-song experiments seize Young's imagination, and in the autumn he drops Crazy Horse in favour of a new 10-piece line-up, all R&B horns and big band swing, called The Blue Notes.

17 JANUARY 1987
Radio station WNEW in New York claims that Buffalo Springfield have re-formed and are recording a new album.

FEBRUARY 1987
Crosby, Stills, Nash and Young are said to be recording in Los Angeles with producer Bill Szymczyk, for an album to be released in June. The problem is that Geffen still own Young's contract; David Geffen remarks, "If they want to make a record with Neil Young, that record can only be made for me, because I will not allow Neil to make a record for anybody while he's under exclusive contract to me, for which I paid a healthy amount of money."

Graham Nash: "Neil is about to hand in a record with Crazy Horse, and when you only have one record left to deliver, you have a lot of bargaining power. Because Neil's contract is virtually up, he could go in and do 'My Way' six different ways and hand it in. If Geffen pisses him off, Neil is liable to do it!"

David Crosby: "We're gonna make a great album. We're gonna kick ass."

Stephen Stills: "It feels like we're a band again."

Neil Young: "There's a very strong chance of the group being better and stronger, and perhaps bigger, than it ever was before. There's an audience out there for CSNY. We could have a huge tour, and if we make a great record... There's a lot more depth and rawness, and a lot more funk and soul, in this band than has ever been heard on record. I just don't feel competition from anyone."

6 FEBRUARY 1987
CSNY: Greenpeace benefit (2 shows) at Arlington Theater, Santa Barbara. Only CSNY performance of 'Nothing Is Perfect'.

MARCH 1987
68 premières in Los Angeles, with NY in a small role. (BA 28/3)

Young denies that CSNY have begun recording, but admits that a reunion album is a distinct possibility.

24 APRIL 1987
Young and Crazy Horse open a European tour at the Palau D'Sports Municipal, Barcelona, Spain. The standard set for the first few shows comprises 'Mr Soul', 'Cinnamon Girl', 'When You Dance I Can Really Love', 'Down By The River', 'Heart Of Gold', 'After The Goldrush', 'Inca Queen', 'Drive Back', 'Opera Star', 'Cortez The Killer', 'Sugar Mountain', 'Mideast Vacation', 'Long Walk Home', 'The Needle And The Damage Done', 'When Your Lonely Heart Breaks', 'Like A Hurricane' and 'Hey Hey My My'. All the material from the

'Landing On Water' LP performed during the recent US tour is dropped from the repertoire.

The Rusted-Out Garage sets are not brought to Europe, supposedly because of excessive transportation costs.

Billy Talbot (Crazy Horse): "We rehearsed for the tour for three hours. We played two new songs, one that had no words yet, and we jammed. And that was it."

25 APRIL 1987
Auditorium Casa Campo, Madrid, Spain.

26 APRIL 1987
Sports Palace, Bilbao, Spain.

28 APRIL 1987
Montpellier, France (cancelled). Instead, Young flies to Rome.

29 APRIL 1987
Young stages a press conference in Rome.

30 APRIL 1987
Palazzo Dello Sport, Rome, Italy.

1 MAY 1987
Arena, Verona, Italy. Young is interviewed before the show by RAI.

2 MAY 1987
Palasport, Genoa, Italy.

4 MAY 1987
Stadio Communale, Turin, Italy.

5 MAY 1987
Arena, Milan, Italy. The first changes to the set: 'Prisoners Of Rock'n'Roll' and

Crosby, Stills and Nash regrouped after David Crosby's release from prison in 1986, and soon the talk was of yet another CSNY reunion. "We're gonna kick ass," Crosby promised.

'Computer Age' make their only appearances of the tour, while Young also performs 'Comes A Time', 'See The Sky About To Rain' and 'The Loner'. The show is marred by an audience riot, which provokes police violence.

7 MAY 1987
Frankenhalle, Nuremburg, West Germany.

8 MAY 1987
Festhalle, Frankfurt, West Germany. 'Surfer Joe And Moe The Sleaze' is added to the set-list, for a show which fills only around 45% of the arena seating. Young abandons his first attempt at 'Powderfinger' after breaking a string, but performs the song successfully later in the set. More seriously, an audience member throws a glass at Young as he finishes 'Cinnamon Girl', hitting him on the head. Young attempts to confront the miscreant, who remains anonymous in the crowd, and the incident affects the atmosphere for the rest of the show.

9 MAY 1987
Sportshalle, Hamburg, West Germany. In a rather lacklustre set, Young alienates sections of the audience by insisting that a fan taping the gig should be ejected.

11 MAY 1987
Tempodrom, Berlin, West Germany.

12 MAY 1987
Sportshalle, Cologne, West Germany.

13 MAY 1987
Mozart Saal, Mannheim, West Germany. Poor ticket sales mean this show is transferred to a smaller venue shortly before the event, and even then the hall is far from sold out.

14 MAY 1987
Kockelscheuerhalle, Luxembourg. A rare outing for 'Too Lonely'.

16 MAY 1987
Eissporthalle, Graz, Austria.

17 MAY 1987
Stadthalle, Vienna, Austria.

18 MAY 1987
Deutscher Museum, Munich, West Germany.

21 MAY 1987
Patinoire de Malley, Lausanne, Switzerland – cancelled because of poor ticket sales.

22 MAY 1987
Hallenstadion, Zurich, Switzerland.

23 MAY 1987
Les Arènes, Fréjus, France – cancelled because of poor ticket sales.

25 MAY 1987
Palais des Sports, Toulouse, France. 'In The Name Of Love' and 'American Dream' make their tour début.

27 MAY 1987
Ahoy Hall, Rotterdam, Holland. In the longest set of the tour, 'Old Man' makes a one-off appearance.

28 MAY 1987
Forest National Stadium, Brussels, Belgium.

29 MAY 1987
POPB, Bercy, Paris, France. A long 'Tonight's The End' appears to end the show, before Young reappears to reprise 'Like A Hurricane'.

30 MAY 1987
Palais des Sports, Lyon, France. Young plays an acoustic 'Everybody Knows This Is Nowhere'.

2 JUNE 1987
NEC Birmingham. 'American Dream' moves to the acoustic set.

3/4 JUNE 1987
Wembley Arena, London. On the opening night Young and Crazy Horse drag out the endings to many of the electric songs, to the displeasure of sections of the audience but on the 4th a remarkably aggressive and passionate show climaxes with a tortured 'Tonight's The Night', followed by the expected 'Like A Hurricane'.

5 JUNE 1987
Young is interviewed in Dublin for Irish radio.

6 JUNE 1987
Royal Dublin Showgrounds, Dublin, Ireland. A sell-out crowd respond to one of the most successful shows of the tour.

mid-JUNE 1987
The 'Life' album is released. Young: "The album was recorded about 85% live. We took the tracks into the studio and worked on them. That's also the way we made 'Rust Never Sleeps'."

25 JUNE 1987
Young takes part in a radiothon organised by San Jose station KSJO FM to benefit AIDS victims, via the charity organisation the Aris Project.

Neil with John Einarson, author of Don't Be Denied, a biography of Young that covers his early years in Canada.

Neil is reunited with The Squires in June, 1987, at The Paddle Wheel restaurant in Winnipeg, left to right: Terry Crosby, Allan Bates, Ken Smyth, Ken Koblun, Jack Harper and Neil, and (bottom) at the Blue Note Cafe.

26 JUNE 1987

To coincide with the publication of John Einarson's book about Winnipeg rock history, the city stages an event entitled 'Shakin' All Over: The Winnipeg Sixties Bands And Fans Reunion'. Neil and Pegi Young arrive in Winnipeg, to stay with the original Squires drummer, Jack Harper.

27 JUNE 1987

Young and Harper return to their alma mater, Kelvin High School, where the first day of the Reunion is being staged. Young signs copies of Einarson's book, and is then reunited with the other ex-members of The Squires: Ken Koblun, Terry Crosby, Ken Smyth and Allan Bates. That evening, Young, Koblun and another former member of the band, Bill Edmundson, ask the owner of a restaurant called the Blue Note if they can play an impromptu live set. "We're The Squires," Young announces proudly from the stage. "This is our first gig in 20 years."

28 JUNE 1987

The city's Convention Center plays host to the Shakin' All Over concert. Young joins in the day's final set, by fellow Sixties veteran Chad Allan, performing 'American Woman' with Burton Cummings and Randy Bachman of Canadian rockers the Guess Who, Bob Dylan's 'Just Like Tom Thumb's Blues', 'Down By The River' (Young duetting on vocals with Bachman), the Guess Who's 'Albert Fisher', and Bachman-Turner Overdrive's 'Takin' Care Of Business'.

9 JULY 1987

Young agrees to a phone interview with radio station WMMR in Philadelphia.

7 AUGUST 1987

Young guests at Crosby, Stills and Nash's concert at the Shoreline Amphitheater, Mountain View, California, on four songs: 'Long Time Gone', 'For What It's Worth', 'Teach Your Children' and 'Daylight Again'.

8 AUGUST 1987

'Life' reaches its US chart peak of No. 75.

13 AUGUST 1987

Pacific Amphitheater, Costa Mesa, California.

Young divides the performance into three sets: a solo acoustic flurry of 'Hey Hey My My', 'Tell Me Why', 'The Old Laughing Lady', 'Nowadays Clancy Can't Even Sing' (having checked the lyrics in a songbook!), 'For The Turnstiles', 'Someday', 'Birds', 'American Dream' and 'Sugar Mountain'; a two-song interlude of 'Don't Take Your Love Away From Me' (last performed in Australia in 1985) and 'Welcome To The Big Room' (first known performance here), with Larry Cragg on sax alongside Crazy Horse; and then, after the intermission, a frenetic Young/Crazy Horse electric set which features 'Mr Soul', 'Cinnamon Girl', 'Prisoners Of Rock'n'Roll', 'Too Lonely', 'Opera Star', 'Down By The River', 'In The Name Of Love', 'Mideast Vacation', 'Long

At the Shakin' All Over reunion, Neil jammed with Canadian guitar hero Randy Bachman.

Walk Home', 'Powderfinger', 'Like A Hurricane' and 'My My Hey Hey'.

Young: "Every night I'd listen to the tapes, and the acoustic set didn't move me very much and the Crazy Horse set I'd just skim through, because it seemed a little obvious. But that little blues set I did with Crazy Horse and our roadie on the baritone sax, well, I liked listening to that. The crowd seemed to like it too, 'cos they were going fucking nuts and no-one was shouting for 'Southern Man' like they've done throughout my whole fucking career."

15 AUGUST 1987
Red Rocks Amphitheater, Denver, Colorado.

16 AUGUST 1987
Sarasota Tornado Benefit at Manor Downs Race Track, Manor, Austin, Texas. This show, also starring Waylon Jennings and Johnny Cash, draws a paltry crowd of a few hundred people, raising only $5,000 for the hurricane victims.

Young's acoustic set features 'Comes A Time', 'Heart Of Gold', 'The Old Laughing Lady', 'Nothing Is Perfect', 'Love Is A Rose', the almost identical 'Dance Dance Dance' ("some people say my music all sounds the same", Young quips) and 'Hey Hey My My' (dedicated to Elvis Presley, on the 10th anniversary of his death).

17 AUGUST 1987
Fox Theater, St. Louis, Missouri.

18 AUGUST 1987
Poplar Creek Music Center, Hoffman Estates, Illinois. Young encores with 'Tonight's The Night', and also performs 'Revolution Blues' in his acoustic set.

19 AUGUST 1987
Riverbend Music Center, Cincinnati, Ohio. First known performance of 'Ain't It The Truth'.

20 AUGUST 1987
Merriweather Post Pavilion, Columbia, Maryland. First known performances of 'One Of These Days' and 'This Note's For You'.

22 AUGUST 1987
Mann Music Center, Philadelphia, Pennsylvania. First known performance of 'Last Of A Dying Breed'. 'This Note's For You' has entered the acoustic set by this point, and is reprised during the brief saxophone set.

23 AUGUST 1987
Riverfront Park, Manchester, New Hampshire.

24 AUGUST 1987
Saratoga Performing Arts Center, Saratoga

Springs, New York. Crazy Horse feature 'Everybody Knows This Is Nowhere' and an astonishing, drawn-out 'My My Hey Hey', with two false endings.

26 AUGUST 1987
Coliseum, Newhaven, Connecticut.

28 AUGUST 1987
Great Woods Performing Arts Center, Mansfield, Minneapolis.

29 AUGUST 1987
Great Woods Performing Arts Center, Mansfield, Minneapolis.

30 AUGUST 1987
Garden State Arts Center, Holmdale, New Jersey.

1 SEPTEMBER 1987
Blossom Music Center, Cuyahoga Falls, Ohio.

2 SEPTEMBER 1987
CNE Grandstand, Toronto, Canada. 'This Note's For You' is performed three times during this show.

3 SEPTEMBER 1987
Pine Knob Music Theater, Clarkston, Michigan. Another exhilarating performance of 'Tonight's The Night' is the highlight of this show.

4 SEPTEMBER 1987
Alpine Valley Music Theater, East Troy, Wisconsin. *It's Only Rock 'n' Roll* on CBC-TV airs an interview with Neil, plus concert footage from The Squires' reunion.

19 SEPTEMBER 1987
Farm Aid 3, in Memorial Stadium, Lincoln, Nebraska. Young appears alongside Willie Nelson, John Mellencamp, Lou Reed and Kris Kristofferson, among others.

2 OCTOBER 1987
Made In Heaven goes on general release.

7 OCTOBER 1987
Geffen Records agree to end their recording contract with Young, who begins negotiations to return to Reprise.

Young: "Elliot Roberts called and told me. I had just smoked this big bomber, and I almost had a heart attack. I was so happy, but I was too high to enjoy it."

31 OCTOBER 1987
Young plays a private show with the Blue Notes for friends at a Halloween party.

NOVEMBER 1987
Plans for a CSNY reunion are rumoured to

have been halted by concerns over Stephen Stills' health.

2-4 NOVEMBER 1987
Coconut Grove Ballroom, Santa Cruz, California. The shows at the Coconut Grove are billed as 'Three Nights with The Fabulous Blue Notes'. They début Young's new band, an R&B combo featuring Crazy Horse plus a six-man horn section.

The opening set of the tour (all shows from which were recorded) features 'Welcome To The Big Room', 'Find Another Shoulder', 'High Heels', 'Hello Lonely Woman', 'Ain't It The Truth', 'Your Love (Is Good To Me)', 'One Thing', 'Don't Take Your Love', 'Sunny Inside', 'Life In The City', 'Soul Of A Woman', 'This Note's For You' and 'Bad News'. The same 13 songs, with variations and deletions in the running order, comprise the repertoire for the entire tour – which is regarded as a disappointment by fans, its array of unreleased songs not matched by musical fireworks. First known performances of 'Bad News', 'Hello Lonely Woman', 'High Heels' and 'Find Another Shoulder'.

Young: "We'd been on the road for two years, and I just decided that was it. I wasn't going to play my hits, I didn't want to play any more coliseums."

6 NOVEMBER 1987
City Limits Club, Salinas, California. Taunted by a heckler demanding familiar songs, Young announces "No old songs will be performed tonight", and accuses the 'fan' of "living in the past", before ensuring that the miscreant is removed.

7 NOVEMBER 1987
Shoreline Amphitheater, Mountain View, California (2 shows).

8 NOVEMBER 1987
The Old Fillmore, San Francisco, California. (2 shows).

10/11 NOVEMBER 1987
The Omni, Oakland, California (2 shows).

13 NOVEMBER 1987
The Cabaret, San Jose, California (2 shows).

MID-NOVEMBER 1987
Young's manager, Elliott Roberts, denies that his next album will be a blues set. "It'll be a rock'n'roll LP, 'cause he's doing it with Crazy Horse," he claims.

19 DECEMBER 1987
NY introduces children's Christmas concert by San Francisco Boys Choir.

1988

Eighteen years after 'Déjà Vu', Crosby, Stills, Nash and Young finally record and release their second studio album in 1988. Before its release, Young waxes lyrical about CSNY's potential; by the autumn, he is trying to distance himself from a project which he has effectively controlled. The record is by no means a disaster, but (as on the Stills/Young album a decade earlier) Young's own contributions are disappointingly slight. Yet once again, he alone of the quartet emerges from the venture with his critical reputation intact.

Ironically, his own far more insubstantial 'This Note's For You', a lightweight, though enjoyable, R&B album featuring the horns of The Blue Notes, wins the rave reviews that elude CSNY's 'American Dream'. But the most significant aspect of that release is the promotional video made for its title track by British director Julian Temple. Its satirical imagery leads to MTV imposing a total ban on the clip, which – combined with the anti-sponsorship message of the song – helps to portray Young as a revolutionary, a true inheritor of the spirit of 1968.

After a brief interlude playing rhythm guitar behind Bob Dylan at the start of the Never-Ending Tour, Young returns to The Blue Notes (who for legal reasons had become Ten Men Workin') by the close of the year. He records gig after gig, for a planned double-LP to be called 'This Note's For You Too'; more importantly, he introduces into the band's repertoire the two longest and most significant songs he's written in a decade, 'Crime In The City' and 'Ordinary People'. In their full-length versions, both songs remain unreleased, as does the live Blue Notes set.

Instead, Young takes a small band to New York in the final weeks of 1988, and cuts a fierce, compelling album called 'Times Square' – with tracks like 'Cocaine Eyes' returning to the raw-nerved realism of 'Tonight's The Night'.

JANUARY 1988

CSNY meet to discuss their reunion album.

Young: "There's a certain energy you get from singing with people you've known for 25 years, who've been through all these changes with you, gone up and down with you. I think CSNY has a lot to say – especially Crosby."

20 JANUARY 1988

NY inducts Woody Guthrie to the Rock & Roll Hall of Fame, and takes part in the closing superstar jam with Jerry Lee Lewis, Chuck Berry, Bruce Springsteen and Bob Dylan, among others – Young leading the ensemble into the final song of the night, 'Satisfaction'.

29 JANUARY 1988

NY is booked to appear at the Olympic Arts Festival in Calgary, alongside Russian band Autograf, but the concert is cancelled shortly before the day.

FEBRUARY 1988

Nearly twelve years after the collapse of the band's last album project, CSNY regroup at Young's home studio to begin work on a new record.

MARCH 1988

NY & The Blue Notes win a Bammy award as Outstanding Blues/Ethnic Artist/Group. The band eventually receive their awards on stage four months later.

Young is one of the guests as an ASCAP Dinner held to present Bob Dylan with the society's second Founders award. He spends some time chatting to Elizabeth Taylor, Dylan's escort for the evening.

Julian Temple directs a video for the title track of Young's new 'This Note's For You' album, in which he satirises recent promo clips by Michael Jackson and Whitney Houston.

EARLY APRIL 1988

Unable to cope with irony, MTV choose to ban the 'This Note's For You' video.

Young: "I was on my sailboat sailing to Hawaii, and I'd just received word that the video for 'This Note's For You' was not going to be played. I hadn't seen anybody for about eight days, so I was pretty spacey out there. In one night I wrote three songs: 'Ordinary People', 'Sixty To Zero' and 'Days That Used To Be'."

13 APRIL 1988

US release date of 'This Note's For You'. Explaining the radical shift of styles that has characterised his recent albums, Young comments: "It's just the way I am. When I was in school, I would go for six months

wearing the same kind of clothes. Then all of a sudden I'd wear something different."

Hollywood Palace, Los Angeles, California (2 shows). The Bluenotes – revised from the late 1987 shows, with Rick Rosas and Chad Cromwell replacing Crazy Horse's Billy Talbot and Ralph Molina – open another US tour, building up to the release of the 'This Note's For You' album.

The first show comprises 11 songs: 'Ten Men Working', 'Welcome To The Big Room', 'Find Another Shoulder', 'High Heels', 'Bad News', 'Ain't It The Truth', 'Your Love (Is Good To Me)', 'Coupe De Ville', 'Life In The City', 'Soul Of A Woman' and 'This Note's For You' (this last track eventually being included on the compilation album, 'Lucky Thirteen').

For the second set, The Bluenotes repeat just five songs, adding 'Hello Lonely Woman', 'Married Man', 'Hey Hey', 'Crime Of The Heart', 'One Thing', 'Twilight', 'Sunny Inside' and 'Don't Take Your Love' to the set. First known performance of 'Crime Of The Heart'. Bootleg: 'Old Nightmares' (1 song).

Young: "I want to make a movie about a blues band. This band, The Bluenotes, are not fashionable and they're not cool and they're unhip and there's no scene around them. That was the movie I had in my head. That little movie evolved into The Bluenotes and we're playing the clubs. The movie will come later."

14 APRIL 1988

Hollywood Palace, Los Angeles, California (2 shows). The set-lists almost exactly duplicate the previous night's performances.

1988 saw Young metamorphose into 'Shaky Deal', leader of a blues big band called the Blue Notes.

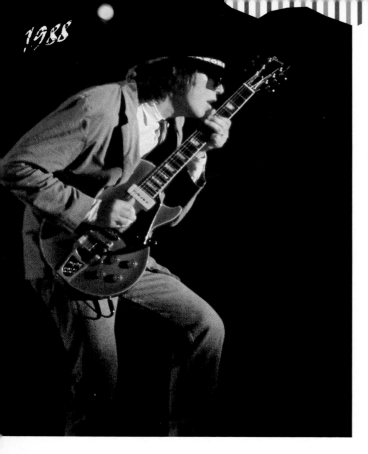

17-19 & 21 APRIL 1988

The World, New York (2 shows). All the World shows were taped for prospective live album, 'This Note's For You Too'. The following songs were recorded: (First Set) 'Ten Men Working', 'Married Man', 'Sunny Inside', 'Hey Hey', 'Bad News', 'Ain't It The Truth', 'Your Love (Is Good To Me)', 'Coupe De Ville', 'Life In The City', 'Soul Of A Woman', 'This Note's For You'; (Second Set) 'Welcome To The Big Room', 'Find Another Shoulder', 'High Heels', 'Hello Lonely Woman', 'One Thing', 'Ain't It The Truth', 'Twilight', 'Life In The City', 'This Note's For You', 'Ten Men Working' and 'Don't Take Your Love'.

The remote recording unit tapes both sets on the 18th: (First Set) 'Ten Men Working', 'Find Another Shoulder', 'Married Man', 'Your Love (Is Good To Me)', 'One Thing', 'Ain't It The Truth', 'Sunny Inside', 'Twilight', 'Life In The City', 'This Note's For You'; (Second Set) 'Welcome To The Big Room', 'High Heels', 'Hello Lonely Woman', 'Bad News', 'Hey Hey', 'Your Love (Is Good To Me)', 'Coupe De Ville', 'Life In The City', 'Soul Of A Woman', 'This Note's For You', 'Ten Men Working'. Bootleg: 'Old Nightmares' (2 songs).

More live recording on the 19th: (First Set) 'Ten Men Working', 'Married Man', 'Find Another Shoulder', 'I'm Goin' ' (first appearance on this tour), 'Crime Of The Heart', 'One Thing', 'Ain't It The Truth', 'Life In The City', 'This Note's For You'; (Second Set) 'Welcome To The Big Room', 'High Heels', 'Sunny Inside', 'Hey Hey', 'Walkin' After Midnight' (Young's only known performance of this song), 'Bad News', 'Your Love (Is Good To Me)', 'Coupe De Ville', 'Hello Lonely Woman', 'Life In The City', 'Soul Of A Woman' and 'This Note's For You'.

'Ten Men Working' is released as a single in the States, backed by the non-album track, 'I'm Goin' '.

The final night of recording sees the following set captured on tape: 'Ten Men Working', 'Married Man', 'I'm Goin' ', 'Find Another Shoulder', 'Ain't It The Truth', 'Bad News', 'Your Love (Is Good To Me)', 'Hey Hey', 'One Thing', 'Coupe De Ville', 'Life In The City', 'Soul Of A Woman', 'This Note's For You', 'Welcome To The Big Room'.

22 APRIL 1988

The Trocadero, Philadelphia, Pennsylvania. A second show was scheduled at this venue, but cancelled. The Bluenotes begin and end the main set with 'Ten Men Working', before encoring with 'Don't Take Your Love'. Bootlegs: 'Life In The City'/'Shaky Neil' (4 songs).

23 APRIL 1988

The Agora, Cleveland, Ohio. Once again, a second show was cancelled; and there's another double dose of 'Ten Men Working'. 'Ain't It The Truth' from this show is issued on the 1993 compilation 'Lucky Thirteen'.

14 MAY 1988

Atlantic Records celebrates its 40th anniversary with a major New York concert – but without Neil Young, who ironically declines to appear alongside Crosby, Stills and Nash at the event, even though he has just completed work on the CSNY album.

LATE MAY 1988

Bob Dylan and his band spend a week rehearsing for their upcoming US tour on Young's ranch; Young agrees to help out at some of the early shows.

JUNE 1988

Both Young and Bob Dylan are reported to be playing cameo roles in Dennis Hopper's new movie, *Backtrack*. Meanwhile, the movie *'68* is released, with Young making another brief appearance as an actor.

2 JUNE 1988

Neil Young appears on the cover of *Rolling Stone* magazine for the third time, accompanying an interview by James Henke.

7 JUNE 1988

Neil Young plays guitar with Bob Dylan's band for the first show of the so-called Never-Ending Tour, at the Concord Pavilion, Concord, California. Young performs for both electric sets and the encore, on the following songs: 'Subterranean Homesick Blues', 'Absolutely Sweet Marie', 'Masters Of War', 'You're A Big Girl Now', 'Gotta Serve Somebody', 'In The Garden', 'Driftin' Too Far From Shore', 'Gates Of Eden', 'Like A Rolling Stone' and 'Maggie's Farm'. Bootleg: 'Homesick Blues'.

10 JUNE 1988

Young performs with Dylan again at the Greek Theater, Berkeley, California, having skipped the previous night's show in Sacramento. This time he only plays the second electric set and encore, on 'It Takes A Lot To Laugh', 'In The Garden', 'Gates Of Eden', 'Like A Rolling Stone', 'Everybody's Movin' ' and 'Maggie's Farm'. Bootlegs: 'Homesick Blues'/'San Francisco Bay Blues'.

11 JUNE 1988

Young makes his third and final contribution to Dylan's 1988 tour, at the Shoreline Amphitheater, Mountain View, California. Again, he appears only for the second electric set and the encore, playing 'I Want You', 'I

Dreamed I Saw St. Augustine', 'Shelter From The Storm', 'Maggie's Farm', 'Like A Rolling Stone' and 'In The Garden'. Bootleg: 'Homesick Blues'.

LATE JUNE/JULY
Young finishes mixing work on the CSNY album.

12 AUGUST 1988
Young opens a month-long North American tour with The Bluenotes at the Riverbend Music Center, Cincinnati, Ohio. He delivers a 17-song set, comprising 'Ten Men Working', 'Hello Lonely Woman', 'I'm Goin'', 'Married Man', 'Coupe De Ville', 'Ordinary People', 'Days That Used To Be', 'After The Goldrush', 'Sixty To Zero', 'Bad

News', 'Ain't It The Truth', 'Your Love (Is Good To Me)', 'Hey Hey', 'Twilight', 'Life In The City', 'Soul Of A Woman' and 'This Note's For You'.

13 AUGUST 1988
Sports Center, Indianapolis, Indiana.

14 AUGUST 1988
Marcus Amphitheater, Milwaukee, Wisconsin. 'Welcome To The Big Room', 'Tonight's The Night' and 'On The Way Home' are added to the end of The Bluenotes' set.

16 AUGUST 1988
Poplar Creek Music Center, Hoffman Estates, Illinois. The Blue Notes perform all

11 verses of 'Sixty To Zero' (heard on bootleg 'Shaky Neil').

18 AUGUST 1988
CNE Grandstand, Toronto, Canada.
Bootleg: 'Depression Blues' (1 song).

19 AUGUST 1988
Lakeside Amphitheater, Buffalo, New York.

20 AUGUST 1988
Cayuga County Fairground, Weedsport, New York.
MTV relents and screens NY's 'This Note's For You' video for the first time.

22 AUGUST 1988
Performing Arts Center, Saratoga Springs, New York.

23 AUGUST 1988
Lake Compounce Festival Park, Bristol, Connecticut. 'My, My, Hey, Hey' makes a rare appearance on a Blue Notes tour.

24 AUGUST 1988
Garden State Arts Center, Holmdel, New Jersey. 'Fool For Your Love' enters The Blue Notes' repertoire, for its first known performance.

26 AUGUST 1988
Mann Music Center, Philadelphia, Pennsylvania.

27 AUGUST 1988
Jones Beach Music Center, Wantaugh, New York. "Well, thanks for doing what you could," Young quips sarcastically to the unresponsive crowd at the end of the show. Bootlegs: 'Old Nightmares' (2 songs)/'Only Once'/'Depression Blues' (1 song).

29 AUGUST 1988
Tanglewood Music Center, Lenox, Massachusetts. First known performance of 'Doghouse', as Young revamps the set, also adding 'Crime Of The Heart', 'One Thing' and 'Sunny Inside' to the band's playlist.

30 AUGUST 1988
Pier 84, New York, New York. The finale of this show is a fearsome performance of 'Tonight's The Night', which culminates with Young tearing all the strings off his guitar.

31 AUGUST 1988
Great Woods Performing Arts Center, Mansfield, Massachusetts. A light plane crashes just outside the arena during the

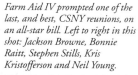

Farm Aid IV prompted one of the last, and best, CSNY reunions, on an all-star bill. Left to right in this shot: Jackson Browne, Bonnie Raitt, Stephen Stills, Kris Kristofferson and Neil Young.

concert, while Young and The Blue Notes rage through 'Tonight's The Night'.

1 SEPTEMBER 1988
Great Woods Performing Arts Center, Mansfield, Massachusetts.

3 SEPTEMBER 1988
Blossom Music Center, Cuyahoga Falls.

4 SEPTEMBER 1988
The Palace Arena, Auburn Hills, Wisconsin. First known performance of 'I'm Just A Passenger' (alias 'Box Car'); Joe Walsh joins the Blue Notes on stage for the encore.

6 SEPTEMBER 1988
Monarch Room, Royal Hawaiian Hotel, Waikiki Beach, Hawaii.

7 SEPTEMBER 1988
Monarch Room, Royal Hawaiian Hotel, Waikiki Beach, Hawaii. BA 34/3 For the first time on this tour, The Blue Notes open their show with 'Welcome To The Big Room' rather than the customary 'Ten Men Working'. During the show, The Blue Notes are presented with their Bammie awards, held over from the ceremony in March.

8 SEPTEMBER 1988
Sheraton Hotel, Honolulu, Hawaii.

OCTOBER 1988
The US indie label No. 6 Records announce plans for a Neil Young tribute album, to raise funds for The Bridge School. Among the tracks commissioned but not included on the final album are Sonic Youth's 'Southern Pacific' and The Butthole Surfers' 'For The Turnstiles'.

25 OCTOBER 1988
Kiva Auditorium, Albuquerque, New Mexico. The shows for this short US tour are billed as 'An Evening With Neil Young', after soul singer Harold Melvin (who has been leading a vocal group called The Bluenotes since 1970) brings a federal court injunction in New York to prevent Young from using the name 'Blue Notes' for his band. By the time the tour commences, Young has renamed his band Ten Men Workin'. These shows open with a lengthy acoustic set, followed by an even longer R&B performance with the band.

26 OCTOBER 1988
Arizona State Fair, Phoenix, Arizona.

27 OCTOBER 1988
Golden Hall, San Diego, California. Despite all the publicity aroused by Young's refusal to accept sponsorship, tickets for this show

suggest that 'Miller Genuine Draft present Neil Young'.

The theatre management are requested by Young to distribute an explanatory leaflet to fans entering the hall: "Neil Young and his current tour have no commercial sponsorship affiliation. Some tickets for this performance were inadvertently printed with sponsorship text included. We apologize to Mr. Young and to you the fan for any confusion this inclusion may have created. Neil Young is 'sponsored by nobody'."

Bootleg: 'Depression Blues' (1 song).

28 OCTOBER 1988
Arlington Theater, Santa Barbara, California.

29 OCTOBER 1988
Community Center Theater, Sacramento, California. The acoustic set comprises 'Comes A Time', 'Look Out For My Love', 'Too Far Gone', 'Lotta Love', a rare performance of 'Stringman', 'After The Goldrush' (complete with horn solo), 'For The Turnstiles', 'This Old House', 'Four Strong Winds' and 'Heart Of Gold'. Ten Men Workin's set begins with their 'theme tune', followed by 'Married Men', 'Find Another Shoulder', 'Hello Lonely Woman', 'Crime Of The Heart', 'Ordinary People' (introduced as being "too long to be a video, too long to be on the radio, and too long to be on an album"), 'Bad News', 'My My Hey Hey', 'This Note's For You' and 'Tonight's The Night'.

30 OCTOBER 1988
Warner's Theater, Fresno, California.

3 NOVEMBER 1988
Release of CSNY's 'American Dream'.

Top: with Kris Kristofferson and Willie Nelson.

12 NOVEMBER 1988
CSNY appear at the Children of the America Hungerthon, organised by Graham Nash and staged at the Palace Theater, Los Angeles, California. They perform 'This Old House', 'Love The One You're With', 'In The Name Of Love', 'Tracks In The Dust', 'Don't Say Goodbye', 'Southern Cross', 'Long Time Gone', 'Teach Your Children' and (with Jackson Browne) 'Crow On The Cradle'. Bootleg: 'Los Angeles 12-11-88'.

14 NOVEMBER 1988
CSNY take part in the live phone-in radio show *Rockline*, Neil and Stephen Stills answering questions in San Francisco, Crosby and Nash in Los Angeles.

17 NOVEMBER 1988
Young attends the Nordoff-Robbins Music Therapy Benefit dinner at the Puck Building, New York, and takes part in a closing jam session with musicians like Phil Collins, Robert Plant and Julian Lennon.

late NOVEMBER 1988
Young begins work on a new recording project at the Hit Factory in New York: originally planned as 'Times Square', the album evolves into the five-track set 'Eldorado'.
   Young: "I recorded a lot of stuff, eight or nine songs, at the Hit Factory in Times Square."

4 DECEMBER 1988
Bridge Benefit II, at Oakland Coliseum, Oakland, California. Young opens the event with 'Comes A Time' and 'Sugar Mountain', before inviting Crosby, Stills and Nash to join him for a ragged 'American Dream'. Neil guests with Nils Lofgren on 'Believe A Little Bit' and with the Grateful Dead on 'Wang Dang Doodle', before CSNY close the evening with 'Helplessly Hoping', 'Love The One You're With', 'This Old House', 'Southern Man', 'Don't Say Goodbye', 'Compass', 'Long Time Gone', 'Southern Cross' and (with Tracy Chapman and Nils Lofgren) 'Teach Your Children'.

17 DECEMBER 1988
Young hosts a children's benefit, 'Friends of Parents Helping Parents', in Santa Clara, California.

Ten Men Workin' evolve into The Restless at the start of 1989, featuring the same core of musicians who'd cut the 'Times Square' LP at the end of the previous year. They tour the States, and then Australia (for which they are renamed The Lost Dogs). But 'Times Square' isn't released: instead, Young tells America and Europe that he's scrapped the project, and then slips five of its tracks onto a mini-LP called 'Eldorado', for consumption in Australasia and Japan only.

Back in America, Young begins to tour as an acoustic solo artist – playing the loudest acoustic guitar anyone has ever heard. There are cameo roles for his support crew in the shows, which reach Europe by December, but the focus is entirely on Young, who prowls the stage like a caged lion, spitting out the lyrics to new songs like 'Rockin' In The Free World' into his radio mike.

'Rockin' In The Free World' duly becomes the key track on 'Freedom', Young's most orthodox album since 'Rust Never Sleeps'. This comparison isn't accidental: by echoing the format of the 1979 LP and enclosing the other songs between acoustic and electric versions of 'Free World', Young obviously means to suggest that 'Freedom' is a complete return to form.

The finished LP eventually includes three of the songs from 'Eldorado', one song from the same sessions ('Wrecking Ball'), and some vintage material that has been written as much as a decade earlier. 'Freedom' sounds like a Neil Young album, ending almost ten years of genre experiments and mysterious blind alleys. Geffen must have wondered why Young couldn't have recorded something similar for them back in 1982.

11 JANUARY 1989
Fox Theater, St. Louis, Missouri. The start of
a mini-tour with a cut-down Bluenotes line-
up, going under the name of The Restless,
featuring Chad Cromwell, R. Rosas, Frank
Sampedro and Ben Keith. Young divides the
shows between gentle acoustic sets, and
deafening electric onslaughts.

12 JANUARY 1989
Memorial Hall, Kansas City.

13 JANUARY 1989
Brady Theater, Tulsa, Oklahoma. The
opening acoustic set features 'Comes A
Time', 'I Am A Child', 'Sugar Mountain',
'The Needle And The Damage Done', 'Four
Strong Winds', 'For The Turnstiles',
'Someday', 'Wrecking Ball', 'This Old
House' and 'Heart Of Gold'. The Restless's
electric repertoire includes 'Heavy Love',
'Don't Cry', 'Cocaine Eyes', 'Eldorado', 'Box
Car' (solo electric), 'Like A Hurricane',
'Cinnamon Girl', 'My My Hey Hey', 'Down
By The River', 'On Broadway' and 'Tonight's
The Night'. Bootleg: 'Tulsa '89'.

14 JANUARY 1989
Bronco Hall, Dallas, Texas. 'Mr Soul' is
performed during both the Texas electric sets.

15 JANUARY 1989
Music Hall, Houston, Texas. Young performs
an acoustic 'Crime In The City', explaining
"This song has something like 30 verses, but
I'm just gonna play a few", and closes with
nearly 25 minutes of 'Tonight's The Night'.

16 JANUARY 1989
Saenger Theater, New Orleans, Louisiana.
Rufus Thibodoux joins the band onstage for
one song.

FEBRUARY 1989
At the Bammies awards ceremony in San
Francisco, Young's song 'This Note's For You'
is voted the Outstanding Song of 1988.

18 FEBRUARY 1989
Municipal Auditorium, Eureka, California.
Young revives the 1977 song, 'Lady
Wingshot' in the electric set of this first show
in a mini-tour of the Pacific North-West.
Also included are 'Bad Fog Of Loneliness',
plus acoustic renditions of 'Silver & Gold',
'Ways Of Love' and 'Days That Used To Be'.
Bootleg: 'In At The Beginning' (2 tracks).

19 FEBRUARY 1989
Hult Center for the Performing Arts, Eugene,
Oregon.

20 FEBRUARY 1989
Civic Auditorium, Portland, Oregon.

21 FEBRUARY 1989
Paramount Theater, Seattle, Washington.

22 FEBRUARY 1989
Orpheum Theater, Vancouver, Canada.

23 FEBRUARY 1989
Opera House, Spokane, Washington. At the
soundcheck to this show, Young performs
'Don't Worry, Be Happy'.

27 FEBRUARY 1989
The Album Network radio transcription
service broadcasts an *In The Studio* show
about the making of the 'Harvest' album,
including much interview material with
Young.

27 MARCH 1989
Young appears on another *In The Studio* radio special, this one covering Crosby, Stills, Nash and Young's 'Déjà Vu' LP.

5 APRIL 1989
Entertainment Center, Perth, Australia. The Australasia/Japan tour was originally to be by Neil Young and The Restless, but the final publicity credited Neil's band as The Lost Dogs – although the musicians are exactly the same as those who had played US shows as Ten Men Workin' and Young & Restless. Australian radio premières the 'Eldorado' EP to coincide with the first Perth show; Young is also interviewed backstage before the concert.

The acoustic sets keep close to recent US shows, while the electric sets typically feature 'Heavy Love', 'Don't Cry', 'No More', 'Cocaine Eyes', 'Box Car', 'Mr Soul', 'Cinnamon Girl', 'Powderfinger', 'Rockin' In The Free World', 'Hey Hey My My', 'On Broadway' and 15-20 minutes of 'Tonight's The Night'.

7 APRIL 1989
East End Markets, Adelaide, Australia.

8 APRIL 1989
Darwin Amphitheatre, Darwin, Australia.

11/12 APRIL 1989
National Tennis Center, Melbourne, Australia. Young performs the epic 'Ordinary People' as a solo acoustic song on the 11th.

14 APRIL 1989
Coffs Harbour, NSW, Australia.

15 APRIL 1989
Entertainment Center, Brisbane, Australia.

17/18 APRIL 1989
Entertainment Center, Sydney, Australia. 'Eldorado' is released in Australia and Japan.
Young: "Just as it was being made ready for release, I changed my mind, because I really wanted to have an album that would make an effect. I felt that 'Eldorado' by itself was a really fine album. But if you don't have a song they can play on the radio... So I took the songs that really created the feeling of 'Eldorado' and put them out as an EP, 5,000 copies, thereby eliminating any of the crap that I have to go through with the radio stations and promotion and record companies. I eliminated all that completely by not even entering the arena. But I still put out a work that was distinctly mine, that I really believed in."
The show on the 18th features another solo performance of 'Ordinary People'.

19 APRIL 1989
Silverdome, Launceston, Australia.

20 APRIL 1989
Entertainment Center, Hobart, Australia.

22 APRIL 1989
Auckland Tent, Auckland, New Zealand. Five days before the show, the date is switched from the previously announced 23 April.

27 APRIL 1989
Bunka Taiikukan, Yokohama, Japan. 'Pocahontas' and 'Sail Away' feature in the acoustic set. Bootleg: 'Japan Tour '89'.

28-30 APRIL 1989
NHK Hall, Tokyo, Japan.
On the 30th Young performs solo renditions of 'This Note's For You' and 'Long Walk Home' at the piano.

2 MAY 1989
Festival Hall, Osaka, Japan.

5 MAY 1989
Shi Kokaido, Nagoya, Japan. Bootleg: 'Japan Tour '89'/'In At The Beginning'.

5 JUNE 1989
Lake Compounce Festival Park, Bristol, Connecticut. The support act for this short East Coast tour – which should have opened the previous night in Wantaugh, a date postponed when Young falls ill – is The Indigo Girls.

Just a month after completing his Far East electric tour, Young débuts an all-acoustic set-list, featuring 'Hey Hey My My', 'Rockin' In The Free World', 'Comes A Time', 'Sugar Mountain', 'Pocahontas', 'Helpless', 'Someday', 'For The Turnstiles', 'This Old House', 'Roll Another Number', 'Too Far Gone', 'This Note's For You', 'No More', the second-ever live performance of 'One Of These Days', 'After The Goldrush', 'Heart Of Gold', 'Ohio' and a rare appearance of 'Four Strong Winds'.

6 JUNE 1989
Waterloo Village Festival Park, Stanhope, New Jersey. 'One Of These Days' is reprised one final time, while 'Crime In The City' replaces 'Someday', and 'The Needle And The Damage Done' and 'Powderfinger' also enter the set-list.

8 JUNE 1989
Lakeside Amphitheater, Darien Lake, New York.

9 JUNE 1989
Great Woods Performing Arts Center, Mansfield, Massachusetts. This show is promoted as part of the Great Woods Folk Festival.

10 JUNE 1989
Bally's Grand Hotel Pavilion, Atlantic City, New Jersey.

12 JUNE 1989
Garden State Arts Center, Holmdel, New Jersey.

14 JUNE 1989
Jones Beach Music Center, Wantaugh, New York. Bruce Springsteen joins The Lost Dogs for the second encore, an extended version of 'Down By The River'. This show is filmed and recorded by Warner Brothers, and 'Crime In The City' and 'This Note's For You' are subsequently released on the home-video *Freedom*. The night's performance of 'Rockin' In The Free World' is also released, as the opening track on the 'Freedom' album. Bootlegs: 'The Loner' (2 songs)/'Alive And Alone'/'Restless'.

2 JULY 1989
Young appears at the Pahasapa Music Festival in Rapid City, South Dakota, on a bill also featuring Willie Nelson, Jackson Browne,

John Denver and Timbuk 3. The show is in aid of Oglala Lakota Sioux Indians in the Rapid City area.

JULY 1989
Young tapes several more songs at his home studio; with three songs from 'Eldorado', plus leftovers from those late 1988 sessions, this material comprises the 'Freedom' album.
Young: "I kept doing different sessions. I did one where I recorded eight old songs that I hadn't recorded yet, some of them 15 years old. I got two that I thought were really good, and the rest I put back on the shelf."

31 JULY 1989
'The Bridge' tribute album to Neil Young is released in Britain, featuring covers of Young songs by Soul Asylum, Victoria Williams, the Flaming Lips, Nikki Sudden, Loop, Nick Cave, The Pixies, Sonic Youth, Psychic TV, Dinosaur Jr., Henry Kaiser & David Lindley, Bongwater and B.A.L.L.
Young: "It's nice that they did that tribute album, but I'm not ready for it. They don't mean to close the book, but to me it's still threatening."

18 AUGUST 1989
Young begins another acoustic tour at the Pacific Amphitheater, Costa Mesa, California.

19/20 AUGUST 1989
Greek Theater, Los Angeles, California. David Crosby and Graham Nash join Young on stage to perform 'Ohio' on the 19th.

22 AUGUST 1989
Santa Barbara County Bowl, Santa Barbara, California.

25 AUGUST 1989
Pine Knob Music Theater, Clarkston, Michigan.

26 AUGUST 1989
Kingswood Music Theater, Toronto, Canada.

27 AUGUST 1989
New York State Fair, Syracuse, New York.

28 AUGUST 1989
Poplar Creek Music Center, Hoffman Estates, Illinois.

30 AUGUST 1989
Riverbend Music Center, Cincinnati, Ohio.

31 AUGUST 1989
Merryweather Post Pavilion, Columbia, Maryland.

2 SEPTEMBER 1989
Veterans Memorial Park, Manchester, New Hampshire.

4 SEPTEMBER 1989
Saratoga Performing Arts Center, Saratoga Springs, New York.

5/6 SEPTEMBER 1989
The Palladium, New York, New York. These concerts are recorded for HBO TV, and performances from the 6th of 'No More', 'Too Far Gone', 'After The Goldrush', 'Ohio' and 'Rockin' In The Free World' are subsequently released on the commercial video *Freedom*. During the show, Neil is presented with the MTV Music Video of the Year award for 'This Note's For You' from the MTV Video Music Awards. Actress Darryl Hannah hands over the trophy, and the presentation is beamed live to the Universal Amphitheater in Los Angeles, where the main ceremony is taking place.

9 SEPTEMBER 1989
Red Rocks Theater, Denver, Colorado.

30 SEPTEMBER 1989
Young performs on *Saturday Night Live*, with Steve Jordan (drums) and Charlie Drayton (bass), musicians best-known from their work with Keith Richards. Frank Sampedro completes the impromptu band. Young

1989

136

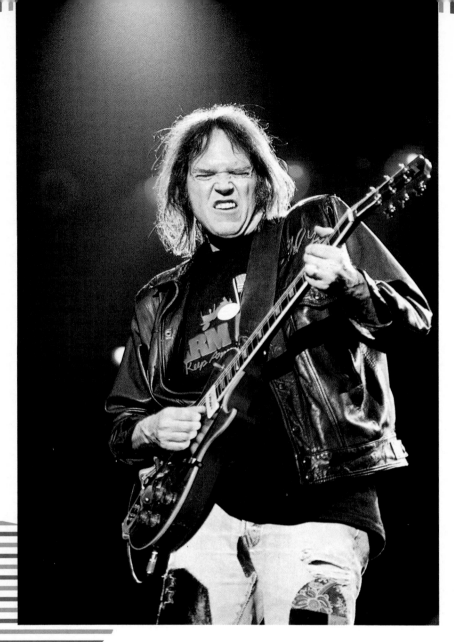

'Pocohontas', 'Crime In The City', 'After The Goldrush', 'The Needle And The Damage Done', 'No More', 'Heart Of Gold' and 'Rockin' In The Free World'.

After brief sets from Hagar, Petty and Chapman, CSN perform, being joined by Young for 'Helplessly Hoping'. CSNY add a ramshackle 'Human Highway', 'Got It Made', a superb 'Silver & Gold', 'Southern Cross', 'Ohio' and the usual Bridge Benefit closer, 'Teach Your Children'.

NOVEMBER 1989

'Freedom' is released.

Young: "I just wanted this one to be a Neil Young album, as silly as that sounds. For years now I've skirted the issue of what was really on my mind by doing stylistic things, genre albums. I wasn't ready to talk about what had happened in my own life. I alienated a lot of fans by doing that. Still, I had a hell of a good time, and you only live once."

10 NOVEMBER 1989

Much Music TV in Canada broadcast *Neil Young: Freedom To Rock*, a one-hour special including footage from several 1988 and 1989 concerts.

26 NOVEMBER 1989

Neil Young performs at a televised concert from the Cow Palace, San Francisco, to raise money for victims of the earthquake that ravaged Northern California on 17 October, but resists the temptation to play with Crosby, Stills and Nash, also on the bill. His solo set comprises 'My My Hey Hey', 'Rockin' In The Free World', 'Comes A Time', 'Homegrown', 'Heart Of Gold' and 'Crime In The City', before Young is joined by The Steve Miller Band, Carlos Santana and The Chambers Brothers for a blues set that included 'Wang Dang Doodle', 'Baby What Do You Want Me To Do', 'Lucille', 'I Want To Be Loved', Miller's 'The Joker' and Wilson Pickett's 'In The Midnight Hour'.

That looks like the end of the show, but Young reappears with an electric guitar and persuades Steve Miller to take part in two lengthy blues jams. During the concert, phone pledges promise more than $1 million for the earthquake victims.

DECEMBER 1989

Young prevents the Lee jeans company from using his song 'Hey Hey My My' as part of an advertising campaign on European cable TV.

5 DECEMBER 1989

Teatro Smeraldo, Milan, Italy. Young opens his brief European acoustic tour with a set comprising 'My My Hey Hey', 'Rockin' In

performs 'Rockin' In The Free World', 'The Needle And The Damage Done' and 'No More'. The last song is subsequently included on a promo-only CD single of the studio version of that number. Young resists the temptation to perform 'Fuckin' Up', which he had written during the afternoon rehearsals for the show. Bootlegs: 'Alive And Alone'/'Shaky Neil'.

OCTOBER 1989

Young's brother Bob pleads guilty in Toronto to conspiring to traffic in hashish – a lesser charge than the one for which he was arrested and originally convicted seven years earlier.

28 OCTOBER 1989

Young tops the bill at the third Bridge Benefit show at the Shoreline Amphitheater, Mountain View, California, supported by Crosby, Stills & Nash, Tracy Chapman, Sammy Hagar and Tom Petty.

The show opens with Young, Petty and Hagar performing Bob Dylan's 'Everything Is Broken', before Neil plays a solo set:

The Free World', 'The Old Laughing Lady', 'Don't Let It Bring You Down', 'Someday', the only performance on this tour of 'Pocahontas', 'Crime In The City', 'Eldorado', 'Too Far Gone', 'This Note's For You', 'The Needle And The Damage Done', 'No More', 'Hangin' On A Limb', 'Heart Of Gold', 'Rockin' In The Free World' and 'Powderfinger'.

7 DECEMBER 1989
Musikhalle, Frankfurt, West Germany. 'After The Goldrush' replaces 'Pocahontas' in the set, though Young resists an audience request for 'Voodoo Chile'. Bootleg: 'Swinging In The Silence'/'Crime In The City'.

8 DECEMBER 1989
Grosse Freiheit, Hamburg, West Germany. German radio record the show, which includes his first European performance of 'Fuckin' Up'. Bootleg: 'NY Over Hamburg 8.12.89'/'This Note's For You'

10 DECEMBER 1989
Stopera Muziek Theater, Amsterdam, Holland. Before the show, Young is interviewed for Dutch radio VRO, who also tape the concert for future broadcast. Bootleg: 'Amsterdam '89'.
  As Young starts to play 'Heart Of Gold',

someone in the crowd calls out, "Is this the song Bob Dylan wrote for you?" Young laughs, and replies: "I love Bob... Now, there's a thing – I ripped off his song, ripped off his whole sound. He didn't say boo..."

11 DECEMBER 1989
Elysee Montmartre, Paris, France. Sections of the show are filmed for the BBC's *Rapido*. 'Stringman' is performed for the first time since 1976.

12 DECEMBER 1989
Hammersmith Odeon, London. Despite (for Britain) overwhelming audience reaction, Young appears dissatisfied with his reception at the end of the show.

13 DECEMBER 1989
Sportpalets Ahoy, Rotterdam, Holland. First and only known performance of 'Dreaming Man', while 'Razor Love' is played for the first time since 1984. Also added to this set for the final date are 'Cocaine Eyes', 'Comes A Time', 'Roll Another Number' and 'Winterlong'.

14 DECEMBER 1989
Young joins The Alarm onstage at the Ritz, New York to perform 'Rockin' In The Free World'.

Young with wife Pegi.

1990

Basking in the reviews for 'Freedom', Young allows himself a few months out of the public eye in early 1990 – emerging only to join CSNY for some fundraising concerts for a former sideman. Meanwhile, he bickers gently with Reprise over the size and contents of 'Decade II', a retrospective project that he'd originally planned to deliver back in 1987.

In the summer, he returns to Britain for a cameo appearance as a soloist to celebrate the life and beliefs of South African freedom fighter Nelson Mandela. But rather than cut an acoustic record, he goes immediately into the studio with the ever-loyal Crazy Horse, and reappears two months later with the tapes for 'Ragged Glory'.

Young has obviously regained his ability to catch the mood of the times. 'Freedom' was released just as Eastern Europe's monolithic Communist régimes collapsed; now the rock world is heading towards the grunge explosion, and Young is there on cue with a rowdy, alcohol-fuelled record, which revives some Crazy Horse favourites from the past (notably 'Country Home', which they'd been playing since 1975), and soaks every song in growls of feedback.

JANUARY 1990
Young appears on 'Splendid Isolation', a track on Warren Zevon's new album, 'Transverse City'.

Crazy Horse release their first new album for many years, 'Left For Dead'. Living up to its title, the record is effectively deleted within a month when the record label goes bankrupt.

14 JANUARY 1990
Dutch TV broadcast a one-hour documentary on Young, including footage from the Amsterdam show in December.

17 JANUARY 1990
An interview with Young is broadcast on the TV show *Rapido*.

25 FEBRUARY 1990
MTV broadcast *Freedom*, a 30-minute Neil Young special taped at the Palladium Theater, New York on 6 September 1989. The show was directed by Timothy Hutton, and included live performances of 'Crime In The City', 'This Note's For You', 'No More', 'Too

Far Gone', 'After The Goldrush', 'Ohio' and 'Rockin' In The Free World'.

Young: " 'Rockin' In The Free World' cuts both ways. Rockin' in the free world, that's what we Americans want to do. But how free is the free world anyway?"

MARCH 1990
The movie *Love At Large*, featuring Young in the role of Rick, a misogynist gangster, opens in the USA. Young's scenes were filmed in March 1989.

Record company insiders report a mild argument between Reprise and Neil Young, over the size and content of Young's 'Decade II' box set, which has been overdue since 1987. Young is said to have revamped his idea as a 15-CD box; Reprise are apparently unwilling to issue more than 8 albums in the package.

17 MARCH 1990
Young attends the Bammie Awards ceremony at the Civic Auditorium, San Francisco, to collect his Bay Area Music awards for the year's best album ('Freedom') and best male

vocalist. During the all-star finale, he performed two blues songs with John Lee Hooker and John Fogerty, among others.

31 MARCH 1990

Crosby, Stills, Nash and Young re-unite at a benefit concert for their former drummer, Dallas Taylor, at the Civic Auditorium, Santa Monica, California. The performance is organised by FREDA (Foundation for Research and Education on Drug Abuse).

Young performs 'Rockin' In The Free World' solo, 'Eldorado' with Frank Sampedro, then two further solo songs, 'Someday' and 'Mother Earth'. Crosby, Stills and Nash play a trio set, before Young joins them for 'Human Highway', 'Silver And Gold', 'Southern Cross', an electric 'Wooden Ships' and 'Teach Your Children'. Dallas Taylor played with the quartet on the last song, his first performance with CSNY since 1970.

1 APRIL 1990

CSNY: Civic Auditorium, Santa Monica, California; a second benefit for FREDA, this one raising money for environmental campaigns in California. Young joins Crosby, Stills and Nash for 'For What It's Worth' during their set, and CSNY replace 'Southern Cross' with an electric 'Ohio'.

7 APRIL 1990

Neil Young appears at Farm Aid IV, at the Hoosier Dome, Indianapolis, Indiana. 48,000 tickets for the event are sold in less than 90 minutes.

After Crosby, Stills and Nash perform 'Suite: Judy Blue Eyes', Young joins them onstage for 'This Old House'. He then plays two solo songs, 'Rockin' In The Free World' and the live première of 'Mother Earth' (a performance which is overdubbed for use on the 'Ragged Glory' LP). Bootleg: 'Farm Aid'.

16 APRIL 1990

The Nelson Mandela International Tribute For A Free South Africa concert is held at Wembley Stadium, London. Young joins Peter Gabriel, Tracy Chapman, Simple Minds and The Neville Brothers on the bill for the show, which is broadcast live on UK TV. His two-song set duplicates his solo performances from Farm Aid IV.

17 APRIL 1990

'Rockin' In The Free World' is issued as a single in the UK.

JUNE-JULY 1990

Young and Crazy Horse record the 'Ragged Glory' album in his home studio. Work on the album is blamed for the delay in Young's long-awaited CD career retrospective.

Young: "About every three years I do something with Crazy Horse. I branch out and do other things but I always come back to Crazy Horse. It's like coming home."

31 AUGUST 1990
'Mansion On The Hill' is sent out to US radio stations as a CD sampler for the 'Ragged Glory' LP.

5 SEPTEMBER 1990
The US TV première of *Ragged Glory*, on the same day that American FM radio stations broadcast a show about the making of the album, with songs introduced by Young and members of Crazy Horse.

11 SEPTEMBER 1990
'Ragged Glory' is released.

18 SEPTEMBER 1990
Reprise in the States release 'Mansion On The Hill' as a CD and cassette single, with the non-LP cut 'Don't Spook The Horse' as the flipside.

Young: "It kinda condenses the whole album. If you buy 'Don't Spook The Horse', you don't have to listen to the album!"

15 OCTOBER 1990
Edna Rassy Young, Neil's mother, dies.

22 OCTOBER 1990
WEA release the *Freedom* home-video in Britain.

26 OCTOBER 1990
Neil Young presents the fourth Bridge Benefit concert at Shoreline Amphitheater, Mountain View, California. Also on the bill are Jackson Browne, Elvis Costello and Edie Brickell.

Young opens the show with Crazy Horse, performing just one song, 'Lotta Love'. He joins Elvis Costello to harmonise on his closing song, 'Alison', then returns with Crazy Horse for the night's closing set: 'Love And Only Love', 'Everybody Knows This Is Nowhere', 'Days That Used To Be', 'Helpless', 'Mansion On The Hill', 'Down By The River' (with Elvis Costello), and an all-star performance of 'Rockin' In The Free World'.

30 OCTOBER 1990
The Catalyst, Santa Cruz, California: show cancelled.

NOVEMBER 1990
It is confirmed that Neil Young is working on a six-CD retrospective of his career, which will include material by CSNY and Buffalo Springfield.

5 NOVEMBER 1990
Young appears on MTV to defend 'Fucking Up'.

6 NOVEMBER 1990
The Catalyst, Santa Cruz, California: show cancelled again, officially because Young has contracted influenza. But Young and Crazy Horse spend the evening filming promo videos for 'Over And Over' and 'Fucking Up'.

13 NOVEMBER 1990
The Catalyst, Santa Cruz, California. A warm-up show for the Ragged Glory tour, featuring (1st set) 'Country Home', 'Surfer Joe & Moe The Sleaze', 'Love To Burn', 'Days That Used To Be', 'Bite The Bullet', 'Cinnamon Girl'; (2nd set) 'Farmer John', 'Cowgirl In The Sand', 'Over And Over', 'Danger Bird', 'Don't Cry No Tears', 'Sedan Delivery', 'Roll Another Number', 'Fuckin' Up'; (3rd set) 'T-Bone', 'Homegrown', 'Mansion On The Hill', 'Like A Hurricane' 'Love And Only Love'; (encore) 'Cortez The Killer'. Bootlegs: 'Don't Spook The (Crazy) Horse'/'Homegrown'/'Love Art Blues' (1 track).

19 NOVEMBER 1990
MTV broadcast a longer Neil Young interview on *The Last Word*.

Edna 'Rassy' Young.

1991

Recruiting 'alternative' bands Sonic Youth and Social Distortion as his support acts, Young takes Crazy Horse out across America in the early months of 1991. The Ragged Glory/Smell The Horse tour provides few surprises for anyone who's been following Young's career; the sound and many of the songs hark back to the Rust Never Sleeps shows of 1978. But the mere fact that Young has returned to playing rowdy rock'n'roll is enough to cement his place as an agreeably wrecked favourite uncle of the MTV generation.

As he had in the late 70s, Young follows a Crazy Horse tour with a double-live album, 'Weld', and adds an optional third CD called 'Arc' – an experimental 37-minute exercise in grunge concrete, a feedback symphony. And with that work complete, he immediately recruits the core of musicians who'd worked with him on 'Harvest' 20 years earlier (minus the rest of CSNY, significantly), and sets to work on a mostly acoustic sequel.

20 JANUARY 1991
The first night of the Ragged Glory World Tour, planned for La Crosse, Wisconsin, is cancelled when Crazy Horse guitarist Frank Sampedro has to be treated for an emergency appendectomy.

21 JANUARY 1991
Young and Crazy Horse hold pre-tour rehearsals at Paisley Park Studios, Minneapolis.

22 JANUARY 1991
Target Center, Minneapolis, Minnesota. First date of *Ragged Glory World Tour '91*, supported by Sonic Youth and Social Distortion.

Young's sets with Crazy Horse last 13 or 14 songs on this tour, with Jimi Hendrix's 'Star Spangled Banner' blaring out over the speakers, before the set begins. 'Hey Hey My My', 'Crime In The City', Bob Dylan's 'Blowin' In The Wind', 'Powderfinger', 'Cinnamon Girl', 'Mansion On The Hill', 'Love To Burn', 'Rockin' In The Free World', 'Love And Only Love', 'Fuckin' Up' and 'Tonight's The Night' are performed during most shows. At this date, 'Country Home' receives its sole rendition for the entire tour, while 'Campaigner' also gets a rare outing.

24 JANUARY 1991
Bradley Convention Center, Milwaukee, Wisconsin. Young introduces 'Cortez The Killer' to the set, where it remains standard hereafter. 'Farmer John' is the night's least predictable offering.

25 JANUARY 1991
Redbird Arena, Normal, Illinois. 'Welfare Mothers' gets its first airing on the tour.

26 JANUARY 1991
Market Square Arena, Indianapolis, Indiana.

28 JANUARY 1991
Fox Theater, St. Louis, Missouri.

29 JANUARY 1991
Rosemont Theater, Rosemont, Illinois.

30 JANUARY 1991
Gardens Arena, Cincinnati, Ohio.

31 JANUARY 1991
Richfield Coliseum, Richfield, Ohio.

2 FEBRUARY 1991
Palace Arena, Auburn Hills, Mississippi.

4 FEBRUARY 1991
Madison Square Garden, New York, New York.

5/6 FEBRUARY 1991
Civic Center, Philadelphia, Pennsylvania.

8 FEBRUARY 1991
Boston Garden, Boston, Massachusetts.

9 FEBRUARY 1991
RPI Auditorium, Albany, New York. 'Roll Another Number For The Road' is performed for the first time on the tour.

10 FEBRUARY 1991
Cumberland Community Center, Portland, Maine.

12 FEBRUARY 1991
Montreal Forum, Montreal, Canada.

13 FEBRUARY 1991
London Garden, London, Canada (cancelled). Replaced by Copps Coliseum, Hamilton, Canada.

14 FEBRUARY 1991
Maple Leaf Gardens, Toronto, Canada.

16 FEBRUARY 1991
Memorial Auditorium, Buffalo, New York. 'Campaigner' receives its second and last airing on the '91 tour. The performances of 'Blowin' In The Wind', 'Mansion On The Hill' and 'Powderfinger' from this show are included on the *Weld* video.

17 FEBRUARY 1991
Civic Arena, Pittsburgh, Pennsylvania. 'Hey Hey My My', 'Crime In The City', 'Cortez The Killer', 'Love And Only Love', 'Rockin' In The Free World' and 'Tonight's The Night' are included in the *Weld* video.

19 FEBRUARY 1991
Hartford Civic Center, Hartford, Connecticut.

20 FEBRUARY 1991
Civic Center, Providence, Rhode Island.

21 FEBRUARY 1991
Civic Center, Providence, Rhode Island (cancelled); replaced by West Point Military Academy.

22 FEBRUARY 1991
Nassau Coliseum, Hempstead, New York.

24 FEBRUARY 1991
Brendan Byrne Arena, Meadowlands,
New Jersey.

25 FEBRUARY 1991
Largo, Maryland (cancelled).

26 FEBRUARY 1991
Hershey Park Arena, Hershey, Pennsylvania.

27 FEBRUARY 1991
Capitol Center, Landover. This show's
performances of 'Cinnamon Girl' and
'Welfare Mothers' are included in the
Weld video.

28 FEBRUARY 1991
Dean Smith Center, Chapel Hill,
North Carolina.

1 MARCH 1991
William & Mary College Hall,
Williamsburg, Virginia.

2 MARCH 1991
Young is nominated in three categories at the
Bay Area Music Awards, held at the Civic
Auditorium, San Francisco: best male
vocalist, best album and best guitarist.

3 MARCH 1991
Omni Auditorium, Atlanta, Georgia.

7 MARCH 1991
Orlando Arena, Orlando, Florida.

9 MARCH 1991
Miami Arena, Miami, Florida.

10 MARCH 1991
Sun Dome, Tampa, Florida.

12 MARCH 1991
UNO Lakefront Arena, New Orleans,
Louisiana. 'Down By The River' makes its
first tour appearance.

13 MARCH 1991
The Summit, Houston, Texas.

14 MARCH 1991
Reunion Arena, Dallas, Texas.

15 MARCH 1991
Convention Center Arena, San Antonio,
Texas.

17 MARCH 1991
Myriad Arena, Oklahoma City, Oklahoma.

CSNY forgot their differences long enough to pay tribute to Bill Graham, who had promoted many of their early shows.

19 MARCH 1991
McNicholls Arena, Denver, Colorado.

20 MARCH 1991
Huntsman Center, Salt Lake City, Utah.

5 APRIL 1991
A show at Lawlor Events Arena, Reno, Nevada continues what has by now become the Smell The Horse tour.

6 APRIL 1991
Cow Palace, San Francisco, California.

7 APRIL 1991
ARCO Sports Complex, Sacramento, California.

9 APRIL 1991
Memorial Coliseum, Portland, Oregon.

11 APRIL 1991
Seattle Coliseum, Seattle, Washington.

13 APRIL 1991
Olympic Saddledrome, Calgary, Canada.

14 APRIL 1991
Saskatchewan Place, Saskatoon, Canada. Arranged at short notice but then cancelled because of transportation problems.

15 APRIL 1991
Northlands Coliseum, Edmonton, Canada.

17 APRIL 1991
PNE Coliseum, Vancouver, Canada.

20 APRIL 1991
Thomas & Mack Center, Las Vegas, Nevada.

21 APRIL 1991
Desert Sky Pavilion, Phoenix, Arizona.

23 APRIL 1991
Sports Arena, San Diego, California.

26 APRIL 1991
Sports Arena, Los Angeles, California.

27 APRIL 1991
Sports Arena, Los Angeles, California. 'Love To Burn' and 'Roll Another Number For The Road' are lifted from this show for the *Weld* video.

SUMMER 1991
Young begins recording what finally emerges as the 'Harvest Moon' album.

7 SEPTEMBER 1991
Intended opening date for a three-show Japanese tour for Amnesty International, in which Young is supposed to appear alongside Tracy Chapman and Warren Zevon. Poor ticket sales and Young's affliction with an ear infection put paid to all three concerts.

17 SEPTEMBER 1991
Robbie Robertson's 'Storyville' LP is released by Geffen; Young appears as guest vocalist on 'Soapbox Preacher'.

21 OCTOBER 1991
The 'Weld' double-live album is released, taken from 1991 shows in New York, Pittsburgh and Baltimore. Also issued is a limited edition three-CD set which includes the 37-minute feedback collage, 'Arc'.
    To promote the set, Young appears on the radio phone-in show, *Rockline*.
Young: "The next thing I'm doing is acoustic – I've already recorded it. It's sort of like 'After The Goldrush' or 'Harvest' or 'Comes A Time', those kind of records."

2 NOVEMBER 1991
Young stages the fifth Bridge School Benefit concert at the usual venue, the Shoreline Amphitheater, Mountain View, California.
    As ever, Young opens the show, performing

Bob Dylan's 'Forever Young' on pump organ. Sets follow from Larry Keegan, John Lee Hooker, Don Henley, Nils Lofgren (joined by Neil for 'Believe'), Tracy Chapman, Sonic Youth (who abandon their performance midway through the second song, plagued by acoustic problems and audience catcalls) and Willie Nelson.

Young closes the evening with The Stray Gators, performing two renditions of 'Long May You Run' (the first having collapsed in a howl of, for once, unwanted feedback), 'Birds', 'Harvest Moon', 'From Hank To Hendrix', 'Comes A Time' and an all-star 'Forever Young'.

3 NOVEMBER 1991
CSNY re-form once again for the Bill Graham Tribute concert at Polo Field, Golden Gate Park, San Francisco, California. 300,000 fans attend the show, held in the memory of the rock promoter who died in a helicopter crash the previous month.

Young: "Bill was around from the very beginning. It kept getting bigger and he was always there. He cared about it being comfortable for the people that came to the show. It's like he was the Godfather of rock'n'roll, and now he's gone it's just a big void."

CSNY's entire acoustic set is broadcast live on local radio, albeit with serious sound problems: 'Teach Your Children', 'Love The One You're With', 'Long May You Run', 'Long Time Gone', 'Southern Cross', 'Only Love Can Break Your Heart' and a brilliant, elongated 'Wooden Ships'. Bootleg: 'Helpless Believers'. Besides CSNY's set, Young also performs 'Forever Young' with The Grateful Dead (on 'Live In Austin, Texas, '84' bootleg).

'**H**arvest Moon' sets the tone for 1992, even though its release – originally announced in January – is postponed time and again in definitive Young style. Never mind that the record isn't yet in the stores: Neil spends much of the year touring to promote it, regularly losing his temper with audience members who've come to party rather than appreciate the delicate tones of an acoustic guitar.

This isn't Young's only complaint of the year: he'd been sniping continually at the move from analog to digital recording since the late 80s, and in 1992 he extends his attack to CDs – though he doesn't have the power to ensure that 'Harvest Moon' appears on vinyl in his adopted homeland.

In October, Young is by popular acclaim the star performer at the tribute concert he termed 'Bobfest'; in his dismissal of Sinéad O'Connor, booed off by the conservative audience for her anti-papist views, he once again aligns himself with the working man rather than the underground. But his new, sub-25-year-old audience is equally conservative, and proves just as willing to take 'Harvest Moon' on board as they have 'Ragged Glory'. Young hasn't enjoyed such universal support across the rock audience since 1970.

JANUARY 1992
Young announces the imminent arrival of a new studio album, recorded the previous summer and autumn; the release of the LP, titled 'Harvest Moon', is postponed throughout the year, until November.

16 JANUARY 1992
Lone Star Roadhouse, New York. At the 1992 Rock & Roll Hall Of Fame ceremony, where Young jammed with The Edge, Keith Richards, Jimmy Page, Johnny Cash and plenty more.

20 JANUARY 1992
Paramount Theater, Seattle, Washington. Bootleg: 'Early Harvest'/'Dreamin' Man'. The set for the first night of Young's acoustic tour includes 'Long May You Run', 'From Hank To Hendrix', 'Silver & Gold', 'You And Me', 'War Of Man', 'Old King', 'Such A Woman', 'Harvest Moon', 'Heart Of Gold', 'Dreamin' Man', 'Natural Beauty', 'Don't Let It Bring You Down', 'Down By The River' and 'After The Goldrush'.

21 JANUARY 1992
Paramount Theater, Seattle, Washington. 'Cowgirl In The Sand' joins the set-list.

23 JANUARY 1992
Civic Auditorium, Portland, Oregon. Both the Portland shows are marred by continual audience conversation while Young is performing.

24 JANUARY 1992
Civic Auditorium, Portland, Oregon.

25 JANUARY 1992
Opera House, Spokane, Washington.

13-15 & 17-19 FEBRUARY 1992
Beacon Theater, New York, New York. Young briefly attempts 'Depression Blues' on the 13th. The following night sees the first known performances of 'I'll Always Be A Part Of You' and 'Unknown Legend'. On the 15th

Young precedes 'Old King' with a five-minute monologue. The set for the 17th includes 'Depression Blues' and 'Home Fires'. Bootleg: 'Live Under Harvest Moon' and on the 18th there's another lengthy monologue.

On the final night, Young performs 'Look Out For My Love", and adds 'Mr Soul' to the set-list. A perceptive audience member notes the similarity between 'You And Me' and 'Old Man', and bellows the old song as Young tries to perform its successor. Young: "Shut up you asshole! Anyone who wants to sing a few songs here, just come on up... When I first came here, I played just as many new songs as I'm doing now. When I was playing those songs, people listened to me because they didn't have any distractions in their head about me, they didn't know who I was. They listened to me."

14 MARCH 1992
Farm Aid V at Texas Stadium, Fort Worth, Texas. Bootleg: 'Solidarity With A Stringman'.

18-20 MARCH 1992
Orpheum Theater, Boston, Massachusetts. The first of three 18- or 19-song shows, during which Young performs a total of 28 different songs. Included in this set are 'Long May You Run', 'Unknown Legend', 'From Hank To Hendrix', 'Silver And Gold', 'You And Me', 'War Of Man', 'Old King', 'Such A Woman', 'Harvest Moon', 'Heart Of Gold', 'Dreamin' Man', 'Natural Beauty', 'Don't Let It Bring You Down', 'Mr Soul', 'Sugar Mountain', 'After The Goldrush' and 'One Of These Days'.

'The Needle And The Damage Done', 'Too Far Gone' and 'Homefires' feature in the set on the 19th. Bootleg: 'Homefires'.

'Stringman' makes one of its periodic appearances in Young's concert repertoire on the 20th – but is overshadowed by renditions of 'Like A Hurricane' on the pipe organ, and 'Tonight's The Night' at the grand piano. Also added to this set are 'Comes A Time', 'The Old Laughing Lady', 'Helpless', 'Are You Ready For The Country' and 'Fuckin' Up'. Bootleg: 'Homefires'.

22-24 MARCH 1992
Tower Theater, Philadelphia, Pennsylvania.
'Down By The River' makes a rare acoustic appearance on the 23rd. Bootleg: 'Like A Musical Ride'.

1 APRIL 1992
Walden Woods Benefit, Los Angeles. Young performs 'Natural Beauty' (on 'Like A Musical Ride' bootleg).

17/18 MAY 1992
Public Auditorium, Cleveland, Ohio.

20-22 MAY 1992
Fox Theater, Detroit, Michigan.
On the 22nd Young performs an acoustic 'Cinnamon Girl', plus a piano rendition of 'Tonight's The Night' and (in deference to the following day's ceremony) 'Four Strong Winds'. As he begins to play 'Old King', someone in the audience shouts out "After The Goldrush!". Young replies: "This isn't 'After The Goldrush'... somebody here has a retentive problem."

23 MAY 1992
Young is appointed an honorary Doctor of Music at Lakehead University, Thunder Bay, Canada.

23 JUNE 1992
Tanglewood Music Center, Lenox, Massachusetts. In a double-play of self-plagiarism, Young introduces the confessional song 'Hitchhiker', incorporating a verse from 'Like An Inca', and plays "two songs that sound alike", a medley of 'Dance Dance Dance'/'Love Is A Rose'.

25 JUNE 1992
Garden State Arts Center, Holmdel, New Jersey. 'On The Way Home' is an unusual inclusion in the set, while 'Cripple Creek Ferry' is performed in response to an unexpected audience request.

26 JUNE 1992
Merriweather Post Pavilion, Columbia, Maryland. Young abandons his performance of 'Cortez The Killer' midway through, noting: "If you forget the words, it's time to stop playing". 'Home Fires' is also played in this set. Bootleg: 'Depression Blues' (2 songs).

28 JUNE 1992
Star Lake Amphitheater, Burgettstown, Pittsburgh, Pennsylvania. 'Such A Woman' is the song aborted in this set, which includes an acoustic 'Down By The River'.

29 JUNE 1992
Performing Arts Center, SPA Park, Saratoga Springs, New York.

Young joined Keith Richards, The Edge and Jimmy Page for the closing jam at the 1986 Rock & Roll Hall Of Fame ceremony in New York.

Young with R.E.M. guitarist Peter Buck.

11 JULY 1992
Young joins Warren Zevon onstage for two songs at the American Music Festival, at the Winter Park Resort.

30 JULY 1992
David Crosby and Graham Nash add backing vocals to Young's recording of 'Silver And Gold' at his California ranch.

SEPTEMBER 1992
Young writes a guest editorial in the latest issue of the magazine *Guitar Player*, complaining about the limitations of digital recording techniques and compact discs: "I would like to hear guitars again, with the warmth, the highs, the lows, the air, the electricity, the vibrancy of something that's real."

11 SEPTEMBER 1992
Erwin J. Nutter Center, Wright State University, Fairborn, Dayton, Ohio. Young's acoustic set for the first night of this short tour comprises 'Comes A Time', 'Long May You Run', 'From Hank To Hendrix', 'The Old Laughing Lady', 'Dance Dance Dance', 'Helpless', 'Unknown Legend', 'Like A Hurricane', 'Heart Of Gold' (aborted after Young mangles the lyrics), 'The Needle And The Damage Done', 'Tonight's The Night',

'Speakin' Out', 'Harvest Moon', a reprise of 'Heart Of Gold', 'Such A Woman' (interrupted when Young stops to lecture the over-boisterous audience), 'Old King', 'Don't Let It Bring You Down', 'Field Of Opportunity', 'Homegrown', 'Sugar Mountain' and 'After The Goldrush'.

12 SEPTEMBER 1992
Deer Creek Music Center, Noblesville, Indiana. 'Roll Another Number', a shortened 'Pocahontas' and 'This Note's For You' join the set.

13 SEPTEMBER 1992
Riverport Performing Arts Center, St. Louis, Missouri. 'You And Me', 'Powderfinger', a piano version of 'Mansion On The Hill' and 'Mr Soul' are added for this show, during which Young's first attempt at 'From Hank To Hendrix' is aborted, and 'Old King' is interrupted for smart-ass one-liners. Young: "I don't think I could start a riot, even if I wanted to – well, maybe if I played 'Tonight's The Night' 25 times in a row and left!"

15 SEPTEMBER 1992
Red Rocks Amphitheater, Red Rocks Park, Morrison, Colorado.

16 SEPTEMBER 1992
Park West Amphitheater, Park City, Utah.

18 SEPTEMBER 1992
Salem Amphitheater, Salem, Oregon. By this point of the tour, 'Everybody Knows This Is Nowhere', 'Down By The River', 'One Of These Days' and 'Old Man' have been added to the set. Young also performs Bob Dylan's 'Just Like Tom Thumb's Blues'.

19 SEPTEMBER 1992
The Gorge, George, Washington. Young abandons his intention to perform 'L.A.' after strumming a few chords.

21/22 SEPTEMBER 1992
Greek Theater, Los Angeles, California.
Another set revamp on the 22nd brings performances of 'Cinnamon Girl', 'Cowgirl In The Sand', 'War Of Man' and 'Southern Man'. Bootleg: 'Riding On Hendrix's Bus'.

23 SEPTEMBER 1992
Summer Pops Bowl, Embarcadero Marina Park, San Diego, California. 'Dreamin' Man' and 'Natural Beauty' are added for this show.

25 SEPTEMBER 1992
Pacific Amphitheater, Costa Mesa, California. Young includes 'Field Of Opportunity' and 'Lotta Love' in his set.

26 SEPTEMBER 1992
Bally's, Las Vegas, Nevada.

27 SEPTEMBER 1992
Desert Sky Pavilion, Phoenix, Arizona.

OCTOBER 1992
Release of the spurious Neil Young CD 'The Lost Tapes', by the Portuguese label Movie Play Gold: the album purports to be a set of demos recorded at Quad Studios in Nashville after The Buffalo Springfield split in 1968, but actually features no Young performances.

16 OCTOBER 1992
Bob Dylan 30th Anniversary Concert, at Madison Square Garden, New York, New York. After Sinéad O'Connor's abrupt abandonment of her performance, Young's renditions of 'Just Like Tom Thumb's Blues' and 'All Along The Watchtower' electrify the crowd, and act as a tacit endorsement of their harsh treatment of O'Connor. Musically, though, Young's two songs are the highlight of the entire multi-artist event, and he is rapturously received when he joins the other cast members for 'My Back Pages' and

'Knockin' On Heaven's Door'. Bootlegs: 'When Friends Are Coming'/'Tribute'/'The Best Of Bob Dylan's Anniversary Concert'/'Celebration Night'/'Shaky Neil'/'Depression Blues'.

Young: "I chose songs that I knew really well that I didn't have to work at, that I could stretch out as much as I wanted to on the spot."

Young on Dylan: "There's nothing really special about him. He's just a great songwriter, he's like the Shakespeare of the Nineties."

21 OCTOBER 1992

Publication in Canada of the first edition of John Einarson's book, *Neil Young: Don't Be Denied — The Canadian Years.*

1 NOVEMBER 1992

Shoreline Amphitheater, Mountain View, California.

3 NOVEMBER 1992

'Harvest Moon' is belatedly released, 10 months after it was first announced. In the *NME*, Steve Sutherland notes perceptively: "There are no great songs on 'Harvest Moon'... It's a forlorn gesture from a decent man who wishes that each and every person would think and act to make the world a better place to live in."

7 NOVEMBER 1992

'Harvest Moon' enters the UK album chart at No. 12, its highest position.
BBC Radio 1 broadcast the first of two interviews with Young about 'Harvest Moon' (part 2 on 14 November).

14 NOVEMBER 1992

Riverside Theater, Milwaukee, Wisconsin. Young begins another short tour, performing 'Long May You Run', 'Lotta Love', 'From Hank To Hendrix', 'Unknown Legend', 'Pocahontas', 'Like A Hurricane', 'War Of Man', 'Old King', 'The Needle And The Damage Done', 'Tonight's The Night', 'Fuckin' Up', 'Such A Woman', 'Heart Of Gold', 'Harvest Moon', 'Don't Let It Bring You Down', 'Roll Another Number', 'Sugar Mountain' and 'I Am A Child'.

15 NOVEMBER 1992

Riverside Theater, Milwaukee, Wisconsin. Young performs seven songs not played the previous night: 'Comes A Time', 'Cinnamon Girl', 'Dreamin' Man', 'Powderfinger', 'This Note's For You', 'Dance Dance Dance' and an unexpected performance of The Buffalo Springfield's 'Broken Arrow'.

Young (introducing 'Roll Another Number'): "Here's one for our new President, Bill Clinton. Did he inhale? We ought to

know that about our leaders."

17 NOVEMBER 1992

Young films a show for the VH1 cable TV series *Center Stage*, at Channel 11 Studios, WTTW, Chicago, Illinois. Young continues his revamping of the set-list, by performing songs like 'Love Is A Rose', 'One Of These Days', 'Natural Beauty', 'Mr Soul', 'You And Me' and 'After The Goldrush'. Bootleg: 'World On A String'/'Centerstage' (entire show).

Young (introducing 'Tonight's The Night'): "It's too light in here to do this song, but it'll look dark on TV."

18 NOVEMBER 1992

Chicago Theater, Chicago, Illinois. Only one new addition to tonight's set: 'Speakin' Out'. Young cuts short his performance, apparently troubled by the noise of the crowd.

19 NOVEMBER 1992

Chicago Theater, Chicago, Illinois. Four new songs for this show: 'The Old Laughing Lady', 'Helpless', a rare performance of 'Love Art Blues' and 'Ohio'. After the previous night's distractions, Young insists on a ban on beer being sold at the venue.

21 NOVEMBER 1992

Orpheum Theater, Minneapolis, Minnesota. 'Too Far Gone' is added to the set. Bootleg: 'Mirror Man'.

22 NOVEMBER 1992

Orpheum Theater, Minneapolis, Minnesota. For the final show of the mini-tour, Young performs 'Everybody Knows This Is Nowhere', 'Old Man' and 'Homefires'.

1 DECEMBER 1992

'Harvest Moon' is released as a cassette and CD single in America.

5 DECEMBER 1992

Young performs on NBC-TV's *Saturday Night Live*, playing 'From Hank To Hendrix' and 'Harvest Moon' (the latter in place of 'War Of Man', which he performed during the rehearsals).

8 DECEMBER 1992

Young is scheduled to appear on the *David Letterman Show*, but cancels shortly before the show.

16 DECEMBER 1992

Young records a performance for *MTV Unplugged* at the Ed Sullivan Theater in New York, but decides after the taping that the show isn't good enough to broadcast. The songs played at this show are 'Love Is A Rose' (2

takes), 'Unknown Legend' (2 takes), 'From Hank To Hendrix' (3 takes), 'You And Me', 'Old Man', 'Harvest Moon' (2 takes), 'War Of Man' (3 takes), 'Comes A Time', 'Old Man' again, 'Silver And Gold' (3 takes), 'Are You Ready For The Country' (2 takes), 'One Of These Days', 'Dreamin' Man', 'Down By The River', 'Last Trip To Tulsa' (2 takes) and 'After The Goldrush'.

LATE DECEMBER 1992

The first *Center Stage* show is broadcast, with Young singing 'Mr Soul', 'Harvest Moon', 'War Of Man', 'You And Me' and 'After The Goldrush'.

Although a handful of unissued songs, notably the confessional 'Hitch-Hiker', emerge during live shows in 1993, Young's activities mostly look towards the past. The release of 'Lucky Thirteen' marks the 10th anniversary of the ill-fated Geffen deal with an air of reconciliation. His second attempt at taping an Unplugged show for MTV not only spawns an album, but also compensates for the increasingly formulaic approach of the acoustic-based TV series.

In the summer, he begins a long, sprawling 'oldies' tour that encompasses the European festival circuit. Rather than reliving old ragged glories with Crazy Horse, though, he fulfills a lifetime's ambition by recruiting Stax soul legends Booker T & the MGs as his backing band. The reviews are appropriately enthusiastic.

Young returns to Crazy Horse at the end of the year for another set of album sessions, three years after 'Ragged Glory' (itself three years after 'Life', which was three years after the aborted 1984 LP, and so on and on back into the mid-70s). The record is completed in January 1994 for late spring release; but then an unnamed member of the band apparently leaks the rough mixes to the collectors' network, with the result that Young vows not to release the album, or to work with Crazy Horse in the future.

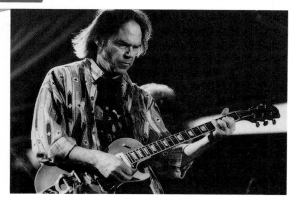

4 JANUARY 1993

The 'Lucky Thirteen' compilation is released by Geffen Records. Young himself assembled the package, which includes five previously unreleased tracks, portentously labelled as coming from 'The Neil Young Archives'.

15 JANUARY 1993

Young guests on the *Tonight Show*, with Jay Leno, performing 'Harvest Moon' and 'Unknown Legend'.

7 FEBRUARY 1993

Young reshoots a performance for MTV's *Unplugged* series, on Stage 12 at Universal Studios, Universal City, California. He performs the following songs (those marked * were aired on March 10): 'The Old Laughing Lady*', 'Mr Soul*', 'World On A String*', 'Pocahontas*', 'Stringman*' (on piano), 'Like A Hurricane*' (on pump organ), 'Tonight's The Night' (begun but aborted, on piano), 'The Needle And The Damage Done*', 'Helpless*' (on piano), 'Sample And Hold', 'Transformer Man*', 'Dreamin' Man', 'Harvest Moon*', 'War Of Man', 'Unknown Legend*', 'Winterlong', 'Long May You Run*', 'Look Out For My Love*' and 'From Hank To Hendrix*'. Bootlegs: 'Back To My Roots' (inc. 'War Of Man')/'Helpless Believers' (1 track).

23 FEBRUARY 1993

Another episode of *Center Stage* is broadcast, featuring Young performing 'Long May You Run', 'From Hank To Hendrix', 'Harvest Moon', 'Love Is A Rose' and 'After The Goldrush'.

28 FEBRUARY 1993

Young appears again on *Center Stage*, with 'Harvest Moon', 'Love Is A Rose', 'War Of Man', 'You And Me' and 'After The Goldrush' repeated from the previous shows.

MARCH 1993

The magazine *Classic Toy Trains* runs an extensive feature about Young and his son Ben,

for whom Neil has constructed a special set which can be operated by a handicapped child.

Young is named as one of the artists who has been asked to contribute to 'Sweet Relief', a tribute album to the songwriter Victoria Williams, who is suffering from MS. In the event, the LP is released without a track from Young.

1 MARCH 1993

Young performs alongside Simon and Garfunkel at a benefit concert for the Children's Health Fund, at the Dorothy Chandler Pavilion, Los Angeles, California. It's Simon & Garfunkel's first live show for a decade, and Young joins them in the unusual role of support artist, to perform 'From Hank To Hendrix', 'Mr Soul', 'World On A String', 'Pocahontas', 'One Of These Days', 'Sugar Mountain', 'Stringman', 'After The Goldrush' and two songs with S&G, 'Helpless' and 'Only Love Can Break Your Heart'. Young also guests on electric guitar during 'The Sound Of Silence' at the close of Simon & Garfunkel's set.

6 MARCH 1993

Young collects the Best Album of 1992 prize at the Bammie Awards, staged at the Bill Graham Civic Auditorium, San Francisco.

10 MARCH 1993

MTV in the States airs Young's edition of *Unplugged*.

1 APRIL 1993

Young takes part in the Old Growth Forests benefit show at the Park by the River, Portland, Oregon, on the same bill as David Crosby. He performs 'Comes A Time', 'Mother Earth', 'After The Goldrush', 'Heart Of Gold' and 'Sugar Mountain' acoustic and solo, and takes the opportunity to remind President Clinton – then attending the Pacific North West Forestry Summit – of his obligations towards environmental causes in the region.

24 APRIL 1993

Farm Aid VI, at the Cyclone Stadium in Ames, Iowa. Soundgarden, The Jayhawks and Alice In Chains are among the more rowdy acts on the bill, along with a host of top country performers.

Young opens his set with 'Mother Earth' at the pump organ, introducing it with a gibe at the politicians not present for the show: "This song is for you, Clinton and Gore – I would have liked to have seen you here today". He then performs 'Helpless' on piano, before being joined by co-organiser Willie Nelson for 'Four Strong Winds'. 'The Farmer', a song written specially for the Farm Aid cause, is preceded by a lengthy rant about the US government's indifference towards their financial problems. Young's final song is 'From Hank To Hendrix', but he is persuaded to perform 'Are There Any More Real Cowboys' as an encore with Willie Nelson.

22 MAY 1993
A brief clip of Young and Willie Nelson performing 'Are There Any More Real Cowboys' is included in Nelson's 60th birthday CBS TV special.

9/10 JUNE 1993
Warfield Theater, San Francisco, California. The first of four warm-up gigs for the European tour, with Booker T & the MGs. These shows have identical set-lists: 'Mr Soul', 'The Loner', 'Southern Man', 'Helpless', 'This Note's For You', 'Motorcycle Mama', 'Like A Hurricane', 'I Believe In You', 'Everybody Knows This Is Nowhere', 'Love To Burn', 'Separate Ways', 'Powderfinger', 'Only Love Can Break Your Heart', 'Harvest Moon', the previously unheard 'Live To Ride' ("a song about my motorcycle"), 'Down By The River', the Otis Redding hit '(Sitting On) The Dock Of The Bay' (co-written by MG's guitarist Steve Cropper) and Bob Dylan's 'All Along The Watchtower'.

12 JUNE 1993
The Pavilion, Concord, California.

13 JUNE 1993
Civic Auditorium, Santa Cruz, California.

26 JUNE 1993
Young begins his European festival tour, supported by Booker T & the MGs, at the Schüttorf Festival, Gilderhaus, Germany. With the exception of 'Everybody Knows This Is Nowhere', which is dropped for this tour, the basic nightly set-list is similar to the warm-up shows.

27 JUNE 1993
Isle Of Calf Festival, Oslo, Norway. Young adds an acoustic version of 'The Needle And The Damage Done' to the set-list.

28 JUNE 1993
Naval Museum Park, Stockholm, Sweden. The show finishes with the tour's first rendition of 'Rockin' In The Free World', supported by the members of Pearl Jam, and also includes extended versions of 'Like A Hurricane' and 'Down By The River'. Bootleg: 'Dream Machine' (1 track).
   The entire Young performance for the *Center Stage* show is finally aired complete for the first time, on Public Broadcast TV in the States.

30 JUNE 1993
Ice Hall, Helsinki, Finland.

1 JULY 1993
Roskilde Festival, Copenhagen, Denmark.

3 JULY 1993
Torhout Festival, Belgium.

4 JULY 1993
Werchter Festival, Belgium. Young abandons 'Love To Burn' a little way into the song, then tries again later in the set.

5 JULY 1993
The Ahoy, Rotterdam, Holland. Bootleg: 'Dream Machine'.

7 JULY 1993
Le Zénith, Paris, France. A below-par night during the Booker T tour.

8 JULY 1993
Riazor Stadium, La Corona, Spain.

10 JULY 1993
Slane Castle, Ireland.

11 JULY 1993
Finsbury Park, London. Bootlegs: 'Finsbury Park, London, 11 July 1993'/'Young's Heart Runs Free'.

12 JULY 1993
Scottish Exhibition Center, Glasgow. First known performance of 'Change Your Mind', added midway through the set.

14 JULY 1993
Young holds a press conference in Milan.

15 JULY 1993
The Forum, Milan, Italy.

16 JULY 1993
The Arena, Corregio, Italy.

18 JULY 1993
Schlosshof, Bad Mergentheim, Germany.
Bootleg: 'Fucked Up'.

19 JULY 1993
Tanzbrunnen, Cologne, Germany.

21 JULY 1993
Paleo Festival, Nyon, Switzerland.

23 JULY 1993
Foro Italico, Rome, Italy. Further shows
planned for Israel are scrapped.

11 AUGUST 1993
Civic Auditorium, Rapid City, South
Dakota. The American tour keeps strictly to
the set-lists Young had been performing in
Europe, with no hint of experimentation.

14 AUGUST 1993
Marcus Amphitheater, Milwaukee,
Wisconsin.

15 AUGUST 1993
World Amphitheater, Chicago, Illinois.

16 AUGUST 1993
Pine Knob Music Center, Detroit, Michigan.

18 AUGUST 1993
CNE Grandstand, Toronto, Canada.

20 AUGUST 1993
Jones Beach Music Center, Wantaugh, New
York.

22 AUGUST 1993
Garden State Music Center, Holmdel, New
Jersey.

23 AUGUST 1993
Great Woods Music Center, Mansfield,
Massachusetts.

26 AUGUST 1993
Star Lake Amphitheater, Pittsburgh,
Pennsylvania.

28 AUGUST 1993
Walnut Creek Amphitheater, Raleigh, North
Carolina.

29 AUGUST 1993
Lakewood Amphitheater, Atlanta, Georgia.

EARLY SEPTEMBER 1993
At the MTV Video Awards, Young and Pearl
Jam reprise their live-in-Stockholm
performance of 'Rockin' In The Free World'.

1 SEPTEMBER 1993
Fiddlers Green, Denver, Colorado.

4 SEPTEMBER 1993
B.C. Place, Vancouver, Canada.

5 SEPTEMBER 1993
The Gorge, George, Washington.

6 SEPTEMBER 1993
The Meadows, Portland, Oregon. Another
Young/Pearl Jam link-up for 'Rockin' In The
Free World'.

8 SEPTEMBER 1993
Shoreline Amphitheater, Mountain View,
California.

9 SEPTEMBER 1993
Pacific Amphitheater, Costa Mesa,
California.

11 SEPTEMBER 1993
Sports Arena, Los Angeles, California.

12 SEPTEMBER 1993
Sports Arena, San Diego, California.

14 SEPTEMBER 1993
Desert Sky Pavilion, Phoenix, Arizona.

16 SEPTEMBER 1993
Woodlands, Houston, Texas.

17 SEPTEMBER 1993
Irwin Center, Austin, Texas.

18 SEPTEMBER 1993
Starplex, Dallas, Texas.

30 SEPTEMBER 1993
At the Canadian Music Video Awards,
Young's 'Unknown Legend' clip is voted the
best Foreign Video by a Canadian Artist.

9 OCTOBER 1993
Young joins Bob Dylan on stage for the final
encore of 'Leopard-Skin Pill Box Hat' at
Shoreline Amphitheater, Mountain View,
California.

6 NOVEMBER 1993
Young stages the 7th Bridge School Benefit
show. Other acts appearing are Simon &
Garfunkel, Melissa Etheridge, Jackson
Browne, Sammy Hagar, Eddie Van Halen,
Warren Zevon, Bonnie Raitt and Ann &
Nancy Wilson.
   Young opens the show with 'Sugar

Mountain' and 'Mother Earth', then returns to duet with Warren Zevon on 'Splendid Isolation'. For the first time at a Bridge Benefit, Young doesn't play the closing set, giving that honour to Simon & Garfunkel. Instead, he appears immediately before them, performing a weirdly tuneless rendition of Rodgers & Hammerstein's 'Stranger In Paradise', 'After The Goldrush' and the unreleased 'I'll Always Be Part Of You'. The night's finale is an all-star rendition of 'Rockin' In The Free World'.

DECEMBER 1993
Young appears with Pearl Jam to perform 'Rockin' In The Free World' at the MTV Video Awards.
   Crazy Horse join Young to begin sessions for his next album.

JANUARY 1994
Young completes work on his next album with Crazy Horse. He is also featured on a new record of trio performances organised by bassist Rob Wasserman.

14 FEBRUARY 1994
Young is nominated as the Best International Male Artist at the Brits Awards in London.

1 MARCH 1994
Neil is nominated for four Grammy Awards.

EARLY MARCH 1994
Young is erroneously reported to have abandoned his forthcoming Crazy Horse collaboration, after discovering that details of the album, and copies of the master tape, have been circulated on a computer network – having been leaked to a collector by a member of Crazy Horse. Claims that Young will never work with the band again are made, but swiftly denied. Meanwhile, Young's lush song 'Philadelphia' appears on the soundtrack of the acclaimed movie of the same name, and is also issued as a single in its own right.

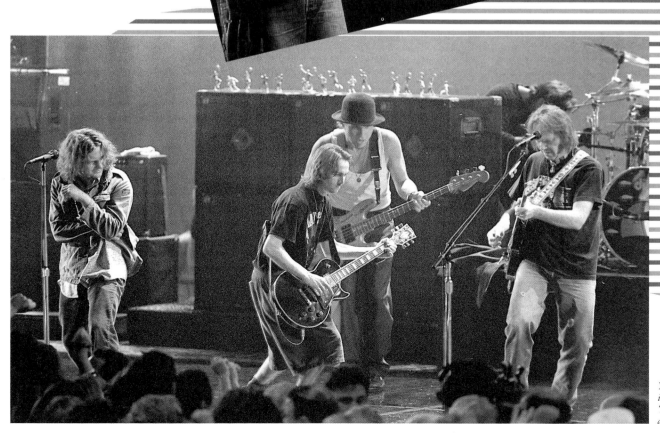

Young joins Pearl Jam for an incendiary performance of 'Rockin' In The Free World' at the MTV Video Awards.

Singles

THE SULTAN/AURORA
(by The Squires)
Canada: V 109 (September 1963)

NOWADAYS CLANCY CAN'T EVEN SING/ GO AND SAY GOODBYE
(by Buffalo Springfield)
US: Atco 6428 (August 1966)

BURNED/EVERYBODY'S WRONG
(by Buffalo Springfield)
US: Atco 6452 (December 1966)
* single withdrawn immediately after release

FOR WHAT IT'S WORTH/DO I HAVE TO COME OUT AND SAY IT
(by Buffalo Springfield)
US: Atco 6459 (January 1967)
UK: Atlantic 584 077 (February 1967)

BLUEBIRD/MR SOUL
(by Buffalo Springfield)
US: Atco 6499 (June 1967)

ROCK'N'ROLL WOMAN/A CHILD'S CLAIM TO FAME
(by Buffalo Springfield)
US: Atco 6519 (September 1967)
UK: Atlantic 584 145 (November 1967)

EXPECTING TO FLY/EVERYDAYS
(by Buffalo Springfield)
US: Atco 6545 (December 1967)
UK: Atlantic 584 165 (February 1968)

UNO MUNDO/MERRY-GO-ROUND
(by Buffalo Springfield)
US: Atco 6572 (March 1968)
UK: Atlantic 584 189 (June 1968)

KIND WOMAN/SPECIAL CARE
(by Buffalo Springfield)
US: Atco 6602 (July 1968)

ON THE WAY HOME/FOUR DAYS GONE
(by Buffalo Springfield)
US: Atco 6615 (September 1968)

THE LONER/SUGAR MOUNTAIN
US: Reprise 0785 (November 1968)
* the B-side is a previously unreleased live recording

EVERYBODY KNOWS THIS IS NOWHERE/THE EMPEROR OF WYOMING
US: Reprise 0819 (March 1969)
*early promo copies feature an alternate take of the A-side

DOWN BY THE RIVER/THE LOSING END
US: Reprise 0836 (July 1969)
* the A-side is an edited version

THE LONER/EVERYBODY KNOWS THIS IS NOWHERE
UK: Reprise RS 23405 (September 1969)

PRETTY GIRL WHY/QUESTIONS
(by Buffalo Springfield)
UK: Atco 226 006 (October 1969)

OH LONESOME ME/SUGAR MOUNTAIN
US: Reprise 0861 (October 1969)
UK: Reprise RS 20861 (September 1970)
* A-side is an extended take

WOODSTOCK/HELPLESS
(by Crosby, Stills, Nash & Young)
US: Atlantic 2723 (March 1970)
UK: Atlantic 2091 010 (May 1970)

OH LONESOME ME/I'VE BEEN WAITING FOR YOU
US: Reprise 0898 (March 1970)
* A-side is an extended take; B-side is an alternate mix

TEACH YOUR CHILDREN/ COUNTRY GIRL
(by Crosby, Stills, Nash & Young)
US: Atlantic 2735 (May 1970)
UK: Atlantic 2091 002 (April 1970)

OHIO/FIND THE COST OF FREEDOM
(by Crosby, Stills, Nash & Young)
US: Atlantic 2740 (June 1970)
UK: Atlantic 2091 023 (August 1970)

CINNAMON GIRL/SUGAR MOUNTAIN
US: Reprise 0911 (June 1970)
* A-side is an alternate mix

DOWN BY THE RIVER/CINNAMON GIRL
UK: Reprise RS 23462 (August 1970)
* the A-side is an edited version; the B-side is an alternate mix

OUR HOUSE/DEJA VU
(by Crosby, Stills, Nash & Young)
US: Atlantic 2760 (September 1970)
UK: Atlantic 2091 039 (November 1970)

BLUEBIRD/MR SOUL
(by Buffalo Springfield)
US: Atlantic OS 13074 (1970)
* 'Oldies' series reissue: Mr Soul is an otherwise unavailable alternate take

ONLY LOVE CAN BREAK YOUR HEART/ BIRDS
US: Reprise 0958 (October 1970)
UK: Reprise RS 20958 (October 1970)
* B-side is an alternate mix

WHEN YOU DANCE I CAN REALLY LOVE/SUGAR MOUNTAIN
US: Reprise 0992 (March 1971)

WHEN YOU DANCE I CAN REALLY LOVE/AFTER THE GOLDRUSH
UK: Reprise RS 23488 (February 1971)

CINNAMON GIRL/ONLY LOVE CAN BREAK YOUR HEART
US: Reprise 0746 (late 1971)
* 'Oldies' series reissue

HEART OF GOLD/SUGAR MOUNTAIN
US: Reprise 1065 (January 1972)
UK: Reprise K 14140 (January 1972)

OLD MAN/THE NEEDLE AND THE DAMAGE DONE
US: Reprise 1084 (April 1972)
UK: Reprise K 14167 (June 1972)

WAR SONG (by Neil Young & Graham Nash)/ **THE NEEDLE AND THE DAMAGE DONE**
US: Reprise 1099 (June 1972)
* A-side is otherwise unavailable

HEART OF GOLD/OLD MAN
US: Reprise 1152 (late 1972)
* 'Oldies' series reissue

BLUEBIRD/MR SOUL/ROCK'N'ROLL WOMAN/EXPECTING TO FLY
(by Buffalo Springfield)
UK: Atlantic K 10237 (October 1972)

TIME FADES AWAY/LAST TRIP TO TULSA
US: Reprise 1184 (November 1973)
* B-side is otherwise unavailable live track

ONLY LOVE CAN BREAK YOUR HEART/ AFTER THE GOLDRUSH
UK: Reprise K 14319 (March 1974)
* reissue

SOUTHERN MAN/TILL THE MORNING COMES/AFTER THE GOLDRUSH/HEART OF GOLD
UK: Reprise K 14350 (May 1974)
* reissue

WALK ON/FOR THE TURNSTILES
US: Reprise 1209 (June 1974)
UK: Reprise K 14360 (August 1974)

LOOKING FOR A LOVE/SUGAR MOUNTAIN
US: Reprise 1344 (September 1975)
UK: Reprise K 14416 (March 1976)

DRIVE BACK/STUPID GIRL
US: Reprise 1350 (January 1976)

DON'T CRY NO TEARS/STUPID GIRL
UK: Reprise K 14431 (May 1976)

LONG MAY YOU RUN/12-8 BLUES
(by the Stills/Young Band)
US: Reprise 1365 (July 1976)
UK: Reprise K 14433 (August 1976)

MIDNIGHT ON THE BAY/BLACK CORAL
(by the Stills/Young Band)
US: Reprise 1378 (October 1976)

HEY BABE/HOMEGROWN
US: Reprise 1390 (August 1977)

LIKE A HURRICANE/HOLD BACK THE TEARS
US: Reprise 1391 (September 1977)
UK: Reprise K 14482 (September 1977)
* A-side is an edited version

THE NEEDLE AND THE DAMAGE DONE/ SUGAR MOUNTAIN
US: Reprise 1393 (December 1977)
* reissue

COMES A TIME/ MOTORCYCLE MAMA
US: Reprise 1395 (October 1978)

COMES A TIME/LOTTA LOVE
UK: Reprise K 14492 (October 1978)
* release cancelled

FOUR STRONG WINDS/HUMAN HIGHWAY
US: Reprise 1396 (December 1978)

FOUR STRONG WINDS/MOTORCYCLE MAMA
UK: Reprise K 14493 (December 1978)

HEY HEY MY MY (INTO THE BLACK)/MY MY HEY HEY (OUT OF THE BLUE)
US: Reprise 49031 (September 1979)
UK: Reprise K 14498 (September 1979)

CINNAMON GIRL/THE LONER
US: Reprise 49189 (December 1979)
* both sides are live recordings

HAWKS AND DOVES/UNION MAN
US: Reprise 49555 (November 1980)
UK: Reprise K 14508 (November 1980)

STAYIN' POWER/CAPTAIN KENNEDY
US: Reprise 49641 (February 1981)

SOUTHERN PACIFIC/MOTOR CITY
US: Reprise 49870 (November 1981)
* also issued as Reprise 49895 on red triangular vinyl

OPERA STAR/SURFER JOE AND MOE THE SLEAZE
US: Reprise 50014 (January 1982)

LITTLE THING CALLED LOVE/WE R IN CONTROL
US: Geffen 29887 (December 1982)
UK: Geffen GEF 2781 (January 1983)

SAMPLE AND HOLD (extended)/ **MR SOUL**
(extended)/**SAMPLE AND HOLD**
US: Geffen 20105 (12") (January 1983)

MR SOUL Part 1/**MR SOUL** Part 2
US: Geffen 29707 (February 1983)

WONDERIN'/PAYOLA BLUES
US: Geffen 29574 (August 1983)
UK: Geffen GEF 3581 (September 1983)

CRY CRY CRY/PAYOLA BLUES
US: Geffen 29433 (October 1983)

ARE THERE ANY MORE REAL COWBOYS/Willie Nelson track
US: Columbia 05566 (July 1985)

GET BACK TO THE COUNTRY/MISFITS
US: Geffen 28883 (September 1985)

OLD WAYS/ONCE AN ANGEL
US: Geffen 28753 (November 1985)

WEIGHT OF THE WORLD/PRESSURE
US: Geffen 28623 (July 1986)
UK: Geffen GEF 7 (7"); GEFT 7 (12")
(September 1986)

MIDEAST VACATION/LONG WALK HOME
US: Geffen 28196 (June 1987)

LONG WALK HOME/CRYIN' EYES
UK: Geffen GEF 25 (June 1987)

TEN MEN WORKIN'/I'M GOIN'
US: Reprise 27908 (7" & cassette) (April 1988)
* B-side is otherwise unavailable

THIS NOTE'S FOR YOU (live)/ **THIS NOTE'S FOR YOU**
US: Reprise 27848 (May 1988)

AMERICAN DREAM/COMPASS
(by Crosby, Stills, Nash & Young)
UK: Atlantic A 9003 (January 1989)

AMERICAN DREAM/COMPASS/ SOLDIERS OF PEACE
(by Crosby, Stills, Nash & Young)
UK: Atlantic A 9003T (12") (January 1989)
*also issued in limited edition with 'Ohio' (A 9003TX)

THIS OLD HOUSE/GOT IT MADE
(by Crosby, Stills, Nash & Young)
US: Atlantic 88966 (January 1989)

ROCKIN' IN THE FREE WORLD (live)/
ROCKIN' IN THE FREE WORLD
US: Reprise 22776 (August 1989)
UK: Reprise W 2776 (April 1990)

ROCKIN' IN THE FREE WORLD (live)/
ROCKIN' IN THE FREE WORLD/
COCAINE EYES
UK: Reprise W 2776T (12"); W 2776CD
(CD) (April 1990)

MANSION ON THE HILL (edit)/
**MANSION ON THE HILL/ DON'T
SPOOK THE HORSE**
US: Reprise 7599-21759-2 (CD)
(September 1990)
*Don't Spook The Horse is otherwise unavailable

**OVER AND OVER/DON'T SPOOK
THE HORSE**
US: Reprise 7599-19483-4 (cassette)
(February 1991)

HARVEST MOON/OLD KING
US: Reprise 9-18685-2 (CD); 9-18685-4
(cassette) (December 1992)

HARVEST MOON/ WINTERLONG
UK: Reprise W 0139 (7"); W 0139C (cassette)
(February 1993)

**HARVEST MOON/OLD KING/THE
NEEDLE AND THE DAMAGE DONE/
GOIN' BACK**
UK: Reprise W 0139CD (CD)
(February 1993)

**HARVEST MOON/DEEP FORBIDDEN
LAKE/ CAMPAIGNER/WINTERLONG**
UK: Reprise W 0139CDX (CD)
(February 1993)

**THE NEEDLE AND THE DAMAGE
DONE/YOU AND ME**
UK: Reprise W 0191 (7"); W 0191C (cassette)
(July 1993)
*A-side is live from 'Unplugged' TV show

**THE NEEDLE AND THE DAMAGE
DONE/ YOU AND ME/ FROM HANK
TO HENDRIX**
UK: Reprise W 0191CD (CD) (July 1993)
*A-side is live from 'Unplugged' TV show

**LONG MAY YOU RUN/SUGAR
MOUNTAIN**
UK: Reprise W 0207 (7"); W 0207C (cassette)
(October 1993)
* A-side is live from 'Unplugged' TV show; B-
side is live from 'Live Rust'

**LONG MAY YOU RUN/SUGAR
MOUNTAIN/ CORTEZ THE KILLER/
CINNAMON GIRL**
UK: Reprise W 0207CD (CD) (October 1993)
* A-side is live from 'Unplugged' TV show;
remaining tracks are from 'Live Rust'

**ROCKIN' IN THE FREE WORLD
(edit)/ROCKIN' IN THE FREE WORLD**
UK: Reprise W 0231 (7"); 0231C (cassette)
(February 1994)
* reissue

ROCKIN' IN THE FREE WORLD (edit)/
ROCKIN' IN THE FREE WORLD (live)/
ROCKIN' IN THE FREE WORLD
(LP version)
UK: Reprise W 0231CD (CD)
(February 1994)
* reissue

**PHILADELPHIA/SUCH A
WOMAN/STRINGMAN**
UK: Reprise W 0242CD (CD)
(March 1994)
* A-side is title song from Tom Hanks movie,
also available on the film soundtrack LP

BUFFALO SPRINGFIELD
(by Buffalo Springfield)
US: Atco 33-200 (January 1967)
UK: Atco 587/588 (February 1967)
*For What It's Worth/Go And Say Goodbye/Sit
Down I Think I Love You/Nowadays Clancy
Can't Even Sing/Hot Dusty Roads/Everybody's
Wrong/Flying On The Ground Is Wrong/
Burned/Do I Have To Come Right Out And
Say It/Leave/Out Of My Mind/Pay The Price*
* original copies included Baby Don't Scold Me in
place of For What It's Worth
* reissued in the UK as 'In The Beginning' in 1971.

BUFFALO SPRINGFIELD AGAIN
(by Buffalo Springfield)
US: Atco 33-226 (November 1967)
UK: Atlantic 587/588 091 (February 1968)
*Mr Soul/A Child's Claim To Fame/Everydays/
Expecting To Fly/ Bluebird/Hung Upside
Down/Sad Memory/Good Time Boy/
Rock'n'Roll Woman/Broken Arrow*

LAST TIME AROUND
(by Buffalo Springfield)
US: Atco SD 33-256 (August 1968)
UK: Atco 228 024 (January 1969)
*On The Way Home/It's So Hard To Wait/
Pretty Girl Why/Four Days Gone/Carefree
Country Day/Special Care/In The Hour Of
Not Quite Rain/Questions/I Am A Child/
Merry-Go-Round/Uno Mundo/Kind Woman*

NEIL YOUNG
US: Reprise RS 6317 (December 1968)
UK: Reprise RSLP 6317 (September 1969)
*The Emperor Of Wyoming/The Loner/If I
Could Have Her Tonight/I've Been Waiting
For You/The Old Laughing Lady/String
Quartet From Whiskey Boot Hill/Here We Are
In The Years/What Did You Do To My Life/I
've Loved Her So Long/The Last Trip To Tulsa*
* the LP was reissued in the USA in late 1969
with different mixes of several tracks

RETROSPECTIVE
(by Buffalo Springfield)
US: Atco SD 33-283 (February 1969)
UK: Atco 228 012 (March 1969)
*For What It's Worth/Mr Soul/Sit Down I
Think I Love You/Kind Woman/Bluebird/On
The Way Home/Nowadays Clancy Can't Even
Sing/Broken Arrow/Rock'n'Roll Woman/I Am A
Child/Go And Say Goodbye/Expecting To Fly*
* compilation of previously issued tracks

**EVERYBODY KNOWS THIS IS
NOWHERE**
US: Reprise RS 6349 (May 1969)
UK: Reprise RSLP 6349 (July 1969)
*Cinnamon Girl/Everybody Knows This Is
Nowhere/ Round & Round/Down By The
River/The Losing End/ Running Dry/Cowgirl
In The Sand*

DEJA VU
(by Crosby, Stills, Nash & Young)
US: Atlantic SD 7200 (March 1970)
UK: Atlantic 2401 001 (March 1970)
*Deja Vu/Teach Your Children/Almost Cut My
Hair/Helpless/Woodstock/ Deja Vu/Our House/
4 + 20/Country Girl/Everybody I Love You*

AFTER THE GOLDRUSH
US: Reprise RS 6383 (September 1970)
UK: Reprise RSLP 6383 (September 1970)
*Tell Me Why/After The Goldrush/Only Love
Can Break Your Heart/Southern Man/Till The
Morning Comes/Oh Lonesome Me/Don't Let It
Bring You Down/Birds/ When You Dance I
Can Really Love/
I Believe In You/Cripple Creek Ferry*

EXPECTING TO FLY
(by Buffalo Springfield)
UK: Atlantic 2462 012 (October 1970)
*For What It's Worth/Expecting To Fly/Special
Care/Hot Dusty Roads/Everybody's Wrong/Pay
The Price/Flying On The Ground Is Wrong/
Burned/Do I Have To Come Right Out And
Say It/Leave/Out Of My Mind/
Merry-Go-Round*
* compilation of previously issued tracks

FOUR WAY STREET
(by Crosby, Stills, Nash & Young)
US: Atlantic SD 2-902 (April 1971)
UK: Atlantic 2657 007 (April 1971)
*Suite: Judy Blue Eyes/On The Way Home/
Teach Your Children/Triad/The Lee Shore/
Chicago/Right Between The Eyes/Cowgirl In
The Sand/Don't Let It Bring You Down/49 Bye
Byes/America's Children/Love The One You're
With/Pre-Road Downs/Long Time Gone/
Southern Man/Ohio/ Carry On/Find The Cost
Of Freedom*
* double-live album; subsequently issued on
CD with four bonus tracks: King Midas In
Reverse/Laughing/Black Queen/The Loner-
Cinnamon Girl-Down By The River (medley)

HARVEST
US: Reprise MS 2032 (February 1972)
UK: Reprise K 54005 (February 1972)
*Out On The Weekend/Harvest/A Man Needs A
Maid/Heart Of Gold/Are You Ready For The
Country/Old Man/ There's A World/Alabama/
The Needle And The Damage Done/Words*

JOURNEY THROUGH THE PAST
(film soundtrack)
US: Reprise 2XS 6480 (November 1972)
UK: Reprise K 64015 (November 1972)
*For What It's Worth/Mr Soul/ Rock'n'Roll
Woman (all by Buffalo Springfield)/Find The
Cost Of Freedom/Ohio (both by CSNY)/
Southern Man/Are You Ready For The
Country/Let Me Call You Sweetheart/
Alabama/Words/God Bless America/ Relativity
Invitation/Handel's Messiah/King Of Kings
(both by the Tony & Susan Alamo Christian
Foundation Orchestra & Chorus)/Soldier/Let's
Go Away For A While (by The Beach Boys)*

TIME FADES AWAY
US: Reprise MS 2151 (September 1973)
UK: Reprise K 54010 (September 1973)
*Time Fades Away/Journey Through The Past/
Yonder Stands The Sinner/ L.A./Love In Mind/
Don't Be Denied/ The Bridge/Last Dance*
* live album

BUFFALO SPRINGFIELD
(by Buffalo Springfield)
US: Atco SD 2-806 (November 1973)
UK: Atlantic K 70001 (December 1973)
For What It's Worth/Sit Down I Think I Love You/ Nowadays Clancy Can't Even Sing/Go And Say Goodbye/ Pay The Price/Burned/Out Of My Mind/ Mr Soul/Bluebird/Broken Arrow/Rock'n'Roll Woman/ Expecting To Fly/Hung Upside Down/A Child's Claim To Fame/Kind Woman/On The Way Home/ I Am A Child/Pretty Girl Why/Special Care/ Uno Mundo/In The Hour Of Not Quite Rain/ Four Days Gone/Questions
* double-album compilation, including unissued version of 'Bluebird'

ON THE BEACH
US: Reprise R 2180 (July 1974)
UK: Reprise K 54014 (July 1974)
Walk On/See The Sky About To Rain/ Revolution Blues/For The Turnstiles/ Vampire Blues/On The Beach/Motion Pictures/Ambulance Blues

SO FAR
(by Crosby, Stills, Nash & Young)
US: Atlantic SD 18100 (July 1974)
UK: Atlantic K 50023 (August 1974)
Deja Vu/Helplessly Hoping/Wooden Ships/Teach Your Children/Ohio/Find The Cost Of Freedom/ Woodstock/Our House/Helpless/Guinnevere/ Suite: Judy Blue Eyes
* compilation of previously issued material

TONIGHT'S THE NIGHT
US: Reprise MS 2221 (June 1975)
UK: Reprise K 54040 (June 1975)
Tonight's The Night/Speakin' Out/ World On A String/Borrowed Tune/ Come On Baby Let's Go Downtown/ Mellow My Mind/Roll Another Number For The Road/Albuquerque/ New Mama/ Lookout Joe/Tired Eyes/ Tonight's The Night

ZUMA
US: Reprise MS 2242 (November 1975)
UK: Reprise K 54057 (November 1975)
Don't Cry No Tears/Danger Bird/ Pardon My Heart/ Lookin' For A Love/Barstool Blues/Stupid Girl/Drive Back/ Cortez The Killer/Through My Sails

LONG MAY YOU RUN
(by the Stills/Young Band)
US: Reprise MS 2253 (September 1976)
UK: Reprise K 54081 (September 1976)
Long May You Run/Make Love To You/ Midnight On The Bay/Black Coral/Ocean Girl/Let It Shine/12/8 Blues/Fontainebleau/ Guardian Angel

AMERICAN STARS'N'BARS
US: Reprise MSK 2261 (June 1977)
UK: Reprise K 54088 (June 1977)
The Old Country Waltz/Saddle Up The Palomino/Hey Babe/Hold Back The Tears/Bite The Bullet/Star Of Bethlehem/Will To Love/ Like A Hurricane/Homegrown

DECADE
US: Reprise 3RS 2257 (November 1977)
UK: Reprise K 64037 (November 1977)
Down To The Wire†/Burned/Mr Soul/Broken Arrow/Expecting To Fly (all by Buffalo Springfield)/Sugar Mountain/I Am A Child/ The Loner/The Old Laughing Lady/ Cinnamon Girl/Down By The River/Cowgirl In The Sand/I Believe In You/After The Goldrush/Southern Man/ Helpless (by CSNY)/ Ohio (by CSNY)/Soldier/Old Man/A Man Needs A Maid/Harvest/Heart Of Gold/Star Of Bethlehem/The Needle And The Damage Done/Tonight's The Night/Tired Eyes/Walk On/For The Turnstiles/Winterlong†/ Deep Forbidden Lake†/Like A Hurricane/Love Is A Rose†/Cortez The Killer/Campaigner†/Long May You Run (by the Stills/Young Band)
*triple-LP compilation, including unissued tracks (marked†)

COMES A TIME
US: Reprise 2266 (October 1978)
UK: Reprise K 54099 (October 1978)
Goin' Back/Comes A Time/Look Out For My Love/ Lotta Love/Peace Of Mind/Human Highway/Already One/ Field Of Opportunity/ Motorcycle Mama/Four Strong Winds

RUST NEVER SLEEPS
US: Reprise 2295 (July 1979)
UK: Reprise K 54105 (July 1979)
My My Hey Hey (Out Of The Blue)/ Thrasher/ Ride My Llama/Pocahontas/ Sail Away/ Powderfinger/ Welfare Mothers/Sedan Delivery/Hey Hey My My (Into The Black)

LIVE RUST
US: Reprise 2-2296 (November 1979)
UK: Reprise K 64041 (November 1979)
Sugar Mountain/I Am A Child/Comes A Time/After The Goldrush/My My Hey Hey (Out Of The Blue)/When You Dance I Can Really Love/The Loner/The Needle And The Damage Done/Lotta Love/Sedan Delivery/ Powderfinger/Cortez The Killer/Cinnamon Girl/Like A Hurricane/ Hey Hey My My (Into The Black)/ Tonight's The Night
* double-LP live album

WHERE THE BUFFALO ROAM
(film soundtrack)
US: Backstreet MCA 5126 (1980)
Buffalo Stomp/Ode To Wild Bill #1/All Along The Watchtower (by Jimi Hendrix)/Lucy In The Sky With Diamonds (by Bill Murray)/Ode To Wild Bill #2/Papa Was A Rolling Stone (by the Temptations)/Home, Home On The Range/Straight Answers (by Bill Murray)/ Highway 61 Revisited (by Bob Dylan)/I Can't Help Myself (by the Four Tops)/Ode To Wild Bill #3/Keep On Chooglin' (by Creedence Clearwater Revival)/Ode To Wild Bill #4/ Purple Haze (by Jimi Hendrix)/Buffalo Stomp Refrain

HAWKS & DOVES
US: Reprise 2297 (November 1980)
UK: Reprise K 54109 (November 1980)
Little Wing/The Old Homestead/Lost In Space/ Captain Kennedy/Stayin' Power/Coastline/ Union Man/Comin' Apart At Every Nail/ Hawks & Doves

RE-AC-TOR
US: Reprise 2304 (November 1981)
UK: Reprise K 54116 (November 1981)
Opera Star/Surfer Joe And Moe The Sleaze/ T-Bone/Get Back On It/ Southern Pacific/ Motor City/Rapid Transit/Shots

TRANS
US: Geffen 2018 (January 1983)
UK: Geffen GEF 25019 (January 1983)
Little Thing Called Love/Computer Age/We R In Control/Transformer Man/Computer Cowboy/Hold On To Your Love/Sample And Hold/Mr Soul/ Like An Inca

EVERYBODY'S ROCKIN'
US: Geffen 4013 (August 1983)
UK: Geffen GEF 25590 (August 1983)
Betty Lou's Got A New Pair Of Shoes/ Rainin' In My Heart/Payola Blues/ Wonderin'/Kinda Fonda Wanda/ Jellyroll Man/Bright Lights, Big City/ Mystery Train/Everybody's Rockin'

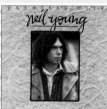

GREATEST HITS
New Zealand: Reprise 252711 (February 1985)
Cinnamon Girl/Old Man/Comes A Time/ Walk On/The Loner/Like A Hurricane/ Heart Of Gold/Southern Man/Down By The River/ Southern Pacific/Hey Hey My My (Into The Black)

OLD WAYS
US: Geffen 24068 (August 1985)
UK: Geffen GEF 26377 (September 1985)
Wayward Wind/Get Back To The Country/ Are There Any More Real Cowboys/Once An Angel/ Misfits/ California Sunset/Old Ways/ My Boy/ Bound For Glory/Where Is The Highway Tonight?

LANDING ON WATER

US: Geffen 24109 (July 1986)
UK: Geffen 924 109-1 (July 1986)
Weight Of The World/Violent Side/Hippie Dream/Bad News Beat/ Touch The Night/ People On The Street/Hard Luck Stories/I Got A Problem/Pressure/Drifter

LIFE

US: Geffen 24154 (June 1987)
UK: Geffen WX 108 (June 1987)
Mideast Vacation/Long Walk Home/Around The World/Inca Queen/Too Lonely/Prisoners Of Rock'n'Roll/Crying Eyes/When Your Lonely Heart Breaks/We Never Danced

THIS NOTE'S FOR YOU

US: Reprise 25719 (April 1988)
UK: Reprise 925 719-1 (April 1988)
Ten Men Workin'/This Note's For You/Coupe De Ville/Life In The City/Twilight/Married Man/Sunny Inside/Can't Believe Your Lyin'/Hey Hey/One Thing

AMERICAN DREAM

(by Crosby, Stills, Nash & Young)
US: Atlantic 81888 (November 1988)
UK: Atlantic WX 233 (November 1988)
American Dream/Got It Made/Name Of Love/Don't Say Goodbye/This Old House/Nighttime For The Generals/ Shadowland/Drivin' Thunder/Clear Blue Skies/That Girl/Compass/ Soldiers Of Peace/Feel Your Love/Night Song

ELDORADO

Japan: Reprise 20P2 2651 (March 1989)
Cocaine Eyes/Don't Cry/Heavy Love/On Broadway/Eldorado

FREEDOM

US: Reprise 25899 (October 1989)
UK: Reprise 925 899-1 (October 1989)
Rockin' In The Free World/Crime In The City/Don't Cry/Hangin' On A Limb/Eldorado/The Ways Of Love/ Someday/On Broadway/Wrecking Ball/No More/Too Far Gone/Rockin' In The Free World

RAGGED GLORY

US: Reprise 26315 (September 1990)
UK: Reprise 7599-26315-1 (September 1990)
Country Home/White Line/Fuckin' Up/Over And Over/Love To Burn/ Farmer John/ Mansion On The Hill/ Days That Used To Be/Love And Only Love/Mother Earth (Natural Anthem)

WELD

US: Reprise 26671 (October 1991)
UK: Reprise 7599-26671-2 (October 1991)
Hey Hey My My (Into The Black)/ Crime In The City/Blowin' In The Wind/Welfare Mothers/Love To Burn/ Cinnamon Girl/ Mansion On The Hill/Fuckin' Up/Cortez The Killer/ Powderfinger/Love And Only Love/ Rockin' In The Free World/Like A Hurricane/ Farmer John/Tonight's The Night/Roll Another Number
* double-CD live album; also available as Arc/Weld, a three-CD set (Reprise 26746)

ARC

US: Reprise 9 26769-2 (October 1991)
Arc
* 37-minute sound collage, only available as a separate CD in the USA

HARVEST MOON

US: Reprise 45057 (November 1992)
UK: Reprise 9362-45057-2 (November 1992)
Unknown Legend/From Hank To Hendrix/ You And Me/Harvest Moon/ War Of Man/One Of These Days/ Such A Woman/Old King/ Dreamin' Man/Natural Beauty

LUCKY THIRTEEN

US: Geffen 24452 (January 1993)
UK: Geffen GED 24452 (January 1993)
Sample And Hold/Transformer Man/ Depression Blues†/Get Gone†/Don't Take Your Love Away From Me†/Once An Angel/Where Is The Highway Tonight?/Hippie Dream/ Pressure/Around The World/Mideast Vacation/ Ain't It The Truth†/This Note's For You†
* compilation, including unissued material (marked †)

UNPLUGGED

US: Reprise 45310 (June 1993)
UK: Reprise 9362-45310-2 (June 1993)
The Old Laughing Lady/Mr Soul/ World On A String/Pocahontas/ Stringman/Like A Hurricane/The Needle And The Damage Done/Helpless/Harvest Moon/Transformer Man/Unknown Legend/Look Out For My Love/Long May You Run/From Hank To Hendrix
* live album from 'MTV Unplugged' TV broadcast

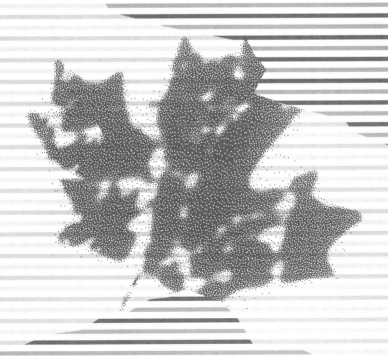